The Racial Crisis in
American Higher Education

SUNY Series,
FRONTIERS IN EDUCATION
Philip G. Altbach, Editor

The Frontiers in Education Series draws upon a range of disciplines and approaches in the analysis of contemporary educational issues and concerns. Books in the series help to reinterpret established fields of scholarship in education by encouraging the latest synthesis and research. A special focus highlights educational policy issues from a multidisciplinary perspective. The series is published in cooperation with the Graduate School of Education, State University of New York at Buffalo.

The Racial Crisis in
American Higher Education

Edited by
Philip G. Altbach and Kofi Lomotey

Foreword by Clark Kerr

State University of New York Press

Published by
State University of New York Press, Albany

© 1991 State University of New York

All rights reserved

Printed in the United States of America

No part of this book may be used or reproduced
in any manner whatsoever without written permission
except in the case of brief quotations embodied in
critical articles and reviews.

For information, address State University of New York
Press, State University Plaza, Albany, N.Y., 12246

Library of Congress Cataloging-in-Publication Data

The Racial crisis in American higher education / edited by Philip G.
  Altbach and Kofi Lomotey.
      p.   cm. — (SUNY series, frontiers in education)
    Includes bibliographical references.
    ISBN 0-7914-0520-6. — ISBN 0-7914-0521-4 (pbk.)
    1. Minorities—Education (Higher)—United States.   2. College
  integration—United States.   3. Universities and colleges—United
  States—Case studies.   4. United States—Race relations—Case
  studies.   I. Altbach, Philip G.   II. Lomotey, Kofi.   III. Series.
LC3731.R255   1991
378.1'982—dc20   90-33700
                                                                            CIP

10   9   8   7   6   5   4   3   2

Contents

CLARK KERR

Foreword

The Racial Crisis in American Higher Education reads to me, in its totality, like the famous passage from the Book of Daniel. In case you have forgotten: "Thou art weighed in the balances, and art found wanting." This volume does not go so far, however, as does the Book of Daniel, and also say: "Thy kingdom [is] finished." The central message is that higher education, in its policies toward minorities and its treatment of them, has been found wanting, and that there have been, and will be even more, serious consequences.

The injunction is that the greatest single imperative before American higher education currently is to improve its performance in this crucial area. I agree that this is one of the great imperatives now before higher education but would suggest that there are others, including but not limited to: (1) responding to the demands of our society for higher education to make greater contributions to our national economic competitiveness and (2) renewing our faculties and facilities in a short period of time to replace those recruited and built in the 1960s and early 1970s. The first of these two poses a great contradiction—it places a very heavy emphasis on merit alone while the treatment of minorities includes an emphasis on compensatory opportunities. The second, however, is a complementary force since it will open up many new faculty positions for possible appointments of minorities.

I have spoken of this volume "in its totality" and will comment further upon it also "in its totality" but this, I fully realize, is somewhat misleading for there are altogether fifteen essays involving nineteen authors. Each essay has, of course, its own themes and emphases. However, they do add up to one overall and consistent impression that: all is not well! This theme is quickly stated by the two editors, Philip G. Altbach and Kofi Lomotey—both at State University of New York at Buffalo—in the first chapter and in the conclusion. Lomotey writes of different racial cultures "living separately, with little knowledge of, or respect for, each other"; and Altbach of how racial issues in American higher education have been and are at "flashpoints of crisis."

A few of the major themes that run through these essays are:

- Racism is a problem of all of American society, not of higher education alone; yet higher education is now on the front lines of the conflicts as were once the buses, the lunch counters, the city streets, the factory employment offices. Too much of a burden, however, is now being placed on higher education to find solutions which it, by itself, cannot possibly find.
- The numbers are better than they once were, as in the early 1960s, but still not adequate either in admissions or in completion rates, except for Asian-Americans. The special case of Asian-Americans splits the minorities among themselves. Their interests and their favored policies are not only not the same but actually opposed to those of other minorities.
- Nothing works as well as it should—not student aid, not affirmative action. The results, consequently, are not commensurate with the efforts. And, additionally, numbers alone are not enough.
- While the numbers are better, the relations are worse. Some minorities get more but they then come to expect more—their own residence halls, their own requested courses, for example, in their own enclaves. Simultaneously, what is called in one essay the "arrogant majority" is becoming more resentful of what it views as special privileges given to minorities. "Hostile stereotypes" of each other are intensifying. The number of racial incidents on campuses is increasing. Both the lash and the backlash are stronger.
- The most preferred new solution is required courses to improve racial understanding. Yet there can always be problems with compulsory courses in a student body intent on individual choices, and the courses may turn out to be counterproductive.
- The central persons in all of these growing conflicts are the college and university presidents, and next, the faculties at large. Neither is as yet taking the intensifying problems with sufficient seriousness.
- Overall, we have been moving from "separate but equal" (de jure) to "equal but separate" (de facto), and separation and some antagonism are still the harsh facts of American life, including life on campus. There is a new situation in the United States: the old ethnic minorities wanted to be included in the mainstream of national life, but some members of the new minorities reject the mainstream culture.

I agree with all of the above. And this volume pulls it together as I have never seen it done before. The episodes I have known about separately are joined together into a more complete and even overwhelming general view. I have taken the situation very seriously for many years but even more so now that I have read these essays. Higher education may well be even closer to "flashpoints" that might ignite a larger flame than I had previously believed to be the situation.

There are also some other and more favorable developments than the ones this volume emphasizes:

- More and more blacks and Hispanics are entering middle-class status—and some of the problems have been of class as well as of race.
- Education, including higher education, has been the chief line of advancement for disadvantaged minorities, and they know this.
- The labor market is now favorable to the advancement of disadvantaged minorities and will continue to be so for demographic reasons, including the demographics of higher education, for at least another decade (a major depression aside).
- Public opinion polls show that there exists among the general public, both majority and minority, a rising mutual understanding and tolerance.
- In handling conflicts, we seem to have learned from the 1960s. The activists and the police both seem to have concluded (so far at least) that the introduction of violence can be counterproductive. Witness the contrast between the generally peaceful handling of anti-apartheid demonstrations in the 1980s as compared with many violent episodes in the 1960s when both sides were more intent on confrontation.

These considerations, if also taken into account, lead to a less alarming view of the developing situation, but still to grave concern. I recognize however that the writers of these essays are generally closer to the front lines than I now am and I did leave this book with even more concern than when I started to read its pages.

Having said this, let me quickly add that some very fundamental philosophical issues are involved here:

- How much to emphasize merit versus how much to emphasize compensatory opportunities? And how much to emphasize opportunity as against comparative results?
- How much to emphasize free speech and free actions associated with free speech versus how much to emphasize and protect the sensitivities of individuals?

These are inherently more difficult issues than ending discriminatory laws or ending the war in Vietnam; it will take much more time to work out solutions that obtain general consent. And experience to date shows how much easier it is to change public policies than private behavior.

These essays place a great deal of responsibility on the leadership of the college and university president in developing policies and in handling crisis situations. They do not demonstrate, however, it seems to me, sufficient understanding of the difficult position of the president. The president can influence many things but can control almost nothing: not the faculty, not the activist students, not the reacting students (including the fraternities), not the external police, not the board of trustees, not the media, not those vagaries of fate that have so often intervened in crisis situations. In a crisis so much can go wrong, and yet everything must go right to get a universally satisfactory result, and it seldom does. I can see a casualty rate ahead higher among presidents than in any other element involved. One way to read the four excellent case studies is from the point of view of the president involved, as I did with great attention to the detail.

*   *   *

The 1990s will not be the 1960s nor the 1980s nor any past decade. A new world is being born. One set of statistics—minority percent of total United States population:

    1950 - 12 percent
    1980 - 15 percent
    2000 - 30 percent (census estimate)
    2150 - 45 percent (census estimate)

The frequently unhappy 17 percent of college students today (the minorities) may become a frequently unhappy 45 percent within the foreseeable future.

The history of the decades ahead will be written by the actions of many people, by the inputs of many forces—both unfavorable and favorable—and by the vagaries of fate. *The Racial Crisis in American Higher Education* alerts us, once again, to how much is at stake for the nation and for higher education; to how complex are the factors at work, the attitudes, and the philosophical issues; and to how elusive are the solutions. May it be true, as William James once said, that "great emergencies and crises show us how much greater our vital resources are than we had supposed."

Acknowledgments

The preparation of a book requires a great deal of cooperation. We are indebted to Ms. Gage Blair for assisting us in editing the manuscript and to Ms. Lalita Subramanyan for editing and proofreading help. Jossey-Bass Publishers provided permission to reprint one of the chapters. Philip G. Altbach wishes to thank the Hoover Institution, Stanford University which provided support during a part of the editing of the volume. The Graduate School of Education, State University of New York at Buffalo provided an appropriate atmosphere for research. Most of all, we are indebted to the contributors to this volume, all of whom are fully engaged with the issues raised here.

PHILIP G. ALTBACH
KOFI LOMOTEY

Part 1

General Perspectives

PHILIP G. ALTBACH

Chapter One

The Racial Dilemma in American Higher Education

Race is one of the most volatile, and divisive, issues in American higher education. The racial situation manifests itself in many ways, from incidents of prejudice on campus to policy decisions concerning affirmative action to debates on the introduction of multicultural elements in the curriculum. This essay focuses attention on the multifaceted, complex and contentious elements of the present racial situation on campus. In order to understand fully this question, one must look not only at campus conditions but also at broader societal trends and policies during the Reagan years. The university is no ivory tower—it is deeply affected by society. It is important to understand campus race relations not only because the potential for real turmoil exists, but also because we can learn a great deal about the nature of contemporary higher education through a examination of this central issue.

The racial mosaic in American higher education is complex. Among college freshmen in 1985, the largest racial minority group was Afro-Americans, who constituted about ten percent of the total student population. Hispanics represented somewhat over two percent of the student population, with Asian-Americans another two percent. Native Americans were under one percent. Foreign students, largely from Asia and Africa, made up another two percent of the student population. Today Asian-Americans are the most rapidly growing minority group on campus; the dramatic growth in Afro-American student numbers which began in the

1960s has slowed in the last several years. The minority student population is not evenly distributed through the academic system. Traditionally black colleges and universities are more than ninety percent Afro-American in their student populations.

Minority issues have had implications for American higher education as never before. In the 1960s, it was possible to support the civil rights movement without this support having any significant implications for the universities. In the 1980s, issues related to race had a direct impact on campus—for intergroup relations, for the curriculum, for the professoriate and perhaps more important, for the allocation of resources.

Campus race relations are of concern not only to the minority community but to everyone involved in the academic enterprise. For one thing, racial and multicultural issues seem, at this time, to have great potential for precipitating campus disruption. More important, racial issues pervade the entire university—from debates about the curriculum to relations in dormitories, from intercollegiate sports to key decisions on admissions. Affirmative action regulations are directly linked to concerns about the representation of racial minorities (as well as women) on the faculties of colleges and universities. Indeed, over the past two decades, racial questions have come to play an unprecedented role in American higher education.

It sometimes appears that few on campus realize the impact of racial issues. Academic administrators, and the faculty for the most part, see racial issues in isolation, as individual crises to be dealt with on an ad hoc basis rather than as a nexus of issues which require careful analysis. Most in positions of authority seem to feel that racial questions are not central to the academic enterprise—that they are individual problems brought to the center stage by small groups and that they are unnecessary distractions from the real business of higher education. Many, in and out of academic life, feel that racial issues were "dealt with" in the 1960s and that minorities should be satisfied with the policies put into place at that time. Policy makers, in the universities and in government, feel that they should not have to be concerned with racial issues, and their reactions to incidents of crisis often reflect a basic unwillingness to take matters seriously or to consider the broader implications.

The student community is also very much part of the campus racial equation. White students in most colleges and universities do not grasp the seriousness of the situation nor do they recognize the feelings and reactions of minority students. Student attitude surveys continue to show that white students remain liberal in their attitudes about race relations, although there seems to be an undercurrent of resentment against affirmative action and other special programs for minorities. There is, indeed, a certain callousness on the part of many white students about race relations, reflecting perhaps broader trends in society.

There has been a trend among students to focus on racial and ethnic identity and, in some cases, to become somewhat isolated in homogeneous communities. Minority students have often reacted by retreating into their own communities and creating self-imposed ghettos. A desire for social familiarity in the sometimes impersonal environment of the university is understandable. It is sometimes argued that the campus simply reflects the social distance and tensions of the broader society.

The faculty needs to be especially concerned about campus relations. At the most basic level, the educational process is diminished by racial tensions and conflicts. Attention is deflected from teaching and learning. The campus atmosphere may be poisoned by racial conflict. The racial and social class composition of the profession puts it at some disadvantage in dealing with students from different racial and cultural backgrounds since the professoriate is overwhelmingly white, male and middle class. It is also fair to say that most faculty members have not been basically concerned with the situation. Professors are often largely concerned with their own careers. The attitudes of the professoriate, on racial matters as well as on politics, tend to be more liberal than the general population in the United States, but at the same time the professoriate is rather conservative on matters relating to change in the university.[1] Thus, there has been a considerable faculty resistance to structural and curricular changes aimed at reducing racial tensions on campus. As Edward Shils has pointed out, the faith of the professoriate in the "academic ethic" and the historical traditions of the university insulates the institution from rapid change.[2]

Where racial tensions have flared into academic crisis, the faculty has been unable to avoid involvement. Students have frequently demanded changes in the curriculum, strengthening of minority studies academic programs and the like. The faculty has had to deliberate on these issues and has had a responsibility, on most campuses, for such academic changes. Campus crisis is disruptive of the faculty in many ways. The costs of dealing with crisis are often high, not only in financial and human terms but also in terms of the reputation of the institution. In general, the academic profession has tried to avoid involvement with campus racial strife. The faculty has been less than enthusiastic about student demands for expanded minority studies programs and more multicultural courses in the liberal arts curriculum.

Those most affected by racial problems are, of course, the minority student communities in American higher education. It should be kept in mind, of course, that there are differences among the various minority groups in higher education and that these groups do not always share the same goals. In recent demonstrations, there has been significant solidarity among minority student groups in terms of goals and demands, but there are nonetheless variations in the communities. Minority students are concerned about a number of campus issues. The bulk of overt campus racism has been directed against Afro-American students, and the greatest amount of protest has been expressed about ensuring that Afro-Americans are not subjected to racial incidents on campus or in other ways made to feel unwelcome. Asian-American students have been more concerned about patterns of perceived discrimination in admissions rather than overt racial prejudice, although some recent incidents have increased consciousness of racism. Chicano students seek to expand the presence of Hispanic culture on campus and to increase the numbers of Hispanic students in American higher education.

A key flashpoint of controversy on which all of the minority communities agree is the presence of multicultural and minority studies in the curriculum. Minority students have dealt with this issue on two fronts—demanding the expansion of minority studies programs such as Afro-American studies and Asian-American studies and calling for the interaction of minority and multicultural perspectives in the liberal arts curriculum. These demands have aroused a good deal of opposition from faculty, who oppose tampering with the traditional curriculum, and often from administrators, who fear increased costs from the addition of new specializations and courses.

Minority students are the ones suffering racial slights, being affected by discriminatory practices in admissions and in general feeling alienated on many of America's campuses. It is also minority students who have, in most cases, stimulated crisis, either by reacting to racism on campus or by demanding that the university take action to meet their demands. In contrast to the volatile 1960s, the activism of the 1980s was in general, free of violence and generally low key in its rhetoric. Administrative reaction was also more measured than in an earlier period, although police were occasionally called to campus and disciplinary procedures were invoked. In a number of cases university administrators reacted to campus racial problems with ill-advised and sometimes heavy-handed actions that exacerbated the problems. For example, the refusal of Stanford's president to informally meet with students, albeit at short notice, resulted in calling in the local police and arrests, and a major confrontation was narrowly averted only when campus administrators muted their reaction. This reflects the failure of senior university leaders to recognize the seriousness of the problems and the potential for crisis.

During the 1980s, the bulk of student activism was related, in one way or another, to racial issues. The most important flashpoint of activism was related to South Africa and its apartheid racial policies. Hundreds of campuses saw demonstrations demanding university divestment of stocks of companies doing business in South Africa. In some cases, these protest movements were successful. In others, academic institutions made token changes and in still others, the movements did not gain much support.[3]

A second focus of campus activism was in reaction to racial incidents or gestures. Afro-American students sometimes protested these incidents to express their outrage and to direct campus attention to racial problems. There were more than two hundred such incidents that received press attention between 1986 and 1988—and very likely many more that were not widely reported. A final, less widespread, stimulus for activism was the demand for curricular reform to increase the multicultural content of the curriculum. Combined, these concerns generated more activism than, for example, issues like American intervention in Central America and the environment.

The campus racial situation tells us something about the society as well as about higher education. If the best-educated community in the United States—institutions of higher learning—has racial problems, then there is cause for considerable worry about the rest of society. And if better educated individuals, of whatever race, harbor racial prejudices which they occasionally express in random outbursts of racism, there are deep-seated problems both on campus and in society.

THE LEGACY OF REAGANISM

Race relations in America are affected by governmental policy, and the racial crisis on campus is very much a part of the legacy of Reaganism—the policies, and the atmosphere, of the federal government during Reagan's eight years in office. There are several key aspects of this legacy. One is a sense of lack of caring about racial issues in particular and social problems in general. The "Willie Horton" messages in George Bush's presidential campaign advertisements were very much part of this pattern. The lack of vigorous enforcement of civil rights laws, the taming of the U.S. Civil Rights Commission and official opposition to new anti-bias initiatives are all part of the social fabric woven during the Reagan years and enduring today. The kinds of appointments made by the Reagan administration to government posts send important messages. Not only were specific policies put into place and budgetary priorities implemented, but a tone was set which has pervaded statements from administration officials. Lack of concern for the problems of minorities, exhibited in high places, has a tendency to trickle down. For example, many campus administrators, never terribly enthusiastic about affirmative action goals, have put issues of racial equality on the back burner.

Specific governmental policies not only signaled a change in mood in Washington, but also directly affected minorities on campus. Governmental funds for virtually every program dealing with education were reduced in response to the double pressures of Reagan's military buildup and the growing budget deficit. Student loan programs were cut back and administrative and financial restrictions relating to them were increased. As a result, access to higher education was made more difficult. Enforcement of anti-bias and affirmative action policies was significantly weakened—so much so that both civil rights organizations and liberals in Congress vociferously complained. In general, funding for research in the hard sciences was protected better than money for minority programs.

The ethos and atmosphere was just as important as the specific policies. In the end, few government programs were actually canceled although many were underfunded or downplayed. The value of individual initiative was stressed and social responsibility downplayed or ignored. President Reagan's remarks questioning whether there were any homeless people in America were indicative of the mentality of the administration and the orientation toward social problems. Public statements by officials directly concerned with education and with law enforcement, such as Education Secretary Bennett and Attorney General Meese, buttressed both the style and the substance of the administration's approach. The combination of policy decisions, statements and orientations from an administration very much concerned with the mass media set a powerful tone for the national debate on issues of social policy and specifically concerning race relations.

Those in positions of academic leadership found themselves strapped for resources for programs relating to minority access and related matters. They also found that civil rights laws relating to affirmative action were not being rigorously enforced. It was easy, in this environment, to ignore campus-based racial issues. Students also noted the change in national policy and direction. For the first time in a number of years, subtle racism was "in." A vague white middle-class resentment against special programs for minorities in higher education and against affirmative action in general could be expressed in public. The meanspiritedness expressed in Washington was, in part, transferred to the campus. While it would be an exaggeration to blame the rise in campus racial incidents entirely on the legacy of the Reagan administration, there is little doubt that white students were affected by the changing national atmosphere regarding race relations. The Reagan legacy, muted but not basically altered by the Bush administration, has been a key factor in shaping the campus debate about race relations as well as both national and university policies affecting race.

MINORITY TRENDS ON CAMPUS

Important to the campus racial situation are developments with regard to the number of minority students and faculty in American higher education. Many of the programs started in the past several decades have been aimed at increasing the number of minorities in the universities, and particularly at raising the Afro-American population in higher education. During the 1970s, the numbers of minorities in the undergraduate student population increased dramatically. By the 1980s, however, the growth rate for most minorities slowed significantly. In 1985, 87.3 percent of the student population was Caucasian, while 8.1 percent was Afro-American, 1.6 percent Hispanic and 2.1 percent Asian-American. The only group showing continued rapid growth is Asian-Americans. Minority participation in graduate education has shown a dramatic decline in growth, with significant implications for future minority participation in the academic professions.

It is necessary to look carefully at these trends, since there are significant variations in the minority population. There are, overall, fewer Afro-Americans in the high-prestige sector of American higher education. Their numbers tend to be concentrated in less selective public colleges, in community colleges and of course in the traditionally black institutions. Urban Afro-American males are especially underrepresented. However, the Afro-American middle class has expanded dramatically in recent years and their rates of college attendance are as high, if not higher, than comparable populations in the majority population.

Asian-Americans overall are overrepresented in the student population in terms of their numbers in the general population, although again there are significant variations within the Asian-American community.[4] Japanese- and Chinese-Americans participate in higher education in extremely high proportions. Some of the newer immigrant groups, however, such as Laotians and Vietnamese, remain underrepresented. In addition, Asian-American enrollments are skewed with regard to fields of study. The large bulk of Asian-American enrollments are in fields such as engineering and the sciences. Very few Asian-Americans major in the humanities or social sciences. Asian-Americans now constitute a significant minority of students at many of the nation's most prestigious and selective schools and this too has caused some controversy. At the University of California there have been charges that university officials discriminate against Asian-Americans so that their proportions in California's most selective state institutions will not rise too high.[5] The Asian-American community itself has also been concerned about perceived discrimination in admissions.

Trends in graduate enrollments of minorities are also a cause for concern. At a time when there has been a renewed emphasis on hiring

Afro-American faculty members, the number of Afro-Americans going on to graduate school has been declining. Afro-Americans are underrepresented in virtually all fields of study; enrollments are especially low in the sciences and in engineering. This creates problems, of course, when it comes to hiring Afro-American faculty, since the pool of doctoral degree holders is very low. Asian-American graduate enrollments have been growing, but mainly in a few fields in the sciences and in medicine.

The patterns of minority student enrollment are complex and at the present time not very optimistic. Not only has Afro-American and Hispanic growth slowed significantly at all levels, and is a particular problem at the graduate level, it tends to be concentrated in certain regions and in particular kinds of institutions.

THE RACIAL BACKLASH ON CAMPUS

The question naturally arises: Why have there been more than two hundred reported incidents of racial confrontation in American colleges and universities in the past several years? Why now? And why in some of the nation's most prestigious institutions? There are some generalizations that can be made.

As noted earlier, there is little doubt that what we have called the "legacy of Reaganism" plays an important role. The idea that racial intolerance is somehow acceptable in society naturally percolates down to the campus level. Academic institutions are caught in the difficult situation of having made a commitment to serve minority students, but then finding it difficult to serve them adequately. The problem is partly fiscal—special educational and other programs for minority students are expensive. The problem is also the lack of staff, particularly teaching faculty, who are familiar with minority issues and who can provide role models. In this situation, minority students are sometimes themselves unable to keep up with their compeers, who often have a better academic preparation in high school. It is difficult for them to obtain the additional assistance that they need. This breeds frustration.

While minority students may be frustrated by their situation, white students may be resentful of what they perceive as special advantages given to minorities. Variable admissions standards designed to permit more minority students to be admitted are widely discussed on campus by majority students. They feel that minority students with fewer qualifications are being accepted, and others with higher test scores and better high school records are denied entry. Majority students may also resent the special programs provided to minorities—programs which are costly and require the use of scarce resources.

In recent years, there has been no lessening of separation of the races in many American colleges and universities. Minority students have often demanded and received separate dormitories or other arrangements. In such situations there is less informal interaction among racial groups. Races mingle in class but only infrequently socially. While there is very little research on the implications of racial separation in colleges, it does not seem likely that these arrangements would contribute to racial understanding and close relationships. On the other hand, separation may have other advantages in terms of self-esteem for minority students and an environment which is less pressured.

In the less political atmosphere of the 1980s, students have less ideological or moral commitment to racial harmony. In earlier decades, the spirit of the civil rights movement and of a moral commitment to a struggle for racial equality in the United States had an impact on campus. Now, the "me generation" is overwhelmingly concerned with careers and with personal matters, and less concerned about social issues.[6] This lack of an ideological and moral anchor for good race relations has had some impact on white students. It has probably affected minority students as well in the sense that there is relatively little political activism in the minority communities as well as in the white communities and, to some extent, that separatist ideologies have had some impact on minority students. On those rare occasions where student activism had been a force on campus, Afro-American and white students cooperated effectively. This was true during the anti-apartheid demonstrations of the mid-1980s. Multiracial coalitions have also been formed when campus racial tensions have boiled over, and these have generally been quite effective in uniting majority and minority students to work for common goals.

In many of the incidents of racial intolerance that have stimulated campus crises, the original incident was relatively trivial. The perpetrator, typically a white student, often from a fraternity, had little idea the reaction the precipitating event, such as defacing a poster or making a racially biased remark, would cause. Such fairly minor happenings generally go unnoticed in today's racially and ethnically charged campus environment. The perpetrators, in general, "meant no harm." In some instances, such as the well-publicized series of events at Dartmouth College, conservative student groups sought to make ideological points relating to South Africa, affirmative action or other issues, and their campaigns became racially oriented, going far beyond the original intention.

What, then, do the racial incidents that have taken place on campus mean in the broader context of American higher education and for campus race relations? It is clear that there is an undercurrent of racial animosity among American students. It is perhaps related to a resurgence of ethnic identity which has characterized the campuses—and much of society as well. Young people seem to value ethnic self-identification now more than in the recent past. On the other hand, American college students are in general liberal on racial questions and in general supportive of assistance to groups in the population needing special help, including affirmative action programs. Yet, when such programs are perceived to affect the opportunities and perquisites of middle-class, white college students, attitudes seem to be significantly less liberal.

Racial incidents have to some extent polarized campuses where they have occurred. Race, at least during the crisis, becomes a key point of debate and identity. There is inevitably a residue of bitterness and disillusionment. Racial incidents have perplexed campus administrators and faculty. Confident of their own goodwill and enlightened attitudes, the crises have come as an unpleasant surprise. How, they think, can this happen on a campus devoted to intellectual inquiry and which has supported civil rights and other campaigns? There is also a feeling of betrayal and perhaps resentment at the "ingratitude" of minority students. At many universities, even where racial incidents have been started by white students, it is often minority students who are first subjected to arrest or other disciplinary procedures. In sum, racial incidents have created confusion in the academic community.

THE ACADEMIC DIMENSION

The racial situation on campus has had important academic implications. The establishment of minority studies programs is without any question a result of the student struggles of the 1960s and later years.[7] There was little enthusiasm by either faculty or administrators for the addition of minority studies departments or programs (or women's studies for that matter) and this lack of support generally remains. In general, minority studies have not been lavishly supported in most universities, and departments and programs are relegated to the periphery of the institution. During periods of fiscal difficulties, minority studies programs have been under attack and often slated for cuts. There is general agreement among faculty and administrators that these programs are not central to the mission of the university.

Yet, through political pressure and activist movements, the number of Afro-American studies programs and departments grew dramatically during the 1960s and early 1970s, although there was a consolidation and some decline in the number of total programs. Somewhat more recently, programs devoted to Hispanic and Asian-American studies have been established and they are still expanding. The even more widespread development of women's studies programs, which grew around the same period, is beyond the scope of this essay.[8] Despite lukewarm academic support, these programs are by now fairly well institutionalized and are perhaps the most important legacy of the campus unrest of the 1960s and the rise of racial consciousness among minority groups in American higher education.

Minority studies programs are, of course, not without their problems. For a period during the vocationally oriented 1970s, they lost significant support from students. To some extent, they have become "ghettoized" low-status programs catering only to members of minority groups. In part because universities have left significant control over faculty appointments in the hands of "mainstream" departments and disciplines, minority studies departments have only limited autonomy.

Race and ethnicity have also become important and highly controversial elements in current debates about the curriculum in American higher education. The first element of the struggle was to obtain recognition and legitimation for the existence of minority studies, both as a concept and then as an administrative entity on campus. Later, and particularly during the debates which led to the reestablishment of the liberal arts curriculum in many academic institutions, race and ethnicity themselves became a part of the debate. Academic traditionalists—including those who led the fairly successful struggle for the primacy of the liberal arts curriculum—were never supportive of minority studies. The focus was on the traditional concept of the liberal arts curriculum.[9]

Since 1987, debate has taken place in many colleges and universities concerning the nature of the liberal arts curriculum and the role of minority studies in it. The struggle over the curriculum at Stanford has been particularly active and has been widely reported in the media. When Education Secretary William Bennett came to Stanford to speak out against "watering down" the traditional liberal arts curriculum, a national debate ensued. Traditionalists at Stanford argued the established "canon" of accepted (and entirely Western) scholarship constituted the appropriate core of studies for undergraduates. Proponents of change favored the inclusion of material that reflected a wider cultural and racial experience, arguing that American culture is no longer solely Eurocentric, and that to understand both an increasingly complex and interdependent world and a nation which has grown more multicultural it is necessary to significantly expand the curriculum. After more than a year of acrimonious debate by the Stanford faculty, the curriculum was expanded amidst considerable grumbling by the conservative faculty.

The Stanford debate, thanks in part to Secretary Bennett, received the widest national attention but it was mirrored at many universities around the country, with the usual result being some expansion in the curricular horizons for undergraduates.[10] These debates have been of considerable importance for the nature of the curriculum because they go to the heart of conceptions of knowledge and what is appropriate for students to learn. It is clear that without pressure from the minority student communities most universities would not have agreed to curricular change since there is considerable faculty support for the traditional curricular view.

A final arena of contention relating to campus racial issues is the complex area of minority participation in the academic enterprise at all levels. Sometimes referred to as "affirmative action," there has been much controversy concerning the admission of minority students, the recruitment and retention of minority faculty and related issues. Due in part to legal requirements from the federal government and, in the case of public universities, to political pressures from state governments, and in part from an institutional sense of responsibility and an understanding of the changing demographics of American life, many colleges and universities have tried to increase minority representation on campus. These efforts have met with some success over the past several decades.

The problems of minority representation in both the student population and in the academic profession are multifaceted. It is fair to say that there has been considerable resistance by departments and programs to the rigorous enforcement of affirmative action guidelines—both for women and racial minorities. Most academics may be in favor of equal access to the academic profession but they are less than enthusiastic about preferential hiring quotas or pressure to hire staff from minority groups. There has also been a serious problem of an appropriate pool of racial minority candidates for many fields. The number of Afro-American doctoral recipients in mathematics, for example, is extraordinarily small and is declining. In part as a result of campus racial unrest, a number of institutions have committed themselves to significantly increasing the numbers of minority faculty members in the coming few years. The combination of demographic realities, traditional faculty resistance and fiscal problems will make reaching such goals difficult if not impossible.

The American student population has become significantly more diverse in recent years; it represents a wider social-class base and includes more racial minorities than ever before. Afro-Americans and Hispanics remain seriously underrepresented at the most prestigious universities and colleges. In some fields (such as engineering and computer science) they are also dramatically underrepresented. Minorities seem to have a relatively high dropout rate and fewer go on to graduate or advanced professional education.

And, as noted earlier, the trajectory of progress in terms of minority enrollments has slowed at the same time that the proportion of racial minorities in the American population is increasing.

The inclusion of a significant number of minorities on campus has had implications for academic institutions—implications that have not been fully understood. In the early period of active minority recruitment, academic institutions were not successful in providing adequate support services for these new students and, not surprisingly, dropout rates were extraordinarily high. Later, it was recognized that minority students often required special assistance to overcome the handicaps of frequently inferior secondary school preparation and to manage in, for them, an unfamiliar and often hostile environment. The provision of such services has proved costly in terms of financial and staff resources and, as noted earlier, has engendered some resentment from majority students.

In a way, the success of academic institutions in increasing minority enrollments and in serving minority student populations has contributed to the racial incidents of the past several years. Minorities on campus have become more visible and the programs to serve them have attracted attention as well. The fact is that it is always easy to express liberal opinions on issues which are distant from everyday realities and have few implications. It is more difficult to combine liberal attitudes and behavior when theoretical issues have concrete reality on campus. Both white racism and Afro-American separation may in part be reflections of this situation.

CONCLUSION

American higher education faces some dilemmas in terms of dealing with race and minority issues. *In loco parentis* was virtually abandoned in the aftermath of the turmoil of the 1960s and students are viewed as adults who should be able to take care of themselves. There are few rules governing student life anymore. At the same time, universities are considered responsible for helping to shape the racial attitudes of students and are widely criticized for racial incidents that take place. Universities cannot solve society's problems nor can they compensate for government policies which have contributed to racial tensions. Yet they are expected to provide a model for other societal institutions in terms of their programs for minorities and the general atmosphere on campus. Ideally, universities are meritocratic institutions, where judgments about individual performance are supposed to be made solely on the basis of qualifications and merit. At the same time, affirmative action programs and special admissions criteria vitiate pure meritocratic ideals, as do sports and social-class background. Universities are key "sorting" institutions in society, providing credentials based putatively on merit for many key positions. But there are pressures to take minority status into account.

In many ways, society has asked colleges and universities to solve deep problems which it is unable or unwilling to solve for itself. It is not surprising that the tensions and sometimes the conflicts that are evident in society are transferred to the campus. The academic community has been surprisingly successful, in the context of fiscal difficulties and a mission that stresses traditional teaching and research rather than the solution of complex social problems, to accommodate the multifaceted challenges of contemporary racial and minority issues. The crises of the past few years, relating to intergroup relations, the curriculum, the academic profession and the mission of higher education as it relates to minorities, have proved to be disruptive and difficult.

The academic community has tried, with some success, to find solutions to racial problems. There is a significant consciousness on campus concerning race and minority questions. After much debate, changes have been made in the curriculum to reflect a wider cross-cultural experience. Minority studies programs have been established and institutionalized. Resources have been found to support minorities. After some initial errors by administrators in reacting to the tensions, it seems that there is a growing commitment to solving intergroup problems on campus and creating a positive campus climate.

NOTES

1. Everett Carll Ladd, Jr. and Seymour Martin Lipset, *The Divided Academy: Professors and Politics* (New York: McGraw-Hill, 1975), pp. 37–52.

2. Edward Shils, *The Academic Ethic* (Chicago: University of Chicago Press, 1982).

3. Philip G. Altbach and Robert Cohen, "American Student Activism: The Post-Sixties Transformation," *Journal of Higher Education* 61 (January–February 1990): pp. 32–49.

4. Jayjia Hsia, *Asian Americans in Higher Education and at Work* (Hillside, New Jersey: Lawrence Erlbaum, 1988).

5. See *Asian Americans at Berkeley: A Report to the Chancellor* (Berkeley: University of California, 1989). See also "Report of the Special Committee on Asian American Admissions of the Berkeley Division of the Academic Senate, University of California, Berkeley, 1989" and, for a national perspective, Julie Johnson," Asian Americans Press Fight for Wider Top-College Door," *New York Times* (September 9, 1989), pp. 1, 8.

6. Arthur Levine, *When Dreams and Heroes Died: A Portrait of Today's College Student* (San Francisco: Jossey-Bass, 1980).

7. See Alexander Astin et al., *The Power of Protest* (San Francisco: Jossey-Bass, 1975).

8. For a discussion of the development of women's studies in American higher education, see Ellen Dubois et al., *Feminist Scholarship: Kindling in the Groves of Academe* (Urbana, Illinois: University of Illinois Press, 1986).

9. For an extreme statement of the traditionalist position, replete with attacks on minority studies, see the very influential book, Allan Bloom, *The Closing of the American Mind* (New York: Simon and Schuster, 1987). E.D. Hirsch, in his book *Cultural Literacy: What Every American Needs to Know* (Boston: Houghton Mifflin, 1987), also argues by implication that minority studies is not a central concern of higher education.

10. For a typical debate concerning trends in the curriculum featured in the American intellectual press, see "Culture Wars: Knowledge, Power and the Loaded Canon," *Voice Literary Supplement* (January–February, 1989), pp. 1–35. The specific situation at Stanford is discussed from the perspective of an Afro-American student in Steven C. Phillips, "When Words Collide," *Voice Literary Supplement* (January–February, 1989), p. 30.

LEWIS C. SOLMON AND
TAMARA L. WINGARD

Chapter 2

The Changing Demographics:
Problems and Opportunities

INTRODUCTION

Before discussing the future trends for minority students and faculty in American higher education, and the policies implied by these, it is important to understand the overall current and future demographics of our nation. Population trends affect demand for higher education, as well as supply of students and faculty available to the various postsecondary institutions. A college-going population which is more ethically and racially diverse than in the past will have different needs than previous generations of higher education participants. The supply of undergraduates depends on the number of students who are able to persist through high school and then enter college. Similarly, the supply of faculty depends on the number of individuals who are able to persist to the doctorate degree and then choose to enter the field of academics. Such academic and career choices are functions of adequate preparation early in the student's educational experiences, the ability of an individual to finance the many years in school, and the values and attitudes of students and society toward higher education.

The increased number of births during the postwar baby boom (1946 to 1964) led to an unprecedented expansion in American higher education seventeen to nineteen years later. In the late 1950s, the number of births began to decline; however, the expected decline in college enrollments eighteen years later was never realized. Rapid growth in the number of 18 year olds ceased in the mid-1970s, yet between that time and approximately 1982 we observed a relatively constant number of eighteen year olds in the population. After 1982, however, the number of eighteen year olds began to decline sharply and will continue to do so until the late 1990s. Clearly, this indicates that enrollments will decline dramatically between now and the end of the twentieth century, but also, the composition of the student body will change greatly. Although birth rates are the most important predictor of college enrollments approximately eighteen years in the future, there are a number of additional influences, so that birth rates do not transform into an exact predictor of subsequent college enrollments. The most significant influence beyond birth rates is the fact that the United States has always been an attractive place to which citizens of other countries immigrate. In general, as long as the standard of living in the United States remains far superior to that in many other parts of the world, there will be serious pressure from foreigners to seek entry into the United States through legal or illegal means.

Factors influencing the relationship between birth rates and college enrollments fall into two basic categories. The first of these is related to economics and the labor market. As we know, there was an increased number of eighteen year olds who entered college during the early and mid-1970s, due primarily to the postwar baby boom. As a result, some argued that since more and more college graduates were entering the labor market each year, the supply of college graduates for the labor force would increase relative to demand for them. Conversely, the availability of those eighteen year olds with less than a college education would decline. This was predicted to result in a relative scarcity of lesser skilled workers, and an increase in the rate of return to a high school education compared to a college education, and so, incentives would arise for individuals to enter the labor market rather than attend college.[1]

The number of jobs traditionally held by college graduates before the baby boom did not grow as quickly as did the number of graduates during the 1960s and 1970s. Nevertheless, the rate of return, or the difference between the earnings of a college graduate and a high school graduate adjusted for the incremental costs of attending college (which include foregone earnings), have not declined as expected.[2] Many college graduates found themselves entering the labor market and accepting jobs that were previously held by individuals with less than a college education. In turn, these jobs expanded to take advantage of the additional skills and talents exhibited by the college graduates and the earnings of college graduates held up.[3] It was also the case that unemployment rates have always been lower for college graduates. These economic factors, as well as the realization that people attend college for reasons other than economic ones, served to support the desire for a post high school education despite the fact that there were so many people with college degrees.

The second set of factors which affect the correlation between birth rates and subsequent college enrollments involve the standards and activities of educational institutions at the pre-collegiate level. Since a larger proportion of individuals were graduating from high school, the proportion of 18 year olds who were eligible for college increased. Moreover, since the system of higher education as a whole had expanded in order to accommodate the growing cohort of baby boom students; however, after the boom, colleges were faced with lower enrollments, and as a result, were forced to admit greater proportions of a smaller high school graduating class simply to survive. It is clear that the signaling effects of a college degree are not weaker than they were in the past when very few people attended college. Now, the mere possession of a college diploma is no guarantee that the innate and acquired talents of the degree recipient are equal to those of college graduates in previous generations. As a result, those students who are truly capable seek to distinguish themselves by attending colleges where prior standards have been maintained. The result is that the more elite public and private institutions get greater numbers of applicants, while the total number of 18 year olds entering college is declining.

Although the post baby boom period was characterized by overall decreasing birth rates, minority birth rates and minority immigration has increased. As a result, the potential number of minority students at all levels of schooling is increasing. Yet, high school completion patterns, progression to higher education rates and college graduation statistics are very different for minority students than for White or Asian students. It is important to note that Asians are not included in this study as "minority" students. This is due to the fact that traditionally, Asians are not underrepresented in the American school system. Secondly, the 1980 Census did not categorize Asians as a group separate from Whites; and, as a result, there is not significant data to generalize on the behavior of Asians as a unique ethnic group. In the future, as the number of immigrants from Asian countries increases and diversifies, Asians as a whole may resemble more closely other ethnic minorities. As a result, the 1990 Census may provide different data which will enable us to explore the behavior of Asians more accurately.

The percentage of minority graduates from high school is lower than that of White or Asian students, and similarly, progression rates for minority students are low. Overall minority enrollment in higher education is extremely low (17% in 1984) and that representation varies greatly from state to state. By graduate school, the number of minority students has decreased even more, and those students who receive graduate degrees are often wooed into the business sector, and so, few remain in academe. There is little financial incentive for any quality Ph.D. to take an academic position when jobs in the private sector are available; however, there is particular competition for minority candidates who are being recruited by the business sector as well as institutions of higher education. There is a limited supply of minority doctorates, yet the demand for these people is very high. As a result, it is difficult for each institution of higher education to meet their faculty affirmative action and diversity goals.

THE NUMBER OF TRADITIONAL-AGED STUDENTS
ENTERING COLLEGE

The most detailed breakdowns of populations by age, race and ethnicity come in the Census years (years ending in zero). Therefore, 1980 is the most recent year from which these statistics are available. Using this information, we are able to learn the number of Whites, Blacks, and Hispanics of each age for the nation, regions, and states. We developed our initial projection of the number of 18 year olds (the modal age of college entrants) by looking at individuals in each specific year of age from "under one" to 18. Ignoring the possibility that some individuals will die before they turn 18 and, for the moment, the fact that there will be immigrants from other nations, we assumed that these age cohorts will translate directly into 18 years old in the future. For example, we assumed that all those who were 17 years old in 1980 would become 18 years old in 1981; those who were 16 in 1980 would be the 18 year olds in 1982 and so on until those under one year of age would be the 18 year olds in 1998(Chart 1).

CHART 1
18 Year Olds

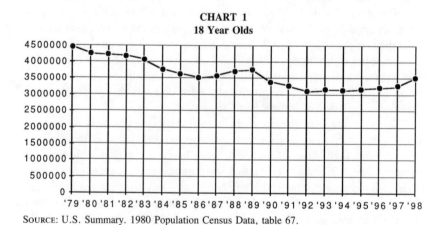

SOURCE: U.S. Summary. 1980 Population Census Data, table 67.

Based on the 1980 Census data, there was a steady decline in the number of 18 year olds between 1979 and 1986 for the nation as a whole. From 1986 to 1989 there will be a slight increase; however, a subsequent decline will occur from 1989 to 1992. Between 1979 and 1992 the total population of 18 year olds in the United States will have fallen from 4,451,724 to 3,109,095. Between 1992 and 1997 the number of 18 year olds will be relatively steady with a very slight increase, from 3,109,095 to 3,269,557. The rate of growth accelerates again after 1997 with the increase resulting in an 18 year old population of 3,533,692 in 1998 (Table 1). During the first seven years between 1979 and 1988 we will have experienced a 21 percent decline in the number of 18 year olds. The next three years will yield a seven percent increase, while a 17 percent decline will be seen in the following three years; finally, an increase of five percent will be experienced over the next five years followed by an increase of eight percent in the last year. The lowest 18 year old population will be seen in 1992 when the number of 18 year olds will be 30 percent below the number in 1979. At the end of the period, in 1998, the number of 18 year olds will be 20 percent less than the number in 1979. Broken down by race, we expect to see a nationwide drop of over 868,000 White 18 year olds, a drop of 69,000 Black 18 year olds, and an increase of almost 34,000 Hispanic 18 year olds by the year 1998.

PATTERNS OF HIGH SCHOOL COMPLETION

The next issue to be addressed is of the potential college-entering cohort, what proportion of these individuals will actually graduate from high school? According to the U.S. Bureau of the Census (1986), we know that 67.6 percent of 18 year olds had completed high school in October of 1985; additionally, 81.5 percent of 19 year olds had graduated from high school. Since the survey from which these figures are based was taken in October, conceivably some 18 year olds could still graduate in their 18th year.

Historically, we know that prior to 1930, graduates as a percentage of the 17 year old population did not exceed 30 percent. This was an increase from roughly two percent in 1869–70 to 29 percent in 1929–30. By 1939–40, our nation had achieved a high school graduation rate (compared to the 17 year old population) of over 50 percent. Also, the share of high school graduates had risen from 50.8 percent in 1939–40 to a peak of over 77 percent in 1968–69. During the 1960's there were particularly high rates of high school graduation, usually over 75 percent. However, beginning in 1973, the proportion of 17 year olds graduating from high school declined steadily until approximately 1980 when the figure was 71.8 percent. Since

TABLE 1

Number and Percent Change in 18 Year Olds

	National Total	Y2/Y1	White Total	Y2/Y1	Black Total	Y2/Y1	Hispanic Total	Y2/Y1
1979	4,451,724		3,587,991		600,008		334,102	
1980	4,251,779	0.9551	3,417,053	0.9524	589,101	0.9818	319,622	0.9567
1981	4,223,848	0.9934	3,380,772	0.9894	600,169	1.0188	324,585	1.0155
1982	4,180,875	0.9898	3,343,837	0.9891	600,439	1.0004	316,742	0.9758
1983	4,059,898	0.9711	3,232,449	0.9667	595,146	0.9912	311,277	0.9827
1984	3,782,784	0.9317	2,992,789	0.9259	567,872	0.9542	297,613	0.9561
1985	3,643,189	0.9631	2,889,432	0.9655	537,569	0.9466	289,555	0.9729
1986	3,518,982	0.9659	2,786,155	0.9643	517,587	0.9628	285,634	0.9865
1987	3,580,644	1.0175	2,846,168	1.0215	513,788	0.9927	292,372	1.0236
1988	3,716,530	1.0380	2,946,378	1.0352	536,456	1.0441	309,824	1.0597
1989	3,760,120	1.0117	2,968,127	1.0074	549,963	1.0252	319,936	1.0326
1990	3,394,998	0.9029	2,658,627	0.8957	506,709	0.9214	301,298	0.9417
1991	3,273,052	0.9641	2,539,701	0.9553	498,320	0.9834	305,492	1.0139
1992	3,109,095	0.9499	2,410,344	0.9491	467,645	0.9384	299,199	0.9794
1993	3,162,691	1.0172	2,456,167	1.0190	468,080	1.0009	311,256	1.0403
1994	3,141,748	0.9934	2,428,232	0.9886	469,947	1.0040	317,896	1.0213
1995	3,179,441	1.0120	2,460,551	1.0133	470,660	1.0015	324,066	1.0194
1996	3,223,816	1.0140	2,497,249	1.0149	477,708	1.0150	324,950	1.0027
1997	3,269,557	1.0142	2,528,598	1.0126	486,890	1.0192	328,216	1.0101
1998	3,533,692	1.0808	2,719,445	1.0755	530,964	1.0905	368,045	1.1213

SOURCE: U.S. Summary. 1980 Population Census Data, table 67.

that time, the share of high school graduates has increased slightly such that in the last few years for which data are available the rate is once again over 73 percent. The National Center for Educational Statistics (NCES) projections of college enrollments are based upon the assumption that 72.6 percent of 18 year olds will graduate from high school between 1983 and 1994.[4]

There are dramatic differences in high school completion rates according to race and ethnic origin. For the total 18 and 19 year old population, the high school graduation rate was 73.4 percent in 1974 and 74.6 percent in 1985. As can be seen, the completion rates were consistent throughout this period. Broken down by race, 18 and 19 year old Whites had a graduation rate of 76.2 percent in 1974 and 76.7 percent in 1985. In the early part of the 1980's, the White completion rate fell to slightly under 75 percent. These figures contrast significantly with high school graduation rates for the same age cohort of Blacks and Hispanics. The completion rate for Blacks was 55.8 percent in 1974 and has risen steadily to achieve a 62.8 percent rate by 1985. The high school completion rate for Hispanics was 48.9 percent in 1974 and 49.8 percent in 1985.

It is important to note that when we look at high school graduation rates as a proportion of 18 to 24 year olds, the rates are substantially higher because the individuals involved have many more years in which to complete high school. The 1974 high school graduation rate for people 18 to 24 years old, for all races, was 80.7 percent and rose to 81.6 percent in 1984.[5] For Whites, the rate increased from 82.7 percent to 83.0 percent. A marked increase from 67.1 percent to 74.7 percent was noted for Black students, while the rate for those of Spanish origin rose from 55.9 percent to 60.1 percent. It is clear that a significant proportion of the non-White population graduates from high school; however, often completion occurs beyond their 18th or 19th year.

A look at historical trends indicates that the proportion of Whites graduating from high school seems to peak at about 80 percent. It is also evident that high school completion rates for both Blacks and Hispanics are substantially below the 80 percent level, but are increasing at a slow, steady rate. Currently, the problem of high school dropouts, particularly among minorities, is one of the most urgent social issues. There is a great deal of discussion about both the economic and social costs when people drop out of high school. The dropout rate has become a measurable target at which politicians, corporate leaders, and other in our society can aim. Due to the increased attention given to this problem, there is every reason to be optimistic that minority rates of high school graduation will rise between now and the end of the 1990's. However, White high school completion rates are most likely to remain constant given their current high levels. This overall improvement, along with the demographics discussed earlier, emphasize that the pool of students available to institutions of higher education will become increasingly dominated by currently underrepresented groups.

It is important to note that due to data limitations, nothing has been said about Asian students. This population has been extremely successful in American schools and colleges. Additionally, Asians have a low high school dropout rate and a high rate of progression into college. They are also the largest component of our immigration from abroad in recent years. Thus, if the Asian population was included in this discussion, the conclusions we have drawn regarding the increasing dominance of minorities in American higher education would be magnified. However, we must caution that there is no conclusive evidence indicating that newly arrived Asians will resemble those already here, or that these immigrants will resemble more closely other minority groups which we have discussed.

RATES OF PROGRESSION INTO COLLEGE

This next issue is how many of the high school graduates actually progress into college. These figures have remained relatively consistent between 1974 and 1985 at levels in the 40 to 50 percent range.

In 1974, approximately 45 percent of White high school graduates entered college as 18 or 19 year olds. This percentage rose to about 49 percent over the next several years. In 1979 the progression rate dropped slightly to 47.5 percent, but rose to 55.9 percent in 1985. The share of Black 18 to 19 year old high school graduates who entered college in 1974 was 41.6 percent. This figure rose for the next two years before falling to 45.7 percent in 1977. The Black progression rate then declined steadily between 1978 and 1985 when it reached a low of 38.5 percent. The Hispanic rate of progression from high school graduation to college entry in 1974 was higher than the ratio for either Blacks or Whites, 49 percent; however, the rate has declined to 44.7 percent in 1985.

The pattern of high school graduation rates for Whites, Blacks and Hispanics is substantially more diverse than that of progression rates of high school graduates into college. When these two ratios are combined, the percentage of the population in college (which is the product of the high school graduation rate and the progression rate) is substantially higher for Whites than for Backs and Hispanics. Until 1983, the share of 18 and 19 year old Blacks in higher education was greater than the share of Hispanics; however, after 1983, the two groups revealed approximately equal shares in college. The proportion of 18 and 19 year old White college attenders rose between 1974 and 1985 from 34.4 percent to 42.9 percent. The proportion for Blacks was 23.2 percent in 1974, rose to 27 percent in 1981, but since then has fallen to 24 percent. For Hispanics, the 1974 share was slightly under 24 percent. After reaching an all-time high of almost 27 percent in 1976, the Hispanic share fell to 22.3 percent in 1985.

It appears that the primary bottleneck which precludes Blacks and Hispanics from entering college when they are 18 and 19 years of age is their low rate of high school completion. Assuming that Blacks and Hispanics are more likely to graduate high school after the age of 18 or 19, we should observe increased rates of college entry once members of these groups reach their twenties. The data clearly reveal that any effort to increase graduation rates for Blacks and Hispanics would be beneficial. However, it is crucial that the standards of education remain at a high level, rather than lowering standards in order to improve the statistics. In the former case, higher completion rates for Blacks and Hispanics would indicate that these students were likely to be more successful in the labor market and other aspects of life than those who drop out. Also, without some type of a high school diploma, these students are unable to attend college.

In recent years, white progression rates have been rising. Consequently, there is hope that this same trend will be evidenced for other groups. Yet, the progression rate of Black high school graduates has fallen in recent years, while the Hispanic high school graduation rate has remained relatively steady.

It is important to identify the reasons for these divergent patterns of progression of high school graduates to college. Economic patterns clearly play a role. The desperate poverty facing many Black and Hispanic communities puts pressure on youngsters from these groups to drop out of high school and find a job. Even those students who complete high school feel the need to work rather than attend college. The ability for minority students to attend college decreases as college costs increase and availability of need-based financial aid declines. As student loan balances build up, so does pressure to drop out and find some type of job to pay them off. This is particularly true for members of low income groups who are less willing to incur large amounts of debt.

Arguments that the truly needy still have access to funds to pay for college fly in the face of the evidence of the declining share of Black high school graduates who are enrolling. Part of the problem is that Black and Hispanic graduates may have access to funds which cover all of the tuition and even perhaps incidental expenses related to college attendance; however, funds are rarely available to cover the earnings foregone by such youngsters when they enter college as opposed to taking even the most menial types of jobs. Many minority high school graduates cannot afford the luxury of deferring income when they see parents and younger siblings living in abject poverty. Thus, even if these high school graduates are qualified for college admittance, and even if they can obtain funds to pay for their college expenses, their need so support their families takes precedence over their desire to enter college. Additionally, as teenage pregnancy rates in the minority communities rise, students who might otherwise have attended college may drop out either to work in order to support their own young families or to stay home and look after their children.[6]

The only positive aspect of such a dismal description is that if policy makers recognize the economic pressures on many minority students, it is at least theoretically possible to begin reducing such pressures. Despite the severe deficits in the federal and some state budgets, it can be argued that the most effective expenditure of public funds and private philanthropy are those directed towards providing the support which would enable minorities to enter college and thereby begin working to break the cycle of poverty.

Clearly, policymakers must look beyond simply providing out-of-pocket college costs to qualified minorities. Until opportunity costs of attending college rather than joining the labor force are taken into consideration, the decision for many low SES and minority youth to enter college will continue to be a difficult one. One of the primary factors explaining minority patterns of enrollment by institutional type is the students' need to work. The community colleges in many states are unique in that they take into account the need for their students to work full-time. Thus, they are the only choice for students who must earn more than is currently available from any scholarship program.

A second set of factors explaining the lower minority rates of progression from high school graduation to college attendance compared to Whites involves the nature of the education obtained during the high school years. From 1974 to 1979, there were few discernible differences among progression rates for Whites, Blacks, and Hispanics. Since 1979, however, progression rates for Whites have risen slowly while those of Blacks and Hispanics have fallen. By 1985, 56 percent of White high school graduates entered college, while only 45 percent of Hispanic graduates and 38 percent of Black high school graduates made that same progression.

Ironically, these gaps have widened precisely during a period when pressure to reduce high school dropout rates and to increase high school graduation rates has mounted. As we alluded to earlier, one way of increasing the probability of high school graduation is to reduce standards. If, in order to increase minority graduation rates from high school, more minorities are tracked into general and vocational programs rather than into college preparatory programs, it is logical to expect a smaller proportion of minority graduates to enter college.

If standards are lowered such that work which previously would have led to failure and termination from high school is now viewed as acceptable to meet graduation standards, then it is also understandable why those who receive a high school diploma do not go on to college or persist there. There has been much effort in recent years to make sure that the high school diploma is not a devalued degree. It is necessary to get beyond the notion of a "quick fix" to the problem of low rates of high school graduation for minorities. Rather, we need to focus political and financial pressure on public high schools to lessen the dropout rates by providing minorities with real preparation for subsequent college study. If college attendance is emphasized, then it is possible that minority progression rates to college will increase over the next decade or so.

Several questions arise with regard to such a potential policy. First, will educational leaders at the high school level ever be able to take the long term view and insist upon appropriate graduation requirements even if that means higher dropout rates and lower graduation rates for minorities in the short run? Second, even if such a longer view were accepted, are the socioeconomic circumstances of many impoverished minorities such that higher standards can result in more graduates with a real preparation for college? Are we really facing a crisis which is purely educational, or are we facing one more deeply ingrained in social problems such as teenage pregnancy, gangs, drugs, the disintegration of the family, and the like? Clearly, some schools are under-funded and the quality and motivation of our teaching force might be lower than it was in previous generations. But can any level of funding and any level of teacher ability and training ever compensate for the dismal circumstances facing many minority youth today? If these problems can be successfully attacked, the representation of minorities in our institutions of higher education can and will increase.

COLLEGE CHOICE

As with high school graduation and college progression rates, first-time enrollment figures have fluctuated over the past two decades. Between 1970 and 1981, the fifty states and the District of Columbia together experienced a 25.8 percent increase in the first-time enrollments in their institutions of higher education.[7] From 1981 to 1984, this trend was reversed as first-time enrollments declined by 9.2 percent. Twice as many states experienced declining first-time enrollments over this time period than experienced increases (table 2). In general, except for in the Rocky Mountain and Far West regions, the decline in the independent sector was greater than the decline in the public sector. Since total college enrollments declined by approximately only 1 percent between 1981 and 1984, it is clear that the decline in first-time enrollments was more than made up by returning students

TABLE 2

Percent Change in First-Time Enrollments
(1981–1984)

State	Change
Nebraska	− 22.7
New Jersey	− 20.4
South Dakota	− 19.8
South Carolina	− 16.3
Colorado	− 16.1
California	21.8
Illinois	30.4
Nevada	84.0

SOURCE: American Council on Education (ACE). *Fact Book on Higher Education* (1987). Tables 92–93.

and by students who attended college beyond the traditional time period. Stability nationally does not necessarily mean that particular states or regions are experiencing that stability.

The NCES has calculated the percent of minorities, by state, enrolled in institutions of higher education for the fall of 1984. The percent is based on United States citizenship enrollment, which is the total enrollment less the enrollment of nonresident aliens. Overall, 17.4 percent of the fall 1984 enrollments in United States institutions of higher education were minorities. The range was from a high of 70.7 percent in Hawaii, to a low of 1.4 percent in Maine (table 3).

As we know, there is a differential distribution of minorities from state to state. This accounts for part of the reason for the wide variations in the minority representation in higher education across states. Related to this is the extent to which various racial/ethnic groups are represented in colleges in the same proportion as they are represented in the overall college age population. To illustrate this point, we will refer to the states of California and Texas. In California, although the college age population was 72.3 percent white, only 68.0 percent of undergraduate enrollments in 1984–85 were white. Similarly, in Texas, 76.1 percent of the college age population was white, while only 71.9 percent of undergraduate enrollments were white. In California, blacks made up 8.5 percent of the college age population, yet 6.7 percent of the actual enrollments were black. The comparable figures for Texas were 13.1 percent and 8.9 percent.[8]

While both whites and blacks are somewhat underrepresented in undergraduate enrollments in California and Texas, the underrepresentation of Hispanics is substantially larger. In California, although 22.6 percent of the college age population was Hispanic in 1984–85, only 10.4 percent of

TABLE 3

Percent of Minorities Enrolled in Institutions of Higher Education
(for Fall 1984)

State	Percent	State	Percent
Hawaii	70.7	Missouri	10.5
District of Columbia	39.3	Ohio	10.1
New Mexico	33.5	Washington	9.8
Mississippi	30.1	Pennsylvania	9.4
California	29.6	Kentucky	8.8
Louisiana	26.7	Kansas	8.7
Texas	25.4	Connecticut	8.3
Alabama	22.8	Indiana	8.2
South Carolina	22.2	Massachusetts	8.0
Georgia	21.5	South Dakota	7.6
Maryland	21.5	Oregon	7.3
Florida	21.3	Montana	6.3
New York	20.8	Wisconsin	6.3
North Carolina	20.6	Rhode Island	5.9
Illinois	19.4	North Dakota	5.2
New Jersey	18.2	Utah	5.2
Virginia	17.3	West Virginia	5.2
Arizona	17.0	Nebraska	5.1
Arkansas	16.8	Idaho	4.7
Tennessee	15.8	Iowa	4.3
Alaska	14.9	Wyoming	4.0
Michigan	12.7	Minnesota	3.9
Oklahoma	12.7	New Hampshire	2.7
Delaware	12.6	Vermont	2.1
Nevada	12.3	Maine	1.4
Colorado	10.8		

SOURCE: Digest of Educational Statistics, 1987, table 133.

enrollments were Hispanic; in Texas, the comparable figures were 21.9 percent and 13.1 percent. In both California and Texas, American Indian enrollments were at least equal to the proportion of American Indians in the college age population. In California, 0.9 percent of the population and 1.3 percent of the enrollments were American Indian, while in Texas, 0.3 percent of both the population and enrollments were American Indian. The situation for Asians is quite the opposite of what we have seen in the white, black, Hispanic and American Indian populations. In California, although 5.1 percent of the college age population is Asian, fully 10.2 percent of college enrollments are Asian. Similarly, although only 0.8 of 1 percent of the college age population are Asian, 2.1 percent of Texas enrollments are Asian.

Another reason which accounts for different states having different shares of minorities in their institutions of higher education is the fact that students, particularly white students, often leave their state of residence to attend college. Since blacks and Hispanics are more likely to be members of low SES groups, they are also most likely to attend college close to home.

One strategy used by institutions to combat declining enrollments is to retain as many of their own residents as possible. In addition, colleges and universities can recruit students from other states. This tactic is particularly useful for private schools. However, public institutions which receive state funding are under pressure to satisfy the enrollment demand from within the state before they begin looking elsewhere; out-of-state students may be viewed as receiving an unwarranted subsidy.

Perhaps the most important question regarding college choice is how first-time, full-time freshmen sort themselves into various types of institutions. The share of minority groups attending very highly selective private institutions, the most elite group of institutions, is small. Overall, approximately 1.2 percent of the minority college-going population attend the most elite schools. The specific minority group most likely to attend the elite colleges was Asians. Between 1976 and 1984, their share of the elite population rose from 1.4 percent to 2.5 percent. Alien residents' share in very highly selective private institutions rose from 1.6 percent to 2.2 percent. The white share of the same population was 1.2 percent in 1976, and this rose to 1.5 percent in 1984. Hispanics, blacks and American Indians generally saw less than 0.5 of 1 percent of their first-time, full-time freshmen attending very highly selective private institutions.

In general, all races, but particularly Hispanics, are most likely to begin their college careers in public two-year colleges. Previous research has indicated that the number of students who begin in two-year colleges and then continue to completion of the baccalaureate degree is very low. As a matter of fact, less than 10 percent of two-year students transfer to the four-year college or university. Thus, one way for four-year institutions to increase their enrollments is to encourage two-year college students to transfer after they receive their Associate of Arts (A.A.) degree. The problem is that high proportions of two-year college students drop out of school before even completing the A.A. degree. A great deal of work must be done to ensure persistence of two-year college students and their subsequent transfer to four-year institutions.

Of course, an underlying question in this regard is whether or not students enrolling in two-year colleges, particularly those who select vocational programs, have an interest in attaining more than a A.A. degree. Indeed, there is the question as to whether or not these students would be better served in the labor market by achieving a higher degree. Although some people in the four-year sector consider any students who do not attain a bachelor's degree to be failures, this certainly is not always the case. If we view some college attendance as being a greater achievement than no college experience, our perspective is very different than if we view one or two years of college as failing to achieve the objective of the bachelor's degree. The fact of the matter is that the bachelor's degree may not be the objective of many high school graduates.

With the exception of Asians, private universities as a whole attract small proportions of minority students. There are many reasons for these patterns, including higher tuition costs, the necessity to leave home and often travel substantial distances to attend, and in certain cases higher admissions standards. In the past, as long as there have been substantial numbers of middle-class whites, private institutions could be rather complacent in their recruiting efforts towards minorities. However, as the number of whites declines between now and the end of the century, it will become necessary for private institutions to reconsider their recruitment patterns. Additionally, these schools will need to strive to obtain more financial aid to support minority applicants.

There will be a great deal of interinstitutional competition for students over the next decade, and much of this competition will be for minority students. However, for a given pool of minority students, such competition is a zero-sum game. It would be much more fruitful to work at enlarging the pool. There will also be continued competition from the military and from the job market. Both of these are becoming increasingly attractive, particularly for low SES high school graduates, because the students are likely to receive job-related training, and are not required to forego a full-time income.

THE FUTURE OF THE FACULTY

As the number of nonwhites attending institutions of higher education increases, most colleges and universities are committed to increasing the minority representation on their faculties. Such efforts reflect in part the commitment by colleges and universities to expand opportunities for minority scholars. Moreover, the conventional wisdom is that by providing minority students with similar-race role models, and by having such role models provide multiracial perspectives in the appropriate disciplines, the interests, motivation and success of minority students will be enhanced.

Although the search for minority faculty often results in bidding wars for accomplished minority scholars and teachers, the result of such efforts do not serve to expand the total pool of minority faculty. If institution "A" moves to attract away a minority faculty member from institution "B", A's statistics are improved and B's are made worse; overall, minority students in this country are not better off because there is no increase in minority faculty. Hence, the population of minority faculty will be enlarged and total efforts regarding affirmative action will be expanded only when the pool of new Ph.D.'s is expanded and these individuals are hired into faculty positions.

Yet despite the gallant efforts of many college and university administrators, casual observation seems to indicate that the net increases of minority faculty have been minuscule. Certainly salaries of some minority stars have skyrocketed as a result of the bidding wars. However, most institutions find it very difficult to identify new minority Ph.D's to hire. Some conclude that if a particular institution does not hire many minorities, it simply is not trying hard enough. Before we agree with such charges, it is important to consider data on new Ph.D. production over the last fifteen or so years. Those data provide an alternative explanation for the lack of success experienced by most institutions of higher education when they attempt to hire nonwhite faculty.

Before looking at the numbers, it is important to ask what "counts" as affirmative action appointments today. The most stringent, and probably the most reasonable, definition of an affirmative action appointment is the hiring of a nonwhite American faculty member. Under such a definition, to hire a foreign-born, non-U.S. citizen who is not white, is not considered an affirmative action appointment. Thus, the discussion here will focus on U.S. citizens rather than on permanent residents or temporary residents or temporary residents who are citizens of other countries.

We focus on data on Ph.D.'s awarded in 1987, the most recent year for which data are available. As a point of comparison, we have selected 1974 for several reasons. That earlier year was a time of oversupply of Ph.D.'s in most fields and of very weak demand for faculty. The hiring boom of the late 1950s and 1960s had peaked several years earlier, and most of those hired during the era of high demand were many years from retirement. By 1987, many institutions were aware of the pending retirements of faculty who were hired in the 1950s and warranted it, but rather in anticipation of future retirements and of a time several years hence when competition for new faculty would heat up as it had in the mid-60s. In essence, some institutions decided that in order to get a jump on the competition, it made sense to appoint new faculty immediately rather than wait until the retirements actually took place and shortages reappeared.

In 1974, the number of Ph.D.'s awarded to United States citizens was 26,827, and this total fell to 22,863 by 1987. Between those years the number of Ph.D.'s awarded to permanent residents in the United States also fell, from 1,853 to 1,570. Non-United States citizens with temporary visas were the only group which saw the number of Ph.D.'s rise (from 3,447 in

1974 to 5,593 in 1987). Of course, not all new doctoral recipients expect to work in colleges and universities. In 1974, 55.6 percent of United States citizens who received Ph.D.'s expected to hold a job in an institution of higher education, and this proportion fell to 44.3 percent by 1987. On the other hand, the number of new Ph.D.'s anticipating a postdoctoral fellowship in 1974 was 13.2 percent and this number rose to 22 percent by 1987. These figures enable us to determine a range of new Ph.D.'s available to academe. On the one hand, a low estimate of the proportion moving into academe is those who already hold academic jobs when they receive their doctorates. A higher estimate is obtained by combining those anticipating jobs in higher education and those with postdoctoral fellowships if we assume that once the postdoctoral fellowships are concluded, the holders of them will move into academic jobs. By combining those with jobs in higher education and those holding postdoctoral fellowships, we see that the proportion of new Ph.D.'s available to academe fell from 69 percent in 1974 to 66 percent in 1987. Hence, using our lower estimate we find that the number of new Ph.D.,'s available for academe fell from 14,916 in 1974 to 10,228 in 1987, or to 68.6 percent of the 1974 figure. Using our higher estimate, the number of new Ph.D.'s available for academe fell from 18,457 to 15,158, or to 82.1 percent of the 1974 figure.

Even though the total pool of Ph.D.'s and those apparently available for academe fell between 1974 and 1987, opportunities for affirmative action appointments might have increased had the proportion of nonwhite United States citizens receiving doctorates risen commensurately with the ethnic distribution of the population. However, the proportion of white United States citizens receiving Ph.D.'s between 1974 and 1987 actually increased from 87.4 percent to 89 percent. By either our high or low estimate, whites were more likely than others to be available for academic jobs, and their proportion stayed relatively constant at about 89 percent over the period under consideration.

The lack of representation of nonwhite groups among Ph.D. recipients is striking despite the fact that the numbers of some minority groups receiving doctorates rose between 1974 and 1987. The number of American Indians who received doctorates decreased from 1974 to 1987; however, Asian-Americans saw an increase during the same time period. United States blacks received fewer doctorates in 1987 than they did in 1974, as did Mexican-Americans. Both Puerto Ricans and other United States Hispanics experienced an increase in doctorates in 1987 (table 4).

The figures just presented are low, and we have not reduced them by a proportion of Ph.D.'s who will take jobs outside of academe. Such a reduction would reduce the numbers dramatically in some fields, such as the physical sciences, which includes computer science, and engineering.

TABLE 4

Number of Doctorates Received

	1974	1987	Change
Total US	26,827	22,863	− 3,964
American Indian	129	116	− 13
Asian-American	293	540	247
Black	846	765	− 81
White	23,442	20,358	− 3,084
Puerto Rican	60	180	120
Mexican-American	195	174	− 21

SOURCE: National Research Council, Doctorate Recipients from United States Universitites, 1974 and 1987.

It is obvious that colleges and universities do not hire generic Ph.D.'s, but rather, particular departments seek faculty members with Ph.D.'s in specific fields. Therefore, the data with greatest relevance to affirmative action hiring policies are the numbers of Ph.D.'s awarded to various ethnic groups in particular groups of fields. For present purposes, we group disciplines into seven categories: physical sciences, engineering, life sciences, social sciences, humanities, education and other professional fields. It should be kept in mind that whatever number of Ph.D's were awarded to a particular ethnic group in, for example, the physical sciences, this still must be allocated among physics, chemistry, mathematics, computer science and so on. That is, the number of new Ph.D.'s available to any specific department is even smaller than the numbers presented here.

The 116 doctorates awarded to American Indians in 1987 reflects a decline from 1974 in degrees awarded in the physical sciences (to 10), in the humanities (to 11), and in education (to 41). American Indians received a few more Ph.D.'s in engineering (8 in 1987), life sciences (16 in 1987) and social sciences (22 in 1987). American Indians received the fewest Ph.D.'s in 1987 of any ethnic group. It seems clear that attempts to hire American Indian faculty by more than just a few institutions are futile at best.

Asian-Americans received 540 doctorates in 1987, almost twice the number that was awarded to this group in 1974. However, Asian-Americans received fewer doctorates in 1987 than in 1974 in humanities (25 in 1987) and education (41 in 1987). They received substantially larger numbers in all other fields: 104 in the physical sciences in 1987, 135 in engineering, 145 in life sciences, 75 in social sciences and 15 in other professional fields. Attempts to increase representation of Asian-Americans in departments of engineering and the physical and life sciences have some prospect of success at this time. It is also noteworthy that in virtually every field, the doctorates awarded to Asians who are permanent residents in the United States, and especially to Asians studying here on temporary visas, far exceed those awarded to Asian-Americans.

American blacks were awarded 765 doctorates in 1987, which is approximately 80 fewer than was awarded to them in 1974, and almost 300 fewer than the number awarded in 1980. More doctorates were awarded to American blacks in 1987 than in 1974 in the life sciences (resulting in 78 in 1987), the social sciences (136) and in other professional fields (58). Fewer doctorates were awarded to American blacks in 1987 than in 1974 in the physical sciences (29 in 1987), engineering (12), the humanities (73) and education (379). The concentration of black doctorate holders in the field of education represents a longstanding tradition, though it is discouraging that the proportion in education has fallen over the last thirteen years. Nevertheless, it is clear that other than in education and possibly the social sciences, the availability of new black Ph.D.'s is small.

As seen in table 5, the number of Puerto Ricans receiving doctorates tripled from 60 to 180 between 1974 and 1987. Except for engineering, where the number of doctorates awarded fell from 7 to 4, every field saw an increase in doctorates awarded to Puerto Ricans. However, the absolute numbers in virtually all fields were very small in 1987:33 in physical sciences, 28 in the life sciences, 21 in the social sciences, 31 in the humanities, 53 in education and 10 in other professional fields. The number of doctorates awarded to Mexican-Americans (174) in 1987 was approximately equal to those awarded to Puerto Ricans; however, this figure represents a decline from 195 in 1974. Except for social sciences (44) and other professional fields (7), all fields saw fewer doctorates awarded to Mexican-Americans in 1987 than in 1974. These included 12 in the physical sciences, 6 in engineering, 15 in the life sciences, 18 in the humanities and 72 in education.

There were 264 doctorates awarded to other U.S. Hispanics in 1987, up from 239 in 1980. These reflected 19 degrees in the physical sciences in 1987, 14 in engineering, 34 in the life sciences, 81 in the social sciences, 47 in humanities, 61 in education and 8 in other professional fields. No one of these Hispanic groups are well-represented in any group of disciplines. However, in combination there does appear to be a small but viable representation of Hispanics in the life sciences, social sciences, humanities and education.

CONCLUSION

This essay has attempted to discern the changes in demographics which will face higher education by the turn of the century. Based on the age

TABLE 5
Number of Doctorates Awarded

	Total US	American Indian	Asian-American	Black	White	Puerto Rican	Mexican-American	Other Hispanic
1987								
Physical Sciences	3,087	10	104	29	2,789	33	12	19
Engineering	1,555	8	135	12	1,323	4	6	14
Life Sciences	4,207	16	145	78	3,807	28	15	34
Social Sciences	4,344	22	75	136	3,888	21	44	81
Humanities	2,721	11	25	73	2,463	31	18	47
Education	5,464	41	41	379	4,743	53	72	61
Other Professional	1,440	8	15	58	1,323	10	7	8
1974								
Physical Sciences	3,648	15	61	46	3,258	6	13	*
Engineering	1,797	7	64	16	1,571	7	7	*
Life Sciences	3,675	15	51	69	3,282	6	22	*
Social Sciences	5,231	19	35	107	4,665	12	27	*
Humanities	4,587	19	28	75	4,055	17	42	*
Education	6,707	46	43	501	5,556	11	78	*
Other Professional	1,180	8	11	32	1,031	1	6	*
Change								
Physical Sciences	−562	−5	43	−17	−469	27	−1	*
Engineering	−243	1	71	−4	−247	−3	−1	*
Life Sciences	531	1	94	9	525	22	−7	*
Social Sciences	−887	3	40	30	−777	9	17	*
Humanities	−1,867	−8	−3	−3	−1,592	14	−24	*
Education	−1,242	−5	−2	−122	−812	42	−6	*
Other Professional	260	0	4	26	292	9	1	*

SOURCE: National Research Council, Doctorate Recipients from United States Universities, 1974 and 1987.
* 1974 figures were not available for this group.

distribution of the population in the United States already born and some reasonable assumptions about immigration from abroad, it is clear that the eighteen year old population available to consider higher education by the year 2000 will be much more ethnically diverse than has been the case historically in the United States. Additionally, the data indicate that the number of minorities entering the potential faculty pipeline is decreasing. By extrapolating current characteristics of minorities, we conclude that the typical eighteen year old college entrant will be less well-prepared for college than has been the case in the recent past. In turn, the pool of minority Ph.D.'s will continue to decrease.

The real question is the extent to which we are justified in extrapolating from the past in making predictions about the nature of minorities by the turn of the century. Clearly, one of the reasons for recent movements to improve secondary education has been the fact that student achievements in that segment have declined. To the extent that these declines have been the result of the changing ethnic composition of the high school class, it might be that improvements aimed at dealing with the new demographics will result in a minority cohort which is better prepared for college. An optimistic view would be that by the year 2000, when minorities comprise a greater share of those considering college, we will see that minorities are better prepared for colleges and more closely resemble their white peers than has been the case to date. On the other hand, if a greater share of eighteen year olds retain the characteristics of minorities as they are today, substantial adjustments will be required by the higher education system.

Such adjustments will include the necessity to change recruiting policies (perhaps including standards for admission) and to increase the availability of financial aid. Commenting on a recent report by the U.S. Department of Education that the level of black enrollments has remained essentially stable over the last decade after a period of great growth from the mid-1960s to the mid-1970s, Patricia Smith, the Director of Legislative Analysis for the American Council on Education said: "The concern is not so much that the number is down (26,000 below the peak of 1,107,000 in 1980), but that we're not making great progress toward increasing it."[9]

It is likely that a larger proportion of resources will have to be spent on remediation, that is, underprepared students will have to be brought up to the level where they can deal with college courses. Greater efforts will have to be made to advise and counsel students in order to retain them until the completion of the programs in which they enroll. And greater concern with the transfer function of two-year colleges will have to be demonstrated.

The next twenty years could be considered a time of crisis in higher education, or they could be considered as a period of opportunity. It is tempting to place the responsibility on institutions other than those in the postsecondary system, such as the family, social service agencies and particularly the secondary schools. However, it is likely that whatever improvements are made in these areas, the responsibility for the post–high school education of our nation's youth will remain with the colleges and universities in this country. As the nature of the student body changes this will be a major challenge.

It is clear, when we look at groups of disciplines, that the prospects of American colleges and universities hiring new ethnic minority doctorate recipients, particularly American Indians, blacks and Hispanics are dismal. If every nonwhite doctorate recipient entered academe, and surely that is unlikely given the push for affirmative action hiring in the government and corporate sectors, still each of our baccalaureate-level institutions in this country would not be able to hire one. And ideally, a department's goal should not be to hire only one minority, but rather to hire a critical mass from one or more ethnic group that is most relevant to its particular student population. Once we account for the disproportionate number of doctorates received by ethnic minorities in education and the social sciences, it is almost futile for other disciplines to spend a great deal of time and money searching out new Ph.D.'s for their faculty. There simply are not any to speak of.

Given the statistics on the small pool of new American ethnic minority doctorate recipients, are our colleges and universities justified in ignoring pleas for affirmative action hiring? The answer is clearly no, for these institutions must play a major role in rectifying the ethnic imbalance in doctorate recipients. However, merely trying harder to hire from the available pool is bound to prove futile. The problem cannot be solved immediately because long-term solutions are required. The proportion of our nation's citizens who are nonwhite is rising dramatically, and we must make certain that nonwhite youth complete high school, progress into college, graduate from college and choose to pursue graduate study and the doctorate. Unless the quality of high school education provided to most minorities improves, too many of them will not complete high school and those who do will not choose to attend college. Unless those who choose to enter college are provided with the counseling and remediation support that are necessary because of the inferior quality of their high school education, and unless the curricula available to them are both stimulating and relevant, too many will drop out before they complete college. There has been extensive literature on causes of dropping out of college and we know that opportunities to live on campus, to get involved in the academic and extracurricular life of the college, and the availability of financial aid are important factors determining the prospects of graduation.[10]

Once a minority youngster graduates from college, the opportunity costs of going further are immense. The efforts by the nonacademic sectors to recruit minorities make it very difficult for minority college graduates to give up the relatively high income of a job in order to pursue further study. This difficulty is magnified for poorer college graduates whose families depend upon their earnings. One way to counteract the high opportunity costs of graduate school is to provide generous fellowship support to those who decide to go on. Quite frankly, graduate programs will have to do substantial selling jobs in order to attract minorities into their programs. In addition to tuition waivers, stipends are necessary to compensate for some of the earnings lost from the workplace. Credible promises of involvement in the scholarly work of leading faculty might help as well. Efforts to bring academic salaries in line with salaries available in other sectors of the labor market are absolutely crucial.

Such deliberate efforts will take time. We simply cannot expect that the available pool of new minority doctorate holders will expand rapidly in the next several years. However, rather than wringing hands, the colleges and universities of this country must be prepared to provide not only the opportunities but the incentives so that bright ethnic minorities make academe their career of choice.

NOTES

1. R.B. Freeman, *The Overeducated American* (New York: Academic Press, 1976); S.P. Dresch, "Democracy, Technology, and Higher Education: Towards a Formal Model of Educational Adaptation," *Journal of Political Economy* 83, no. 3 (1975): 535–569.

2. D. O'Neil and P. Sepielli, *Education in the United States: 1940–83* (Washington, DC: U.S. Government Printing Office, 1985).

3. L. Solmon and N. L. Ochsner, *College Education and Employment—The Recent Graduates* (Bethlehem, PA: CPC Foundation, 1979).

4. U.S. Department of Education, National Center for Educational Statistics *NCES), Digest of Educational Statistics* (Washington, DC: U.S. Government Printing Office, 1987), table 133.

5. U.S. Bureau of the Census, "School Enrollment—Social and Economic Characteristics of Students: October, 1985" *Current Population Reports*, ser. P-20, no. 409 (Washington, DC: U.S. Government Printing Office, 1985).

6. R. W. Rumberger, "Dropping Out of High School: The Influence of Race, Sex, and Family Background," *American Educational Research Journal* 20, no. 2 (1983): 199–220.

7. American Council on Education (ACE), *Fact Book on Higher Education* (London: Collier MacMillan, 1987), tables 92, 93.

8. Kaufman in E. Grosman, "Population Characteristics and College Attendance" (unpublished manuscript, 1986).

9. "Minorities' Share of College Enrollments Edges Up," *Chronicle of Higher Education* (March 9, 1988).

10. A. Astin, *Preventing Students from Dropping Out* (San Francisco: Jossey-Bass, 1975); R. Ekstrom, M. Goertz, J. Pollack and D. Rock, "Who Drops Out of High School and Why?," *Teachers College Record,* 87, no. 3 (1983): 356–373.

SUCHENG CHAN AND
LING-CHI WANG

Chapter Three

Racism and the Model Minority: Asian-Americans in Higher Education

INTRODUCTION

The racial incidents that have occurred in recent years on the nation's campuses have spawned a large body of commentary by journalists and scholars. Some have analyzed the causes of these outbreaks while others have moralized over their meaning.[1] Since the students of color victimized by such incidents have been largely African-Americans, most of the writings have treated the topic as an issue in black-white relations. In reality, however, other students of color, including those of Hispanic and Asian origins, have likewise been affected by rising racial tensions in colleges and universities. Moreover, the social dynamics of the incidents involving nonblack students of color are very similar to those involving blacks, as the incident described below will show. With regard to Asian-Americans, more subtle kinds of racism have also surfaced, and it is these emergent forms of racism in American higher education that this essay addresses.

The Incident at the University of Connecticut

In December, 1987 six or seven white male students spat tobacco juice on the hair of eight Asian-American students and called them "Oriental faggots," "Chinks" and "Gooks," as both groups rode a crowded bus to a

43

dance sponsored by the University of Connecticut. There were two student proctors on the bus, but they ignored the harassment aimed at the Asian-American students. After arriving at the dance, the white students shoved and screamed at the Asian-Americans, while one indecently exposed himself to the group. The four Asian-American women present were so upset that they hid in a closet for the rest of the evening. They received little comfort from the proctor, who told them to "relax" and not to mind the white male students, who, according to him, were "just having fun."

In the face of such indifference from someone in authority, the Asian-American students felt quite helpless, but the older sister of one of the women students decided to bring the matter to the attention of the campus administration. She was told that no investigation could proceed without "solid evidence," which meant that the students had to provide the names of their tormenters. This task proved difficult because, other than her sister, none of the other Asian-American students wanted to pursue the matter, for fear of reprisal. But she did gather sufficient evidence of misconduct to compel campus administrators to hold a disciplinary hearing. Two white students were found guilty of harassing the Asian-Americans. One was suspended for a year while the second was placed on probation for the same length of time.[2]

The Model Minority Myth

This incident, which represents but the tip of the iceberg of rising anti-Asian hostility in the United States, stands in sharp contrast to the widespread depiction of Asian-Americans as a "model minority"—a nonwhite group whose members have managed to "make it" in America despite a long history of being subjected to myriad forms of discrimination. As more and more Asian-American students enroll in the nation's colleges and universities, and as their scholastic achievements are increasingly publicized, a backlash has developed against them.

Media attention paid to Asian-Americans can be divided into two phases. In the late 1960s, published articles focused on the high family income, high educational attainment and low rates of deviance among Asian-Americans.[3] In the 1980s, the positive image was cast primarily in terms of the dazzling academic achievements of Asian-American students at all levels of education,[4] although sociologists and economists—in quieter fashion—have continued to present statistics showing the high incomes of various subgroups of Asian-Americans.[5] So relentlessly has the model minority stereotype been presented that the work of writers who have challenged the veracity of such a depiction has received scant attention.[6]

The model minority portrayal is at best an incomplete picture; there is a flip side to the situation that the media has ignored. Many Asian-American students experience immense psychological stress when they cannot live up to the "whiz kid" stereotype.[7] They also suffer from the fact that their non-Asian classmates tend to ostracize them, resenting the fact that they "drive up the grade curve" and taunting them with the allegation that students who do well scholastically must be "nerds" socially. Meanwhile, teachers and administrators neglect the difficulties faced by Asian-American students on the grounds that youngsters who are doing so well academically cannot possibly need any special help.

Hidden Racism in Academia

Disturbing as the surface expressions of racial antagonism against Asian-Americans may be, they are not as important in the long run as certain masked forms of racism that are far more invidious because they are embedded in the very structure of American higher education and in society at large. To understand such hidden racism, we focus on two problems that Asian-Americans have encountered in the last two decades: the enormous obstacles students and faculty have faced in trying to build Asian-American studies programs, and attempts by some of the nation's elite universities to limit the number of Asian-American students on their campuses.

With regard to both issues, although the roadblocks do not appear to be racially motivated on the surface, they in fact have a disproportionately adverse impact on Asian-American students. We believe it is important to understand these emerging forms of racial disenfranchisement, because even though they have so far been directed primarily at Asian-Americans, in time, they will very likely also be used against other racial minorities.

Writings on each of the above two topics have been published.[8] However, the present essay is the first attempt to analyze them within the wider context of how American higher education is organized. Both of us have participated actively in building Asian-American studies on the Berkeley campus of the University of California. One of us (Chan) has done the same at two other universities, while the other (Wang) has led a campaign against the attempts by various leading universities to restrict Asian-American enrollment. Thus, much of our discussion is based on personal knowledge. We argue that because Asian-Americans are relatively powerless in academia, their glittering scholarly achievements notwithstanding, they have had to struggle every step of the way—alongside other people of color—for educational equality.

ASIAN-AMERICAN STUDIES

Origins of Asian-American Studies

The first Asian-American studies programs in the country were established at San Francisco State University and at the University of California (UC) at Berkeley, as the result of massive student strikes in 1968 and 1969. There, Asian-American students joined forces with other students of color to demand the creation of ethnic studies programs that would highlight the historical and contemporary experiences of nonwhite groups in the United States, in order to counter the existing Eurocentric curriculum that either failed to include any information about people of color, or worse, badly distorted the latter's history. The students insisted that the new courses be taught by faculty of color from a perspective that did not denigrate nonwhites, women or working-class people. By gaining greater control over their own education, these activists hoped that they could also exercise greater power over the course of events in society at large.

The program at San Francisco State University was set up within the School of Ethnic Studies, which remains the only school or college of ethnic studies in the country to this day. That at Berkeley became a constituent part of the Department of Ethnic Studies reporting directly to the chancellor's office. The Berkeley academic senate resolution that created the department envisioned its evolution into an autonomous Third World College, but to date, nothing of the sort has developed. Acting under similar coercion, administrators and faculty at other campuses—mostly on the West Coast—also allocated some meager resources for the development of Asian-American studies courses and programs in the early 1970s, but virtually none of these programs has experienced any growth. In fact, all of them have had to fight very hard for their survival.

In terms of location within the university structure, the Asian-American studies programs in existence can be grouped under five categories: 1) relatively autonomous programs housed within a larger ethnic studies entity, such as those at the University of California at Berkeley, San Francisco State University and the University of Washington; 2) subunits within preexisting departments, such as that at City College in the City University of New York; 3) research centers that sponsor a limited number of courses, such as those at the University of California at Los Angeles (UCLA) and the University of Colorado; 4) programs that have a separate office but whose faculty hold joint appointments in disciplinary departments, such as those at the University of California at Santa Barbara and Cornell University; and 5) scattered courses (or in some instances just a single course) housed in whatever units are willing to accommodate them.

Key Issues

Despite their different organizational settings, Asian-American studies programs, like other ethnic studies departments or programs, have experienced similar difficulties. At issue have been several questions. First is the matter of governance: Who could or should control Asian-American and ethnic studies? Second is the issue of academic legitimacy: What constitutes an acceptable curriculum and what should Asian-American and ethnic studies courses cover? Third is the question of professional certification: What kind of qualifications must faculty teaching such courses possess and what kind of research must they do and publish in order to get tenure? Last is the debate over educational mission, which consists of two parts: a) What functions can, do and should Asian-American and ethnic studies programs perform within the university and in minority communities? and b) How do these roles fit into or conflict with the traditional understanding of the functions of the American university?

To see how these issues have manifested themselves, we shall review briefly the history of the programs at UC Berkeley and UCLA.

Asian-American Studies at Berkeley

Governance and curricular legitimacy have been the two main issues that the program at UC Berkeley has fought hardest over. The Berkeley program has not been the scene of any protracted struggle over tenure-track faculty appointments and tenure review, while the question of mission has been hotly debated but never resolved. The program received five tenure-track faculty positions in 1969 as a result of the settlement of the student strike. The Afro-American, Chicano and Native American studies programs likewise each received five positions. It took the Asian-American studies program six years to fill its five positions with faculty holding the Ph.D. However, despite the hiring of individuals whose academic credentials had passed the scrutiny of the academic senate's Committee on Budget and Interdepartmental Relations (known elsewhere as the Committee on Academic Personnel), as late as 1975 only one out of the fifty courses the program was attempting to offer had received permanent approval.

Indeed, throughout the early 1970s, a constant battle raged between the academic senate's Committee on Courses of Instruction and the Ethnic Studies Department. Only after one of us (Chan) was appointed to serve on the committee did the differences between the committee and the department eventually get ironed out. It took extraordinary effort over a two-year period to convince fellow members of the committee that the courses submitted for approval were academically sound and not "mere political rhetoric," that the readings were relevant and the writing assignments rigorous, and that each of the faculty slated to teach those courses had the "proper" academic training.

While the quiet negotiations between the program and the Committee on Courses were going on, a more intense and volatile sectarian struggle took place internally. In conjunction with efforts to gain permanent approval for the entire Asian-American studies curriculum, the tenure-track faculty in Asian-American studies reexamined every course, reorganized the entire curriculum, and reassessed the qualifications of the part-time lecturers and supportive academic staff teaching some of these courses. These faculty were severely criticized—and at times threatened with violence—by others in the program for their seeming desire to cater to the dictates of the university in order to acquire academic legitimacy.

The roots for part of the difficulty the Asian-American studies tenure-track faculty encountered lay in a development that had occurred a few years earlier. In 1973, a review committee had recommended that instead of developing a third world college, each ethnic studies program at Berkeley should be allowed to grow at its own pace, with each becoming a separate department within the College of Letters and Science (L & S) in time. The committee thought that the Afro-American studies program was ready for such a move. Accordingly, it was pulled out of the Ethnic Studies Department to become an independent Afro-American Studies Department within L & S the following year. As this change was made without consulting the other three programs, charges that the move was a "sellout to the establishment" arose. So much recrimination was engendered that everything the Asian American Studies faculty tried to do in 1977 to strengthen their own program was considered suspect.

Several years later, another review committee recommended that the Asian-American, Chicano and Native American studies programs also be subsumed under L & S. The faculty debated the pros and cons of this recommendation at length and concluded they did not wish to join L & S. They believed that maintaining the status quo as a unit without any college affiliation gave their department greater control over curriculum and faculty review. Symbolically remaining autonomous was also important, for it implied that at some future date, the department could still evolve into a college of its own.

After some inconclusive discussions, the dean and the executive committee of L & S, as well as other administrators on campus, gave up their efforts to bring ethnic studies into L & S. They recognized that forcing the issue would only have created another disruptive situation. More important, some administrators seemed to have suddenly realized that they could use the existence of ethnic studies opportunistically. The fifteen tenure-track faculty in the department represented a sizable fraction of the minority faculty at Berkeley, whose presence boosted the campus' faculty affirmative action statistics. Thus, the administrators thought it wisest to let sleeping dogs lie. The college also did something unexpected: Without any fanfare, it amended its governing legislation to make it possible for L & S students to receive a B.A.

not only in Afro-American studies but also in Asian-American, Chicano, ethnic or Native American studies.

The *modus vivendi* so achieved allowed the ethnic studies faculty to turn their attention to more constructive matters. One was a proposal to establish the first Ph.D. program in ethnic studies in the country. Their efforts bore fruit in 1984, when the first graduate students were admitted. The department awarded its first two Ph.D.'s in 1989—the first Ph.D.'s ever granted explicitly in ethnic studies anywhere.

Another hard-fought but victorious struggle resulted in the passage of an American Cultures Requirement on the Berkeley campus in the spring of 1989. Beginning in 1991, every undergraduate at Berkeley, as part of his or her graduation requirement, must take and pass a course that is "integrative and comparative and address[es] theoretical and analytical issues relevant to understanding race, culture, and ethnicity in American history and society. Each course will take substantial account of groups drawn from at least three of the following: African Americans, American Indians, Asian Americans, Chicano/Latinos, and European Americans."[9]

Despite these accomplishments, the Asian-American studies program at Berkeley has received no additional resources since its founding. Even with the addition of a Ph.D. degree, the number of tenure-track faculty remained the same for twenty years. In 1989, the administration finally granted the program a sixth position. It did so not because of programmatic considerations, but purely as a counteroffer to an excellent tenure-track offer that a full-time lecturer, who had taught in the program for five years, had received from another UC campus. In short, Berkeley's Asian-American studies program manages only to maintain a steady state.

Asian-American Studies at UCLA

Asian-American studies at UCLA has operated under a different structure. Instead of a program, the UCLA administration funded a research center in 1970. The problems the center has encountered have been the mirror image of those faced by the program at Berkeley. The center managed to put more than a dozen courses into the catalog without too much trouble but has met enormous resistance in terms of faculty appointments and promotion. Like the program at Berkeley, the UCLA center received five tenure-track faculty positions in 1970, but these had to be placed in existing departments. It took seventeen years for these positions to be filled, despite the fact that from the beginning, the center has emphasized the importance of research and has administered an M.A. degree program in Asian-American studies.

One reason for the long delay is that those affiliated with the center seldom agreed with their departmental colleagues on what kind of candidates would be acceptable for the available faculty positions. The center wanted individuals with strong ties to the community and a leftist political perspective; the departments were concerned not only about the quality of the scholarly work that a particular prospective appointee had done, but often also passed negative judgment on Asian-American studies as a field of academic inquiry per se. In the end, all but one of the positions were filled by assistant professors—individuals with Ph.D.'s from first-rate institutions who had not yet published enough to make their scholarship controversial. The first assistant professor to come up for tenure review fought an uphill battle that lasted for more than three years. He was granted tenure in 1989 only after a showing of widespread student and community support and under the threat of litigation.

On other campuses where Asian-American studies programs exist, the going has been equally rough. Though the particulars on each campus differ, the fundamental issues are similar. The conflicts always revolve around who gets to decide, according to whose standards, what courses can be offered, who is allowed to teach them, and what kind of research is legitimate. Underlying all such arguments are philosophical and political disagreements over what the missions of the university should be.

Different Conceptions of the Missions of the University

Among the educators who have written about the missions of the university, Robert Wolff has distinguished most clearly the different functions the American university is called upon to serve, each of which function conforms to a particular model of the university and shapes how its faculty interact among themselves, with the administration and staff and with students. According to Wolff, first, the university serves as a sanctuary for scholarship. Second, it is a training camp for the professions. Third, it is a social service station that must meet the various "needs" of society, which in a capitalist society, as Wolfe points out, often means simply the market demands for various skills. Lastly, it is an assembly line for establishment men—men groomed to lead and control the social, political and economic institutions of society.[10]

The pioneer generation of Asian-American and ethnic studies faculty and students accepted none of these goals. Rather, they believed that community service and anti-establishment political action should be at the heart of any ethnic studies program. Such a stance clashed head-on with the ideal of the university as an ivory tower—a place for scholarly contemplation and basic research away from the rough hustle and bustle of real life. As for professional training, although advocates of ethnic studies recognized that technical and managerial skills could be used in community service, they insisted that the only acceptable form of service was one that promoted fundamental (i.e., revolutionary) social change. Being a service station that educated masses of students to meet the needs of an exploitative economic system was likewise anathema: If that was all higher education strived to do, then, in the eyes of the activists, education was but a form of "brain drain" that took students *away* from the very communities they should aspire to serve. Finally, the founders of ethnic studies thought the role of the university as an assembly line for nurturing establishment men the most unacceptable of all. In short, because faculty and students in ethnic studies vehemently criticized every aspect of the American university, those who controlled decision-making on campus considered the very presence of ethnic studies faculty and students subversive. Accordingly, they repeatedly refused to approve, or severely questioned, courses and faculty appointments proposed by the fledgling ethnic studies programs.

The point that needs to be made is that even though the conflict between ethnic studies and the university was (and continues to be) basically a *political* one, the criticisms of ethnic studies have more often than not been couched in *racial* terms. It is alleged that minority faculty—either because of their ethnic origins or cultural upbringing—somehow lack whatever intellectual ability it takes to do good research. Even when they publish, what they write, it is said, is mostly "rhetoric," because they cannot be "objective" about the topics they write about, since these so frequently deal with the history, sociology and culture of their own groups. (One wonders why the same charge is never leveled at white historians, social scientists or literary critics who specialize in European or US history and culture.) And if ethnic studies faculty prove popular with students—many of whom come from the same ethnic backgrounds—it must be, it is alleged, because they give easy grades or their courses lack academic rigor.

Given such widespread racist perceptions, it took enormous student pressure to get even a few courses offered. Not surprisingly, these have received very little continual support. Having to defend their embattled programs has taken a toll on the faculty teaching in them. Time and energy are diverted away from research and publications into fighting political battles. Such a state of affairs has hampered the development of the field everywhere.

In the last two years, however, an important turning point has been reached. As an increasing number of colleges and universities seems to be embracing "diversity" not only in their curriculum but in faculty ranks, faculty positions have suddenly been allocated for specialists in Afro-American, Asian-American, Chicano/Latino and Native American studies. Ironically, due to the lack of support for training in those fields in the last two decades, there are at present more positions available than there are individuals to fill them.

ATTEMPT TO RESTRICT ASIAN-AMERICAN ADMISSIONS

Difficult as the struggle to establish Asian-American studies programs has been, its impact on the Asian-American community in general has not been as great as the attempt by several elite universities in recent years to restrict the number of Asian-American students on their campuses. At the heart of this controversy is the notion of "overrepresentation" and whether there should be a "reasonable" upper limit to the percentage of Asian-Americans enrolled on any single campus. This debate has been couched within two frameworks: 1) the idea of meritocracy, which mandates that students be accepted purely on the basis of their academic performance; and 2) the *Bakke* decision, which prohibited racial quotas on the one hand, but approved the use of other criteria to promote affirmative action, on the other hand.

How the Issue Emerged

Social commentators have repeatedly observed that Asian-Americans place a heavy emphasis on education. They usually attribute this to the fact that in traditional Asian cultures, educated men were not only revered but they ruled society. What non-Asian observers often fail to understand, however, is that from the point of Asian-Americans themselves—especially the immigrants who have come to the United States after the earlier immigration quotas based on "national origins" were abolished in 1965—education seems to be the only means at their disposal for overcoming racial discrimination in the labor market. That is to say, they believe a good education will guarantee job security, upward mobility, and better yet, wealth and privilege in America. In their eyes, preparing their children for entrance into the more prestigious universities is an all-important goal. Unfortunately, their aspiration does not always jibe with the role that these institutions play in selecting and training the country's elite.

Historically, the Ivy League colleges have been central in recruiting and training future leaders in the United States. Since the end of World War II, some public universities, especially UC Berkeley and UCLA, have also participated in the process. These institutions, therefore, control an important societal resource: access to the kind of education that leads to prestige, high-paying jobs and powerful positions.

Competition to partake of this resource has been keen. To gain admission to these elite-grooming universities, applicants must meet rigorous academic standards and, just as importantly, be able to pay the high tuition they charge. After enrolling, the students must be able to survive in an environment that promotes class, race and gender hierarchy. For about two hundred years in the nation's history, only white, male gentiles from the Eastern establishment enjoyed this scarce resource. Asian-Americans, like other minorities, including women of all ethnic backgrounds, were kept out. Those Asians who did gain entrance in the early decades of the present century were mostly foreign students, who presented no threat because they were required to return to their homelands after completing their studies under the then-existing immigration laws.

In the 1960s, under the intense political and legal pressures exerted by the civil rights movement, the doors to these elite institutions were partially opened. Asian-Americans were among the groups benefiting from the affirmative action programs that came into being, especially in the private Ivy League colleges and universities. By the late 1970s, their numbers were rising so sharply that campus officials began to worry about the influx. Especially worrisome to the gatekeepers was the fact that Asian-American students began entering in increasing numbers without the benefit of affirmative action programs. Three sets of data will illustrate the rise and subsequent efforts to curb it: increases in the number of Asian-American applicants, increases in the number of Asian-American freshmen enrolled and discrepancies between the admission rate for whites and for Asian-Americans. (Since the statistics thus far disclosed by various universities are incomplete, our reference to them will not be in a uniform format.)

Asian-Americans constituted only 2 percent (168 students) of Brown University's applicant pool in 1975; that percentage rose to 10 percent (1,451 students) in 1983. Similarly, whereas only 217 Asian-Americans applied to Yale in 1976, 1,597 did so in 1987. Harvard and Princeton have not disclosed figures going back to the 1970s, but in 1985, Asian-Americans made up 16 and 17 percent, respectively, of their applicant pools. At UC Berkeley, 1,936 Asian-Americans applied in 1977, but 6,698 did so ten years later.

The percentage of Asian-Americans in the freshman class likewise rose. The increase between 1976 and 1986 at Harvard was from 3.6 to 12.8 percent; at MIT from 5.3 to 20.6 percent; at Stanford, from 5.7 to 14.7 percent; and at Berkeley, from 16.9 to 27.8 percent. However, the gain in Asian-American freshmen enrollment has been much less dramatic than the expansion in the applicant pool. One reason, as a 1983 survey of twenty-five top private universities on the East Coast revealed, is that the percentage of Asian-Americans admitted lagged behind those of all other ethnic groups,

including whites. At Brown, the overall rate of admissions for all freshmen
was 20.4 percent, compared to 14.0 percent for Asian-Americans. The
comparable rates were 15.9 versus 12.5 percent at Harvard; 17.0 versus 14.0
percent at Princeton; and 18.0 versus 16.7 percent at Yale. At Stanford, the
admission rate for Asian-American applicants ranged between 66 to 70
percent of the rate for whites between 1982 and 1985. That there should be
such consistency in the differential found among these institutions has led
critics to charge that informal quotas on Asian-American admissions must
have been imposed some time in the early 1980s.

The Controversy at Berkeley

The apparent curb on Asian-American admissions has created the
greatest controversy at the University of California at Berkeley. Consequently, the situation there has received the most in-depth investigation. In
1983, the 1,240 Asian-American freshmen at Berkeley comprised 27.8
percent of their class. The projected number for 1984 was about 1,400.
However, the actual figure turned out to be only 1,008. With the exception of
Filipino-Americans, who were protected by affirmative action programs,
every Asian-American subgroup registered a decline. The sharpest reduction
occurred among Chinese-American freshmen, whose numbers dropped from
609 in 1983 to 418 in 1984—a 30 percent nose-dive within a one-year
interval. The number of white freshmen also declined, but by a mere 4
percent, from 2,425 to 2,327.

To see how subtly such a limitation was achieved, it is necessary to
understand the procedures Berkeley uses to choose its freshman class.
Nowadays, the campus follows a complicated formula based on grade point
average (GPA), scores on College Entrance Examination Board standardized
tests, the kind of courses and number of years of certain subjects taken in
high school, family socioeconomic status, ethnicity, extracurricular activities, and personal characteristics to determine its mix of freshman admits.
Before 1984, however, things were simpler: the upper 50 percent of the
students were admitted on the basis of *either* high GPA *or* high standardized
test scores; the lower 50 percent were admitted on the basis of more complex
criteria. Students who were UC-eligible but who could not be accommodated
at Berkeley were "redirected" to other UC campuses, but underrepresented
minorities were exempted from redirection.

Unbeknownst to the public, during the 1984 admissions cycle, the
university made three policy changes: 1) it raised the high school GPA for
regularly admissible applicants from 3.75 to 3.9; 2) Asian-American
students who qualified as Educational Opportunity Program (EOP) students,
with the exception of Filipinos, were no longer exempted from redirection;

and 3) a minimum score of 400 on the verbal part of the Scholastic Aptitude Test was proposed for permanent resident aliens.

All three changes had a disproportionately negative impact on Asian-Americans. First, Asian-American students in general tend to have higher GPAs but lower scores in their English aptitude and achievement tests than white students. Thus, by raising the GPA but not standardized test scores, proportionately more Asian-American than white students were denied admission. Second, since some three-quarters of the EOP students who were not from underrepresented minority groups were Asian, by removing the protection they previously received vis-a-vis redirection, more Asian-American than white EOP students had to find someplace else to go. By definition, students are granted EOP status only if their family income falls below a certain amount and if their parents are not college educated. When Asian-American EOP students who might have lived at home in the San Francisco Bay Area were forced to enroll at a campus out of town, the cost of their education increased considerably—in some instances, to such an extent that they could no longer afford to attend a UC campus. Third, the proposed (but never implemented) "floor" on the SAT verbal test would also have affected a disproportionate number of Asian-Americans, for many of whom English is not a native tongue and who, consequently, do not do well on the aptitude and achievement verbal tests. There were also a good number of Spanish-speaking resident alien students, but as members of an underrepresented group who qualified for affirmative action consideration and who could be admitted under the criteria used for the lower 50 percent of the total batch of admittees, this proposed change would not have affected them. Asian immigrant students, on the other hand, did not have similar recourse.

The Racial Meaning of the Admissions Controversy

Quite apart from the technical details of the situation at Berkeley, what must be understood is that none of the changes *overtly* targeted Asian-American students. All of them were couched in terms of problems related to teaching too many non-native speakers of English. Since federal laws now make it illegal to discriminate against groups and individuals on racial grounds, those who look askance at the increased influx of non-European immigrants have seized upon language and cultural differences as pretexts for exclusion. At Berkeley, faculty and teaching assistants tired of grading papers written in poor English asked why it was necessary to take in students with language problems when thousands of high school graduates with superb academic records who need no remedial instruction of any sort are trying to get into Berkeley. Meanwhile, administrators expressed concern over the cost of providing remedial instruction in English—an expense for which the university does not get state funds.

Supporters of nondiscrimination against Asian-Americans argued that as a publicly supported university, Berkeley has a moral obligation to admit a *mix* of students—including those with English problems—so that its student body reflects the ethnic and socioeconomic diversity of California's population as a whole. Under intense public scrutiny, advocates of "diversity" eventually won out. After five years of acrimonious debate, Berkeley's chancellor, without admitting culpability for any intentional discrimination, apologized publicly for the insensitive way in which his colleagues and staff had responded to the issues raised by Asian-Americans. The vice-chancellor set up mechanisms for ensuring that admissions criteria and procedures, as well as any proposed changes in them, will henceforth always be made public before they are implemented. Asian-American campus and community leaders accepted the administration's gesture of goodwill by issuing a statement that declared the matter settled.

Similarly, at Stanford, a faculty committee, while finding no deliberate discrimination against Asian-Americans, acknowledged that "unconscious" bias may have been at work. At Brown, a Committee on Minority Affairs of the board of trustees, after conducting an investigation into allegations of discrimination, concluded unanimously that "an extremely serious situation exists and that immediate remedial measures are called for." Meanwhile, Asian-American faculty, students and community activists continue to remind administrators and decision-making faculty committees that any measures that affect *immigrant* students who are not native speakers of English adversely are in fact a form of anti-Asian discrimination. They vow that covert policy changes with negative effects on any subgroup of Asian-Americans will never again be tolerated.

Why are Asian-Americans So Threatening?

Why do the elite universities suddenly feel so threatened by the presence of Asian-American students? After all, since the late nineteenth century, schools such as Harvard, Yale, Cornell, Princeton, Stanford, Berkeley and UCLA have educated quite a number of students of Asian ancestry. But in the early decades, the presence of Asian students posed no threat: Those who were foreign-born were required to return to their homelands after they finished their studies, while the American-born never could find jobs commensurate with their educational attainment. In other words, while these renowned universities served as an "assembly line for [white] establishment men," they did not perform the same function for nonwhite youth.

World War II changed the situation somewhat. Because of severe manpower shortages in the defense industries, some well-educated Asian-American scientists and engineers, for the first time, found the kind of jobs for which they had been trained. But like their predecessors, the foreign students, these professionals were not particularly threatening to anyone. As technicians, they served the interests of the government or of industry without in any way challenging the latter's supremacy. This situation held true until the mid-1970s.

Since Asian immigration increased in the 1970s, bringing in its wake not only well-educated individuals but also large amounts of capital for investment, Asian-American professionals have become a group to be reckoned with, for two reasons. First, many of them have combined their professional knowledge with entrepreneurship. They now own and operate companies that make products and provide services that compete effectively against white-owned enterprises. Second, a number of Asian-American professionals have entered the political arena—the career of S. B. Woo, physicist turned lieutenant governor of Delaware, is but the most visible example—which means that finally, after more than a century of disenfranchisement, Asian-Americans can now hope to have some say over public policy.

University officials have tried to limit the number of Asian-American students in their institutions because they understand all too well the pipeline function that higher education performs. They are wary of seeing too many Asian-Americans acquire the very professional training that will catapult them into the middle stratum of society. They know that as the number of middle-class Asian-Americans increases, some of them will be in a position to exercise a modicum of power. By so doing, they will enable their entire group to finally break out of the legal barriers that have hitherto kept its members silent, suppressed and powerless.

The defensive reaction to the emergence of Asian-Americans is racist because those who have hitherto monopolized power and privilege do not want to share their elite status with nonwhites. There is simply not enough room at the top. Whereas having a small number of Asian-Americans succeed is a confirmation that the American dream still works, seeing "hordes" do so is too frightening. Those who guard the gates into the elite stratum of American society feel they must keep the doors closed against a "new yellow peril." Unlike the historical "yellow peril" that came in the form of "cheap labor," the new menace is embodied in highly competitive professionals and entrepreneurs. The immigration bill introduced by Senator Edward Kennedy represents one attempt to plug up the opening in the dike; the botched attempts to impose "quotas" on Asian-American university admissions represents another. It seems that even as many enlightened white

Americans affirm the desirability of cultural pluralism, they nevertheless hope to keep their own privileged status just a little bit longer.

THE STRUCTURE OF POWER IN AMERICAN HIGHER EDUCATION

The true meaning of the battles that Asian-Americans in higher education have fought can be understood fully only by looking at the nature of the American university. Because the American university is called upon to serve more functions than its counterparts elsewhere in the world,[11] scholars have differed in the models they have proposed to explain its organization.[12] In addition to performing those functions discussed by Wolff, writers have also recognized that the university is a vast bureaucracy containing many subunits.[13] Furthermore, during the 1960s, observers began to think of the college campus as an important arena in which many of society's political conflicts were being fought out and adjudicated.[14] As a number of scholars have noted, what makes the essence of the American university so difficult to grasp is that its missions have at times corresponded with, but at other times contradicted, the goals of American society as a whole.[15]

We believe that no single model can explain adequately the structure of the American university because, in fact, it is a social system within which a community of scholars, a bureaucracy and a political arena coexist. Within such a multifaceted system, power takes different forms and is exercised in diverse ways. Six kinds of power in the academy are relevant to our discussion of the position that Asian-Americans occupy in higher education: collegial, reputational, administrative, bureaucratic, personal and agitational power. Asian-Americans in higher education today possess and exercise these different forms of power to different degrees.

Collegial and Reputational Power

Collegial power is exercised by faculty—primarily the senior faculty— through their control of the curriculum, the faculty review process and the definition of what constitutes legitimate scholarship. Embedded in the standards by which they judge and reward each other's work is a set of values which graduate students and junior faculty are supposed to absorb through an informal apprentice system with subtle and often unarticulated rituals of deference. In the old days, when the faculty was relatively homogeneous, there were few challenges to the decisions based on supposedly purely meritocratic values. Institutional practices, such as confidentiality in the peer review process and barring junior faculty from certain kinds of decision-making, shore up the power of the senior faculty, while power based on scholarly reputation gained as a result of research and publications further undergird their authority. Whenever outside forces threaten to impinge on the authority of the tenured senior faculty, they invoke the sanctity of academic freedom to protect their entrenched position within the academy.

In the last twenty years or so, serious challenges have arisen to the collegial and reputational power of the senior faculty in the form of new courses that embody a critique of the existing scholarship and the hiring of minority and women faculty who insist on their right to do research on issues that fall outside prevailing paradigms. Despite the lip service paid to creativity, however, innovative courses and research that call into question the existing social and intellectual arrangements of privilege and power are strenuously resisted, if not condemned outright. Junior faculty—especially those in ethnic studies or women's studies programs—have often been denied tenure or merit increases because their scholarship does not fit within the acceptable parameters of discourse.

The communication channels through which collegial and reputational power are exercised form an "old boys' network" which outsiders, such as Asian-Americans, other minorities and women, find very difficult to penetrate. Because this network is an informal one, it hinges on personal friendship and influence-trading. Very seldom does a nonwhite or female faculty member feel free to talk to colleagues "off the record" about important matters concerning their departments, their colleagues or their fields. Consequently, those who are not plugged into this interpersonal network simply do not participate in (and in most instances are not even aware of) some of the most important decisions that are made in the university—decisions that affect their own careers in profound ways. Asian-American studies programs have had so much trouble obtaining resources, getting their courses approved and their recommendations for faculty appointments accepted precisely because their faculty have never found their way into the inner circles that govern the university.

It would be a mistake, however, to assume that lack of access to collegial power is the same across the board. Minority entrée into the charmed circles dominated by the senior faculty differs considerably in the different disciplines. In general, those in the natural sciences find it slightly easier to participate in the day-to-day social interaction that accompanies academic work because scientific research routinely requires teamwork. That is to say, the social organization of academic inquiry in the natural sciences seems to be more conducive to drawing in colleagues of diverse backgrounds than is the situation in the humanities and social sciences. But who gets accepted into the inner circles is very selective: Those who won't rock the boat are the most likely to be allowed entry. The presence of such individuals is not threatening because they will help to perpetuate the system, and not change or destroy it.

However, despite the fact that a notable number of Asian-American scientists and engineers have achieved international recognition for their work and thus possess reputational power, seldom has it been translated into other forms of power. No Asian-American has yet been appointed to the governing boards of the major national organizations that influence educational policy, such as the National Science Foundation, the American Council on Education, the Carnegie Commission on Higher Education and the College Entrance Examination Board.

Administrative and Bureaucratic Power

A third form of power, administrative power, comes from occupying formal positions of authority within the university structure. As such, it is highly visible. But unlike the situation in Asian countries, or even in other American institutions, administrative power in the American university is often more circumscribed than meets the eye. Because the university is cherished as a *community* of scholars, academic administrators in the United States must act cordially—that is to say, collegially rather than dictatorially— towards their faculty and staff colleagues. Just as important, they have to balance multiple and conflicting demands on the limited resources they control. In major research universities, they share decision-making in particular with senior faculty. On those campuses where shared governance exists, there is usually a stable corps of faculty who routinely participate in committee work and perform quasi-administrative functions. These very same individuals are the ones who maintain an ongoing "old boys' network" among themselves.

Very few Asian-Americans have attained high administrative positions in the university. The handful who have done so tend to be concentrated in engineering and the natural sciences—fields in which their reputational power is sufficiently great to overcome the barriers in their path. In universities, as in corporations, it is often alleged that Asian-Americans lack leadership qualities. The real obstacle, however, is that many whites refuse to accept nonwhite supervisors with the power to hire, review and fire them. The inability of Asian-Americans to advance beyond a certain level in the hierarchy is now popularly referred to as the "glass ceiling."

In general, minority administrators are found most often in the student services part of the university bureaucracy. They head units such as EOP, student affirmative action programs, student learning centers (where tutorial services are offered) and offices overseeing multicultural activities—all of them units in which the majority of the staff are usually people of color. In such units, the issue of nonwhites supervising whites does not arise to the same degree as elsewhere in the university bureaucracy. The small number of minority administrators in the academic sector of the university tend to hold staff, and not line, positions—carrying out decisions made by others rather than exercising independent decision-making power of their own.

Far less visible than administrative power is the bureaucratic power possessed by administrative and clerical staff members, who influence the outcome of decisions more than is sometimes realized. They do so by virtue of their role in the day-to-day implementation of decisions, by their intimate knowledge of university rules and regulations, and by the position they occupy as gatekeepers controlling access to administrators. The sizable number of Asian-Americans in this white-collar sector of the university represents a vast reservoir of untapped power with considerable potential to bring about change within the university. So far, however, not too many individuals occupying staff positions seem willing to break out of the docile, hardworking mode into which they have been cast. Before they can do so, they must acquire a consciousness of their own political importance.

Personal and Agitational Power

A fifth form of power based on the ability of particular individuals to influence other people is not embedded in the organizational structure per se. Rather, it comes from the interpersonal skills an individual possesses. In American society, where there is considerable room for people to charm and manipulate others, individuals with personal power but not always formal positions of authority can nevertheless accomplish a great deal, so long as they are assertive without being abrasive. Such individuals possess great self-confidence and do not hesitate to turn opportunities to their own advantage. But because exercising this kind of power requires Asian-Americans to be brazen in a manner that is contrary to the way many have been brought up, relatively few of them have made use of it to promote the causes in which they believe.

A sixth kind of power is based on the ability to agitate, wherein by militance and the sheer force of numbers, hitherto powerless and voiceless groups manage to make themselves heard and to get their demands taken seriously. Until the late 1960s, students had no access to the structure of governance in the university at all, but as a result of mass demonstrations, they won the right on many campuses to seat representatives on faculty committees. As a matter of fact, student leaders have often gained greater access to administrators and senior faculty than have minority faculty.

Asian-American students and faculty first tasted agitational power when they joined coalitions of students in the civil rights and antiwar movements, but soon—on East and West coast campuses, at least—they focused their efforts increasingly on the movement to establish Asian-American and ethnic studies programs. Agitational power is perhaps the only form of power Asian-Americans in higher education have consistently enjoyed in the last twenty years. The presence of a few Asian-American faculty who are willing to act militantly in conjunction with students and community groups has at times served as an effective check on the tendency of administrators and senior faculty to abuse their power.

CHALLENGE AND REACTION

Emerging Coalitions

In the last two or three years, a new and subtle development has taken place in terms of the role that Asian-American faculty play on some campuses. One example is the sort of coalition that has emerged at UC Berkeley. There, as a result of the administration's intransigent refusal to respond candidly and cordially to public inquiries about its undergraduate admissions policies, a tentative working relationship has formed between the radical faculty in Asian-American studies and their more moderate colleagues in other departments. The effort to curb Asian-American enrollment—including denying admission to students with high school GPAs of 4.0 (straight As or higher, i.e., A+)—struck at the very heart of what Asian-Americans, regardless of their political persuasions, hold most dear: upward mobility through education. As a result, some of the Asian-American faculty in the natural sciences, engineering and other professional schools who had hitherto eschewed campus politics started to speak out and, more important, to show a willingness to serve on campus committees—not just administrative ones appointed by the chancellor's office to deal specifically with minority affairs, but also standing committees of the academic senate, through which faculty formulate university policies and govern themselves. In short, a small Asian-American presence finally appeared in Berkeley's structure of power, and it did so in the form of collegial power which had thus far eluded the grasp of most minority faculty.

Ironically, it was the Berkeley administration's bungling that brought this change about. Moderate Asian-American faculty, who for two decades had wanted nothing whatsoever to do with the militant, anti-establishment stance of their colleagues in ethnic studies, are, however, willing to fight against policies that *block* what they see as the most important channel of upward mobility for themselves and their children. Meanwhile, one or two of Berkeley's top administrators have shown enough political savvy to encourage this trend, for it has suddenly become possible to showcase

Asian-American participation in university governance without having to deal with left-leaning militants.

The New Racism

But the nature of white racism is such that a development as the above is inherently unstable. What has happened to Asian-Americans in higher education in recent years is but the forerunner of a larger pattern. Historically, whites have kept people of color and females "in their place" by allegations of biological and intellectual inferiority. Now that blatantly racist reasons can no longer be used, other measures—such as poor skills in English or so-called feminine irrationality—are substituted as reasons for efforts to continue excluding nonwhites and women from the citadels of power. When these criteria, too, are exposed for what they are—that is, covers for the underlying racism and sexism—then a few "controllable" members of the excluded groups are invited to join "the boys." In time, however, as the number of these token individuals increases, and especially if they outperform their white, male colleagues in myriad ways—as measured by the very criteria that the establishment males themselves have set up—they, too, will become a threat, and yet another tactic will have to be devised to uphold a system of power and privilege with an increasing number of cracks.

For now, at least, the white power structure—in academia as in other areas of public life—is still willing to support affirmative action because its underlying premise is paternalistic: Look at these poor, inferior creatures— only by our largess and with our help will a few of them make it. But once some minority-group members—in this case, Asian-Americans—show that they can not only perform academically and economically, but that they also intend to stay (i.e., become part of the American body politic, rather than remain as sojourners pining to return to their homelands once they've made some money), then the survival of the existing racial hierarchy is called into question and affirmative action will no longer be in vogue.

The bottom line is this: One of the basic principles of the new racism is that when nonwhites or women manage to "win" on the basis of existing rules, then the rules must be changed. Though unarticulated, this is precisely the logic behind the efforts of the elite universities to limit Asian-American enrollment. A second principle is that there are two main ways to ensure and perpetuate Euro-American cultural dominance: racial exclusivity and assimilation. If, for pragmatic or political reasons, nonwhites and females cannot be kept out, then they must be assimilated, for members of minority groups who internalize Euro-American male values, and docilely follow the norms that flow from such values, can be absorbed into the existing social system without undermining it. On the other hand, advocates of Asian-American and ethnic studies programs and other minority radicals who oppose assimilation are most unwelcome, because part of their agenda consists of efforts to overturn the existing system of racial and cultural dominance.

CONCLUSION

Fathoming these principles brings us full circle to the model minority myth. The accomplishments of those Asian-Americans who are doing well are widely celebrated because having a model minority in its midst is proof that the United States is still a land of opportunity, where *individual* hard work, perseverance and talent pay off. We are not denying that some Asian-Americans indeed have made it; what we challenge is the implication that *all* Asian-Americans have done so. The Asian-American population is highly heterogeneous; the plight of the poor, the underemployed and unemployed, the uneducated or miseducated, the sick and those in suffering should not be neglected. Moreover, the political use to which the model minority stereotype has been put is insidious. In effect, by holding up Asian-Americans as paragons, other people of color are told that if they would only follow in the same footsteps, their lot, too, would improve. ("Work hard, be satisfied with the small rewards you've been receiving, educate your children at any cost, and above all, don't protest.") The widespread dissemination of such a message is a divide-and-conquer tactic; it pits one minority group against another, thereby reducing the chances of their forming a coalition to challenge the existing structure of power in society in general and in higher education in particular.

It is possible, however, for Asian-Americans to use the model minority myth to their own advantage. In the last twenty years, though they and other people of color have become more numerous and visible on university campuses—at least as students and as white-collar workers—they have not gained commensurate power. Whatever inroads they have made are not uniform—they have had a greater impact on the bureaucratic and the political sectors of the university than on the community of scholars. The reason is that the first two sectors are much more vulnerable to pressure than the third. But there is a way for Asian-American faculty to gain entry into the highly insulated community of scholars: they must continue to be model scholars (i.e., be a model minority in terms of academic performance) *but without stopping there*. Instead, they must learn to turn their reputational power into collegial and administrative power by participating in the making of decisions that affect the distribution of academic resources and rewards.

Asian-American staff should also learn to flex their muscles and exercise more of the bureaucratic power they inherently possess. Asian-American students and community groups, for their part, can continue to use their agitational power judiciously, working in tandem with faculty and staff to bring about the changes that will benefit not only themselves, but all other minority groups which have, for far too long, been excluded and exploited in America.

NOTES

1. Commentaries may be divided broadly into two camps. Representative of the white liberal view, which faults the general anti-affirmative action climate of public opinion sanctioned by the Reagan and Bush administrations, is Jon Weiner, "Racial Hatred on Campus," *The Nation*, February 27, 1989, 260–264. Two varieties of conservative black views, which place the onus on students of color, are clearly articulated in Thomas Sowell, "The New Racism on Campus," *Fortune*, February 13, 1989; and Shelby Steele, "The Recoloring of Campus Life: Student Racism, Academic Pluralism, and the End of a Dream," *Harper's*, February, 1989, pp. 47–53.

2. Kay Tan and Jeff Yang, "The Incident at U. Conn," *Asian American Spirit* 3 (1988): 14–17; and Mark Haruma, "Racism in Connecticut," *Tozai Times,* August 1988, p. 5.

3. William Petersen, "Success Story, Japanese-American Style," *New York Times Magazine,* January 8, 1966, pp. 20 ff., and "Success Story of One Minority in the U.S.," *U.S. News and World Report,* December 26, 1966, pp. 73–78, set the precedent for this literature.

4. "Asian Americans: A 'Model Minority'," *Newsweek*, December 6, 1978, pp. 39 ff.; "Confucian Work Ethic," *Time*, March 28, 1983, p. 52; "A Drive to Excel," *Newsweek on Campus,* April 1984, pp. 4 ff.; "A Formula for Success," *Newsweek*, April 23, 1984, pp. 77–78; "Asian Americans: Are They Making the Grade?" *U.S. News and World Report*, April 2, 1984, pp. 41 ff.; "To America with Skills," *Time*, July 8, 1985, pp. 42–44; David Bell, "The Triumph of Asian Americans," *New Republic*, July 8 1985, pp. 24–31; Fox Butterfield, "Why Asians are Going to the Head of the Class," *New York Times Magazine*, August 3, 1986, pp. 19–24; Robert Oxnam, "Why Asians Succeed Here," *New York Times Magazine,* November 30, 1986, pp. 74 ff.; and Anthony Ramirez, "America's Super Minority," *Fortune*, November 24, 1986, pp. 148 ff.

5. Barry Chiswick, "An Analysis of the Earnings and Employment of Asian-American Men," *Journal of Labor Economics* 4 (1978): 197–214; Charles Hirschman and Morrison G. Wong, "Trends in Socioeconomic Achievement among Immigrant and Native-Born Asian-Americans, 1960–1976," *Sociological Quarterly* 22 (1981): 495–513; Victor Nee and J. Sanders, "The Road to Parity: Determinants of the Socioeconomic Achievements of Asian Americans," *Ethnic and Racial Studies* 8 (1985): 75–93; Franklin Goza, "Income Attainment among Native and Immigrant

Asians in the United States, 1960 to 1980" (unpublished paper); and U.S. Commission on Civil Rights, *The Economic Status of Americans of Asian Descent* (Washington, DC: U.S. Commission on Civil Rights, 1988).

6. Works that challenge and criticize the model minority stereotype include: Amado Y. Cabezas and Harold T. Yee, *Discriminatory Employment of Asian Americans: Private Industry in the San Francisco–Oakland SMSA* (San Francisco: ASIAN, Inc., 1977); David M. Moulton, *The Socioeconomic Status of Asian American Families in Five Major SMSAs with Regard to the Relevance of Commonly-Used Indicators of Economic Welfare* (San Francisco: ASIAN, Inc., 1978); Amado Cabezas, "Myths and Realities Surrounding the Socio-Economic Status of Asian and Pacific Americans," in *Civil Rights Issues of Asian and Pacific Americans: Myths and Realities,* compiled by U.S. Commission on Civil Rights (Washington, DC: U.S. Commission on Civil Rights, 1979), pp. 389–393; Keith Osajima, "Asian Americans as the Model Minority: An Analysis of the Popular Press Image in the 1960s and 1980s," in *Reflections on Shattered Windows: Promises and Prospects for Asian American Studies,* ed. Gary Y. Okihiro et al. (Pullman: Washington State University Press, 1988), pp. 165–174; and Won Moo Hurh and Kwang Chung Kim, "The 'Success' Image of Asian Americans: Its Validity, Practical and Theoretical Implications" (Paper presented at the eighty-first Annual Meeting of the American Sociological Association, 1986).

7. Stanley Sue and Nolan Zane, "Academic Achievement among Chinese and Caucasian American University Students," *Journal of Counseling Psychology* 32 (1985): 570-579; and Laird Harrison, "The Flip Side of 'Success'," *Asianweek,* June 27, July 4, and July 11, 1986.

8. The earliest manifestos on Asian-American studies that are readily available are "AAPA [Asian American Political Alliance] Perspectives," "Understanding AAPA," and "Concept of Asian American Studies," in *Roots: An Asian American Reader,* ed. Amy Tachiki et al. (Los Angeles: Asian American Studies Center, University of California, Los Angeles, 1971), pp. 251, 252 and 264–265. Longer studies of the development of Asian-American studies include Mike Murase, "Ethnic Studies and Higher Education for Asian Americans," in *Counterpoint: Perspectives on Asian America,* ed. Emma Gee et al. (Los Angeles: Asian American Studies Center, University of California, Los Angeles, 1976), pp. 205–223; Don T. Nakanishi and Russell Leong, "Toward the Second Decade: A National Survey of Asian American Studies Programs in 1978," *Amerasia Journal* 5:1 (1978): 1–20; Russell Endo and William Wei, "On the Development of Asian American Studies Programs," in *Reflections on Shattered Windows;* ed. Okihiro et al. pp. 5–15; Chalsa Loo, "The Middle-Aging of Asian American Studies," in ibid., pp. 16–23; " 'Unknown Jerome': Asian American Studies in the California State University System," in ibid., pp. 24–30; and Michael Omi, "It Just Ain't the Sixties No More: The Contemporary Dilemmas of Asian American Studies," in ibid., pp. 31–36.

Writings on the Asian-American university admissions controversy include Thomas E. Hassan, "Asian-American Admissions: Debating Discrimination," *College Board Review,* no. 142 (Winter 1986–1987), pp. 19–21 and 42–46; Lawrence

Biemiller, "Asian Students Fear Top Colleges Use Quota Systems," *Chronicle of Higher Education*, 33 (November 19, 1986): 1 and 34–36; Jeffrey K. D. Au, "Asian American College Admissions—Legal, Empirical, and Philosophical Questions for the 1980s and Beyond," in *Reflections on Shattered Windows*, Okihiro, pp. 51–58; and Ling-chi Wang, "Meritocracy and Diversity in Higher Education: Discrimination Against Asian Americans in the Post-*Bakke*- Era," *The Urban Review* 20, no. 3 (1988): 189–210.

The following relevant documents are available on request: California State Legislature, Assembly Subcommittee on Higher Education, "Asian-American Admissions at the University of California—Excerpts from a Legislative Hearing, January 26, 1988" (Sacramento, CA: California State Assembly, 1988); "Report of the Special Committee on Asian American Admissions of the Berkeley Division of the Academic Senate, University of California, Berkeley" (Berkeley: Academic Senate, University of California, Berkeley, 1989); and "Asian Immigrants: Victims of Language Discrimination at the University of California, Berkeley" (San Francisco: Chinese for Affirmative Action, 1989).

Newspaper coverage is too extensive to cite here. Interested readers should consult the *Daily Californian* (Berkeley), *Oakland Tribune, San Francisco Examiner, Los Angeles Times, Sacramento Bee*, and *Washington Post*.

9. University of California, Academic Senate, Berkeley Division, "Minutes of the Special Meeting," April 25, 1989, p. 6.

10. Robert P. Wolff, *The Ideal of the University* (Boston: Beacon Press, 1969).

11. For a concise comparison of different systems of higher education, see John H. Van de Graff et al., *Academic Power: Patterns of Authority in Seven National Systems of Higher Education* (New York: Praeger Publishers, 1978).

12. James A. Perkins, *The University as an Organization* (New York: McGraw Hill, 1973) contains a series of essays comparing universities to other kinds of organizations, including corporations, government bureaus and large foundations.

13. See, for example, John D. Millett, *New Structures of Campus Power* (San Francisco: Jossey-Bass, 1978); and William R. Brown, *Academic Politics* (University, AL: University of Alabama Press, 1982).

14. J. Victor Balbridge, *Power and Conflict in the University: Research in the Sociology of Complex Organizations* (New York: John Wiley, 1971).

15. Samuel Bowles and Herbert Gintis, *Schooling in Capitalist America: Education Reform and the Contradictions of Economic Life* (New York: Basic Books, 1976); Martin Carnoy and Henry M. Levin, *The Limits of Educational Reform* (New York: David McKay, 1976); Martin Carnoy, *Schooling in a Corporate Society: The Political Economy of Education in America*, 2nd ed. (New York: David McKay, 1975); and Stanley Aronowitz and Henry A. Giroux, *Education under Siege: The Conservative, Liberal and Radical Debate over Schooling* (South Hadley, MA: Bergin and Garvey, 1985).

ALAN COLÓN

Chapter Four

Race Relations on Campus: An Administrative Perspective

INTRODUCTION

Recent years have seen a rise in racial tension and overt conflict on the campuses of collegiate institutions in the United States. From the fall of 1986 through December, 1988, at least one incident of ethnoviolence has been reported at 250 colleges and universities.[1] These acts, which are part of a widening pattern of racial animosity demonstrated across the country, have occurred on the campuses of such schools as the University of Massachusetts at Amherst, The Citadel, Michigan, Dartmouth, California at Berkeley, Texas and Columbia. These incidents and the attention paid to their causes, character and consequences have forced a general recognition that there is a racial crisis in American higher education.[2] What does this crisis mean? What are its sources? What are its long-range and more immediate future implications for the education process and for society? What policies, programs and behaviors are needed to respond to this crisis?

In this essay I examine race relations at predominantly white colleges and universities in the United States. My purpose is to address the questions raised above by: (1) highlighting the culture of African-American people and that of the academy in dynamic interaction; (2) focusing on some of the modal experiences of African-American people in the pursuit of a higher education; (3) exploring the ramifications of the crisis; and (4) making suggestions for research, for policy and decision-making and for generating curricular and co-curricular approaches that might be applied toward the resolution of the crisis.

CONCEPTUAL FRAMEWORK

Race relations on campus tend to reflect and often correspond with and reproduce the power relations among groups on that campus and in the wider society. Power relations and other manifestations of social reality are defined and explained historically and situationally by key concepts. These concepts, and the analytical models which stem from them, include race, class, gender and, significantly for this essay, culture. When approaches to defining and describing social reality are employed in competition with or contradiction to each other, as has been the case in the historic struggle in this country over the production of knowledge and the positioning of racial/ethnic minorities in social theories and educational policies, our fuller understanding of social reality is obscured and our ability to constructively engage it is stifled. For, as McCarthy has stated, " . . . dynamic relations of race, class or gender do not unproblematically reproduce each other. These relations are complex and often have contradictory effects, even in similar institutional settings."[3]

The conceptual polarization which paralyzes the capacity to effectively (i.e., holistically) illuminate social reality has extended to the task of confronting the complexities of campus race relations. A more useful analytic strategy—one that is attempted here—is to synthesize the relevant and applicable constructs. Viewing and comprehending them interacting dynamically with one another as they fit historical and contemporary events can contribute to our search for meaning and prescriptions in the present and coming race relations on campus.

DEMOGRAPHIC TRANSFORMATIONS IN THE UNITED STATES

In addition to the increase in number and variety of immigrants entering the country legally and illegally, population changes are being accelerated by internal developments. The United States is witnessing dramatic demographic shifts which by the twenty-first century will yield a growing and more diversified, visible and accentuated plurality of cultures.[4] For example:

- We are seeing the emergence of another "one-third of a nation"—the African-Americans, Hispanics, Native Americans and Asian-Americans who constitute America's minority population. Many persons in these groups are poverty-stricken.[5]

- In 1988, 14 percent of all adults in the country and 20 percent of children under seventeen were members of these groups of people of color.[6] By the year 2000, one-third of all school-age children will be members of these groups.[7]
- In twenty-five of our largest cities and metropolitan areas, already half or more than half of the public school students come from these groups.[8] By the turn of the century about 42 percent of all public school students will be from groups of people of color or children of poverty.[9]
- From 1985–2000 people of color will constitute one-third of the net additions of the United States labor force. By the turn of the century, 21.8 million people in the labor force will be people of color.[10]
- Also by the year 2000, 80 percent of the new entrants to the labor force will be minorities, women and immigrants.[11]

The realities of these data confront us with a distinct challenge. People of color suffer disproportionately from an array of social and economic handicaps, including unemployment, inadequate education and poor health. The changes in the makeup of the population will ultimately require a more broadly culturally democratic response if the nation is to avoid a compromised quality of life, lower standards of living and escalating social conflict on and off the campus. In the complex of variables in the emerging social reality of the United States, culture and the need to address the differentness of human groups will continue to demand greater attention in the higher education enterprise.

PERSPECTIVES ON CULTURE

Definitions

One need only conduct a cursory review of the literature to recognize the variety of approaches to analyzing culture. While a commonly accepted definition of culture remains elusive, the core of culture is shared beliefs, values and behaviors. The notions of culture are crystallized by the National Alliance of Black School Educators, who have stated that "culture consists of the behavioral patterns, symbols, institutions, values and other human-made components of society and is the unique achievement of a human group which distinguishes it from other groups."[12]

If, as Kuh and Whitt contend, culture is holistic, context-bound and subjective, then the meaning of events and actions cannot be interpreted out of the institutional or group context in which the events and actions occur. "Behavior that seems to be effective in one institution," these authors write, "may or may not be effective in another; what appear to be similar actions and events will mean different things in different settings."[13]

Functions

It is important to note that culture can be a stabilizing and homogenizing force in a social context. This function of culture adds cohesion and continuity to the group or organization, enhances its processes and facilitates the achievement of its goals and objectives. However, because culture is bound, as indicated, to a social context, the culture of every institution or group is different. Since culture has its own internal dynamic it is constantly evolving. In this evolution it is shaped by newcomers and by the bearers of tradition within the group or institution as well as by the influences from the external environment.[14] This means that within groups and institutions, subcultures and countercultures may exist. These variations of or departures from the larger culture may reflect and produce significant organizational and group divisiveness and conflict. Under certain circumstances within and between and among cultures, the potential for conflict, or cultural clash, is heightened.

Culture in Higher Education

For purposes of this essay and expanding on the framework of culture outlined above, I share the definition of culture in higher education offered by Kuh and Whitt as "the collective, mutually shaping patterns of norms, values, practices, beliefs and assumptions that guide the behavior of individuals and groups in an institute of higher education and provide a frame of reference within which to interpret the meaning of events and actions on and off campus."[15]

Colleges and universities, though they have their own unique cultural identities, are inclined to transmit the dominant societal culture. That is, in the main, these institutions parallel, purvey and reproduce the prevalent social, economic and political tenets and structure of what C. Eric Lincoln calls the "overculture.[16] They normally resist the essential task implied when Counts asked *Dare the School Build a New Social Order?*[17] The transformation that has begun in the population of the United States will bring a new significance to Counts' question and the search for its answers will have profound ramifications for the culture of higher education. A sampling of these ramifications can be drawn from an overview of the African-American struggle for a higher education.

THE AFRICAN-AMERICAN PURSUIT OF HIGHER EDUCATION

Through 1865, the dominant experience of African-Americans was slavery. Although the process of enslavement was a far-reaching socialization experience, African people brought a cultural heritage with them which was continued in the New World.

West Africa was the home of most of the 1 million Africans who came to North America and of the ten to fifty million Africans who were forcibly transported out of Africa between 1619 and 1808.[18] In West Africa, formal education under the influence of Muslims flourished from at least the sixteenth century in the large cities. West African urban universities promoted literacy and provided exposure to a broad range of scholarship. In the hinterland almost no formal education existed but traditional informal education, with an emphasis on oral instruction, was available to all. Through the eighteenth century this education ensured the continuation of traditional West African social and cultural life.[19] Between the sixteenth and mid-nineteenth centuries, when this continuity was interrupted by the world trade in African slaves, the Americas became an outpost of West African culture. As Berry and Blassingame have noted,

> . . . That culture continued to be reflected in the United States in the last decades of the twentieth century in music, folktales, proverbs, dress, dance, medicine, language, food, architecture, art, and religion. African cultural patterns also influenced the development of American slavery as an institution.[20]

In order for slavery to work smoothly, control over the slave was a requirement, and imposing ignorance and illiteracy upon the slave was the custom for meeting that requirement. Starting with South Carolina's law of 1740, the states adopted the policy and practices of compulsory ignorance, which made it a punishable crime to teach slaves to read and write and for them to become literate on their own.[21] With compulsory ignorance, as Woodson has observed, "the problem of holding the Negro down . . . is easily solved. When you control a man's thinking you do not have to worry about his actions."[22]

A corollary tactic used for subordination that was a hallmark of the slavery experience was the attempt to de-Africanize those who were enslaved. Africans newly arrived in the Americas had new names imposed upon them; were prohibited from speaking their native language and were made to adopt the English language along with the European view of the universe and conceptual apparatus which defined them and their culture as inferior;[23] suffered disruption of their economic, political and social organization, including their family structure; and were forced to abandon their traditional forms of worship in favor of variations of Christianity which rationalized their enslavement. The adaptive vitality of the Africans born of their experiences as slaves in the United States produced a cultural amalgamation which embraced African cultures and European-American cultures.[24] As Blassingame further explains,

> Antebellum black slaves created several unique cultural forms which lightened their burden of oppression, promoted group solidarity, provided ways for verbalizing aggression, sustaining hope, building self-esteem, and often represented areas of life largely free from the control of whites. However oppressive or dehumanizing the plantation was, the struggle for survival was not severe enough to crush all of the slave's creative instincts. Among the elements of slave culture were: an emotional religion, folk songs and tales, dances, and superstitions. Much of the slave's culture—language, customs, beliefs, and ceremonies—set him apart from his master. His thoughts, values, ideals, and behavior were all greatly influenced by these processes. The more his forms differed from those of his master and the more they were immune from the control of whites, the more the slave gained in personal autonomy and positive self-concepts.[25]

Despite prohibitive laws and customs, some benevolent masters educated their slaves and there were some African-Americans, free and enslaved, who taught themselves reading and writing, as well as the survival mechanisms with which to endure slavery.[26] Nevertheless, the impact of deculturation and miseducation on slaves was substantial. The system of compulsory ignorance was effective enough that 95 percent of the Africans in this country were illiterate at the close of the Civil War.[27]

As the nation sought to heal its wounds of internal war, part of the Reconstruction (1865–1877) was to make formal education available to the freed men and women and their children. (This emphasis stimulated the creation of public education in the South and other regions of the country.) Colleges and universities for African-Americans were necessary because, even with the end of slavery, options for pursuing a higher education in mainstream European-American schools remained restricted or closed to the masses of African-Americans. Three schools—Cheney State (1837), Lincoln University (1854) and Wilberforce (1856)—had been founded before the war. It was not until the years immediately after the war that the establishment of institutions for higher learning of African-Americans began to proliferate, however. These schools included Atlanta University (1865), Fisk University (1866), Howard University (1867) and Hampton Institute (1868). The catalysts in creating and funding these schools were the federal Freedman's Bureau, philanthropic organizations, religious bodies such as the African Methodist Episcopal Church and various missionary groups, and the state governments. Significant as well were the attempts made by African-Americans themselves to obtain a college education.

It was only in the Reconstruction era, as Carnoy has pointed out, that African-Americans had input into the kind of schooling they would receive or the type of role they would play in the planning of their education. For the most part, "Black education after the Civil War depended on the social and economic utility that education was believed to have for the class of *white* persons in control of southern political and economic structures."[28] Carnoy adds that the priority for black education when "radical" northern humanitarians controlled it was for the ex-slaves to be brought into modern industrial "meritocracy" in which their race would not be an inhibiting factor. The major economic role for those released from bondage, however, was as tenant farmers and when political control of the economy reverted to the planters, education for those who worked the land came to be seen as an unnecessary evil. Education for blacks and nonblacks became stagnated as white industrialists saw the ex-slaves as a stable, docile force whose industrial labor could be exploited more efficiently than whites. In their new role blacks were trained primarily for manual and skilled manual work, and confined to a status by northern capitalists as well as southern planters that differed only legally from slavery.[29]

Against this backdrop, by the end of the Reconstruction, black education—elementary, secondary and collegiate—took on a separate and unequal character, one which all the pronouncements of the 1896 Supreme Court decision of separate but equal which followed could not camouflage in practice. Black schools were allocated fewer dollars per pupil or student by state and municipal governments; did not have equal access to or receive comparable grants from private or federal funding pipelines; had substandard facilities, space and supplies; and suffered qualitatively and quantitatively in administration, faculty and support staff. Moreover, many African-American colleges and universities had to contend with the racism, condescension and cultural imperialism that were frequently found among those governments, churches and philanthropies which provided and perpetuated through the curriculum the ideological bases for white supremacy.

The philosophy of industrial education for blacks won wide support among them due largely to the ubiquitous influence of its major advocate, Booker T. Washington. Washington and his followers were opposed by proponents of liberal education. Spearheaded by W. E. B. DuBois, who challenged Washington in his 1903 classic, *The Souls of Black Folk*,[30] and whose scholarship-activism epitomized the achievement and potential of the liberally educated person, attempts were made to accelerate the production of a broadly educated black person who would, in service to his/her people, and to humanity, wage an expanded, no-holds-barred struggle against injustice, exploitation and domination. This was a variation of the model of liberal education upon which some black higher learning institutions had been founded. It should be pointed out, however, that much of the curricula at these schools was duplicative or imitative of what was taught and studied at the white schools. For example, as explained by Bond, "at Fisk University in Nashville, Erastus Milo Cravath instituted a curriculum taken bodily from the classical course of study at Oberlin College where he had studied. At Atlanta University, Edmund Asa Ware and Horace Bumstead adopted without change the curriculum which they had studied at Yale."[31]

It is fair to say, then, that many, if not most, of these black institutions of higher learning were not founded with any particular conscious emphasis placed on or allegiance paid to African-American culture. Such a focus, though, has been infused, in varying degrees, as part of their historical evolution.

Black Students at European-American Institutions

At the white colleges and universities obstacles to African-Americans' attempts to lead meaningful, useful lives through education have abounded. From 1826, the year the first African-Americans graduated from college, to 1890, about 80 blacks graduated from northern white colleges. By 1910 about 693 blacks had graduated from predominantly white colleges. Into the twentieth century some schools relaxed their ban against admitting black students as others increased the quota of African-Americans they would accept. By 1954 about 1 percent of the freshmen admitted to predominantly white colleges were black.[32]

Those black students who attended many northern white schools were usually segregated in living arrangements. They were limited in the number and type of co-curricular activities in which they could participate. Also, they were faced with administrators, teachers and students who discriminated against them, and they had to use racially demeaning books with which historians, sociologists, political scientists and anthropologists popularized derogatory and distorted treatment of their culture. The strain of this existence resulted in intense isolation, alienation and confusion for black students.[33] They sought relief from the cultural environment they were expected to master by immersing themselves in nearby black communities, especially churches; establishing, beginning in 1906, a number of fraternities and sororities which became oases from racism and cultural estrangement and vehicles for leadership development; passing, for some mulattos, as white; and seeking out the rare black professors available. In 1940 none of the 330 black Ph.D.'s in the United States taught at predominantly white colleges. In 1968, blacks constituted only 0.13 percent of the faculties at white higher learning institutions.[34]

Driven by the demands on American society to open up during the civil rights phase of the African-American freedom movement, by the intensity of the black consciousness movement which was spawned by the emphasis on civil rights, and by other forces of change, predominantly white schools began rapidly integrating their student bodies in the mid-1960s. Sudarkasa has observed that federal legislative initiatives during that time led to an unprecedented extension of opportunity for black and other racial minority students to enter predominantly white colleges and universities.[35] The Economic Opportunity Act of 1964 authorized funding of the college work-study program to assist academically and financially disadvantaged students. The Civil Rights Act of 1964, which prohibited the granting of federal funding to institutions that discriminated on the basis of race, was tantamount to the mandate that colleges and universities admit students of color. Moreover,

> Under the Higher Education Act of 1965, work-study programs were expanded, a program of need-based student grants established, federal assistance to struggling colleges provided and a broad set of egalitarian educational objectives outlined. In 1968, the TRIO outreach and academic support programs (Upward Bound, Talent Search, and Special Services for Disadvantaged Students) were created. The 1972 amendments to the Higher Education Act provided additional financial assistance to needy students through the Basic Educational Opportunity Grants, later known as Pell Grants.[36]

It is significant that the successes of organizations such as the Congress of Racial Equality and the Southern Christian Leadership Conference had resulted in the desegregation of southern public accommodations by 1964. Young African-Americans were at the heart of these southern campaigns. Many of them, by the mid-1960s, had grown disillusioned with the electoral politics of the post-Kennedy era. They had become alienated from the northern white liberal youth who were their civil rights allies in Mississippi. They became attracted to the philosophy and strategies of Black Power. They were mindful of the independent, spontaneous rebellions in northern cities of the masses who had realized no tangible gains in their lives from civil rights won or rewon. They were bewildered by the murder of Malcolm X, in 1965, and saw Martin Luther King and Stokely Carmichael come north to fill the void left by Malcolm's death. The coup de grace was King's assassination. All of these influences had a traumatizing and radicalizing effect on African-Americans, especially urban youth.[37]

Coinciding with these developments, waves of ghetto youth began to flow into college campuses. As Berry and Blassingame report, by 1978, more than 50 percent of all black college students were attending white colleges,[38] reversing for the first time the historical pattern of black institutions having enrolled the majority of African-Americans who went to college. Once there, these black students, whose representation in the total student body rose from 5 to as much as 10 percent on many campuses during the late 1960s, made their collective presence profoundly felt. They became a militant social force inside the university by disrupting the normal state of affairs. They held different aspirations and articulated new demands for the content of their education and the treatment of their race. As collegians, some of them were extending the movement they had generated for cultural relevance in high school. According to Drake,

> These high school students of the northern Black ghettos wanted . . . courses for very specific reasons—to aid them in their identity quest; to bolster a sense of pride of being Afro-Americans; to supply them with facts and myths to defend their ethnic group against its detractors and to reinforce bonds of solidarity between Black people in their struggle for equality and respect.[39]

Concurrently, similar demands were being issued by black students and their faculty and administrator allies in California as concessions were forged there for a new, culturally relevant education. Also between 1967 and 1972 students at black schools such as Howard, Fisk, Southern and Jackson State pressed for curricular and other changes at those institutions. The major struggles though, involved black students in the predominantly white schools and the common denominator across the country was the push for documenting and projecting African heritage and the African-American experience that became popularly referred to as black studies.

By 1971, five-hundred white colleges had established programs in black studies.[40] The status of programs in this fledgling field largely paralleled that of African-American people on the campuses. It was one thing for these programs to be tolerated out of political expediency. It was another matter altogether for them to be accepted as legitimate academic enterprises. As with the people whose historical experiences it is organized around, black studies remains very much as the margin in higher education.

Contemporary Trends

It is clear by some indices that some progress has been made in African-American higher education since the mid-1960s. Though grudgingly, the study of the black world has been incorporated into the curriculum of some institutions. As already indicated, federal legislation did pave the way for greater access—momentarily—for African-Americans and other people of color to attend college. Since the mid-1970s, however, the numerical gains in the black presence on campus have been eroding. Affirmative action programs, whose premise is that compensatory measures are needed to overcome past injustices, were begun in 1967 when the federal Department of Health, Education and Welfare started requiring colleges and universities to adopt plans setting goals for the hiring of women and racial minorities. Thus far, while sound in concept, affirmative action programs have not yet appreciably worked. They have not broadly produced equal educational opportunities for students, increased the representation of African-Americans in the work force or reduced the racial discrimination which exists in the academy or in the larger society. (Their shortcomings aside, the legal basis for affirmative action programs has been undercut by recent Supreme Court decisions.[41]) In fact, education opportunities have been diminishing for African-Americans, the only group whose undergraduate enrollments went down between 1980 and 1984.[42] This has been occurring as the rate of blacks graduating from high school has been increasing.

The overall decline of black participation in higher education, Wilson asserts, is most clearly but not completely explained "by a combination of circumstances accompanied by an alarming increase in tuition costs and a lessening economic viability of the Black community in being able to afford college education."[43] Other causes for the decline in enrollment of African-Americans in college include the enticements of military service and proprietary schools and the societal trauma of high black youth unemployment, an increase in crime, the ravages of the drug epidemic and family disintegration. The negative impact of these and related phenomena is pervasive and African-American men have become an endangered species.[44] A conspicuous lack of effective national leadership and a truncated national attitude and will in issues related to the education of people of color are other factors which contribute to the downturn in the overall educational progress of African-Americans.

With these developments, cases of hostility against blacks on white campuses have dramatically risen during an era of increased campus tension and conflict. Coincidentally, enrollments at black colleges have increased somewhat. This trend is explained at least in part by the generally greater affordability of black schools, their capacity to offer a more amicable and supportive learning and living environment and a more desirable cultural experience, and the tradition they have sustained in cultivating black leadership. Despite enrolling only 17 percent of black college youth, historically black colleges and universities awarded 34 percent of the college degrees obtained by African-Americans in 1987.[45] The attractiveness of black collegiate institutions to many African-American students and their families to the contrary, we may expect the bulk of black collegians to experience higher education in preponderantly European-American institutional settings. It is these settings that provide a stage on which will unfold the continuing drama of the conflicts, challenges and imperatives of the new diversity in higher education in the United States during the 1990s.

SOME NOTES ON THE PROBLEM

Student populations in American higher educational institutions will be more colorful, older, more female and more educationally and occupationally "at risk." The new diversification will offer unprecedented implications for the curricular, co-curricular and policy decisions educators must make over the next decade and beyond.

Can higher learning institutions mount an affirmative response to the conflicts and challenges brought on by the new realities of diversity? Can colleges and universities open themselves to multicentered perspectives to produce and reflect a holistic view of the world? These questions are part of the current debate of national proportions in education circles as to whether institutions should adapt their culture and, if so, how. (The debate has been ongoing, but has been sharpened with the publication in 1987 of Bloom's *The Closing of the American Mind* and Hirsch's *Cultural Literacy*).[46] Seeking the answers to these questions will be a major preoccupation in the near future and this will require a reexamination of the modal structure and character of the American higher education enterprise.

The issue of whether the American academy can modify its culture to accommodate the new diversity in its student body cannot be adequately addressed without coming to terms with the social-political-economic lines on which it has been historically organized. Universities, we must recognize, are at the center of the social construction of reality. What people come to believe is real is influenced and determined by scholars, who are the producers, distillers and transmitters of knowledge. That gives the university, where the scholars are based, tremendous power which must co-exist with the exercise of social responsibility for human development. Three salient features of American higher education that have stood as impediments to people of color and women are that it has been monocultural, Western Eurocentric and male dominated.[47] In coming years, the academy will increasingly be called upon to (1) open itself up to the other ways of seeing and doing derived from a plurality of cultural experience; (2) acknowledge the diminishing dominion of Western (or any single) cultural ideology as the universal determinant, conveyer and interpreter of heterogeneous human experience; and (3) challenge the gender chauvinism in the production of knowledge which restricts fuller individual and societal development.

Beyond the need for generating a new thrust for actualizing the human service component of their mission, it is in their own self interests that colleges and universities play a central role in the movement for cultural democracy in education. Neither the academy, nor the larger society, can afford the social-political chaos that would result from people from disparate cultures remaining outside, or at the margin, of society.

The remainder of this essay will be devoted to suggestions for ways colleges and universities might address the new diversity.

TOWARD AN ACTION AGENDA FOR A TRULY HIGHER EDUCATION: PROBLEMS AND PROSPECTS

We need, as Atwell has implored, a new momentum.[48] The new diversification of the American population in higher education, in the workplace and in other sectors of society will require moving from the condition of diversity (the mere presence of multiple racial and ethnic groups and women in a given setting) to the point where different groups actively explore, understand and appreciate others' cultures. In higher education, the struggle to democratize the cultural component of the education process could manifest itself in several overlapping areas, as discussed in the listing of issues and problems below.

Reconceptualization and Planning

We must acknowledge our limitations. Many of the structures and values we accept on our campuses are actually obstacles to the educational and wider success of people of color and women. As I have argued, the defacto ethos of the European-American academy is often at odds with this goal. A critical reexamination of our assumptions and conventions is needed to determine which ones are worth preserving and which ones are now counterproductive. Among the questions which a broad-based dialogue must address here are: What values are to receive top priority? What—and whose—traditions should be perpetuated? What skills are most needed to build society? What should be the relationship of the values espoused for the new diversity in education to the economic system? How is progress measured in the movement toward democratic pluralism in the academy?

Preparing for both the quantitative and qualitative infusion of diversity in higher education will increasingly be a central part of the long-term and short-term planning of American colleges and universities.

Leadership

Campus leaders will be faced with the task of articulating a sense of urgency in their commitment to put the goal of increasing and enhancing the participation of people of color and women high on the institutional agenda. This sense of urgency needs to permeate all levels of the institution (the board of trustees, the president and other top officers of administration, faculty, staff, students, parents and alumni) and others such as legislative bodies, foundations and various governmental agencies that interact with the school.

Verbal commitments on the part of decision makers to a more culturally democratic pluralism in higher education can be concretized by securing adequate staffing patterns and providing other human resources, adhering to established timetables for attaining objectives, following accountability procedures, evaluating ongoing efforts to ensure desired results and spending personal time in various projects undertaken by an institution. Also, many leaders of education in institutions do not have the knowledge base for dealing with diversity. They do not grasp the essence of the problem and the possibilities for constructively responding to it. For them to exercise effective leadership they will have to retool for the tasks that lie ahead. Further, educational leadership must reaffirm and project commitment to ethnic studies and women's studies at the undergraduate and graduate levels.

Adapting Styles of Teaching and Learning

The curriculum must be targeted for change. "We must extend the traditional curriculum," in the words of Atwell, "beyond western civilization as a clear signal that we not only tolerate but cherish the diversity of our society."[49] Prevalent assumptions about a generic approach to scholarship, teaching and learning, curriculum formation and development, and certain types of cognitive functions being more valuable than others will be scrutinized and proven restrictive for, if not dysfunctional to, a more holistic human development. Demands for pedagogical reform to take various culture-based learning styles into account may heighten and we will be required to rethink overall curriculum and instructor competence. Many of us will have to substantially redesign our approach to educational problem-solving.

The curriculum guides the production of knowledge. A readily available, yet heretofore largely distorted, ignored and underutilized, knowledge base already exists that can both expand and correct the traditional curriculum where it is deficient in its treatment of the broader human experience. Concerted efforts need to be made to integrate that base of knowledge with the production of new knowledge.

Partnerships

The racial problems evident in our colleges and universities did not start from and will not be resolved on the campus alone, of course. The new diversification will call for a comprehensive, massive societal approach toward producing a truly educated citizenry. Alliances, which will be needed on all levels and across many sectors, must be strengthened if they already exist and created where they do not. Pioneering linkages will have to be made involving education, various levels of government, business and industry, foundations, etc. in chartering the new territory of teaching, learning about and guiding the realities of race and gender-specific diversity. Cooperative ventures already proven successful need to be fortified and replicated.

Also, diverse groups will have to do more to support one another to infuse cultural democracy into the higher education enterprise. A new dialogue must be struck and functional unity built, for instance, between women's studies and ethnic studies, if we are to incorporate cultural diversity into gender-related scholarship.

Additionally, the crafting of a viable infrastructure as a mechanism for ensuring the continuity of movement toward democratic cultural pluralism is a task the various schools, associations and agencies must bring their resources to bear on.

Evaluation

Systematic assessment as part of long-range institutional and organizational planning for diversity must involve inquiry as to why and how past and current approaches to increase and enhance diversity in higher education have not worked. Scholars who have expertise in their disciplines and in a knowledge of their people are too often an untapped resource as consultants to the schools. Revising the evaluative criteria for promotion, salary increases and tenure decisions, so that those who make the greatest contribution to cultural democracy on campus are rewarded, will be necessary. Relatedly, new approaches and systems of peer inquiry in the production of knowledge among diverse groups need to be put in place.

Research and Scholarship

Who will retool established professionals in matters of gender and cultural diversification? Who will train those who will be the new producers of knowledge and how will we produce them? Who will decide what inquiry is most important? Government, foundations and business and industry will increasingly have an obligation to address these and similar questions. They, as well as colleges and universities, must support and reinforce the work of researchers and writers on culturally diverse and gender-specific concerns. A bottom line responsibility in this area is the synthesizing of old with new data on culturally diverse groups and women.

Academic Summit

As already indicated, a national effort will be needed to advance the aims of cultural democracy on the campus. Hilliard has called for an academic summit to catalyze moving forward with new speed and determination to open up higher education for needed change. Such a summit could stress:

- Clarifying politics and sociology of knowledge issues, especially with respect to the way the curriculum has hindered exposure to and understanding of diversity
- Setting the research agenda for achieving democratic cultural pluralism in education
- Developing new literature to support curriculum reconstruction
- Producing new audio-visual materials and techniques
- Establishing new communications networks
- Monitoring what is taught
- Securing commitment from key partners in the education process
- Attracting dual specialists—those who know their people and have mastered their disciplines
- Stimulating co-curricular developmental activities aimed at modifying the campus learning environment.

According to Hilliard, we also need a national curriculum organization that will oversee the charge to produce culturally democratic curricula from kindergarten through secondary school.[51] This organization would be a key link to state and national leadership. It would play a vital role in reviewing and changing, as necessary, the curriculum, particularly in liberal arts and general education, and its members would interface as well with representatives of the established disciplines.

In conclusion, the growing diversification of the nation's population will usher in a new social reality which will offer profound challenges to higher education. Colleges and universities will have two essential choices in the way they respond to these challenges: They may remain blindly on the course of tradition, thereby perpetuating an intolerable status quo and the chaos which attends it, or they may undergo the introspection and modification of their character, structure and process, i.e., of their culture, that will be necessary to make the higher education enterprise more culturally democratic. The times—now more than ever, I have argued—require the latter choice. For some, the changes in higher education that are needed for preparing for the twenty-first century may be viewed as a lowering of standards. This need not be. It is our collective responsibility to evolve a truly higher education which can accommodate both diversity and excellence. The alternative, as reflected in the chaos that is evidenced in race relations on campuses across the country over the last few years, runs counter to individual, community, group and societal well-being and development. The difficulties associated with advancing cultural democracy in higher education are surpassed by the need to do so. To be remiss in continuing and winning that struggle would be national catastrophe none of us can afford, with consequences that future generations ought not have to bear.

NOTES

1. Telephone interview with Howard Ehrlich, Executive Director of the National Institute Against Prejudice and Violence in Baltimore, MD, July 31, 1989.

2. See Allen R. Gold, "Campus Racial Tensions—and Violence—appear on Rise," *New York Times,* February 21, 1988, p. E6; Lena Williams, "Officials Voice Growing Concern Over Racial Incidents on U.S. Campuses," *New York Times,* December 15, 1986, p. 13; Denise K. Magner, "Blacks and Whites on the Campuses: Behind Ugly Racist Incidents, Student Isolation and Insensitivity," *Chronicle of Higher Education,* 35, (April 26, 1989): A1, 28–32; María de la luz Reyes and John J. Halcón, "Racism in Academia: The Old Wolf Revisited," *Harvard Educational Review* 58 (August 1988); 299–314; Barbara Vobejka, "Report Cites Race Bias in Virginia Colleges," *Washington Post,* October 1, 1987, p. 1; *Newsweek on Campus*, February 1987.

3. Cameron McCarthy, "Rethinking Liberal and Radical Perspectives on Racial Inequality in Schooling: Making the Case for Nonsynchrony," *Harvard Educational Review* 58 (August 1988): 275.

4. See Harold Cruse, *Plural But Equal: A Critical Study of Blacks and Minorities in America's Plural Society* (New York: William Morrow, 1987); William B. Johnston et al., *Workforce 2000: Work and Workers for the 21st Century* (Indianapolis: Hudson Institute, 1987); The Commission on Minority Participation in Education and American Life, *One Third of a Nation: A Report of the Commission on Minority Participation in Education and American Life* (Washington, DC: American Council on Education, 1988); and Price M. Cobbs, "Valuing Diversity: The Myth and the Challenge," in *The State of Black America, 1989,* (New York: National Urban League, 1989), pp. 151–159.

5. *One Third of a Nation*, p. 2.

6. U.S. Bureau of the Census, "United States Population Estimates by Age, Sex and Race: 1980 to 1987," *Current Population Reports,* ser. P-25, no. 1022 (Washington, DC: U.S. Government Printing Office, March, 1988), table 1:12, in ibid.

7. U.S. Bureau of the Census, "Projections of the Hispanic Population: 1983 to 2080," *Current Population Reports*, ser. P-25, no. 995 (Washington, DC: U.S.

Government Printing Office, November, 1986), table T: 14, in *One Third of a Nation*, p. 2.

8. *Demographic Imperatives: Implications for Educational Policy* (Washington, DC: American Council on Education, 1983), p. 10, in *One Third of a Nation*, p. 2.

9. U.S. Bureau of the Census, "Money, Income and Poverty States of Families and Persons in the U.S.: 1986," *Current Population Reports*, ser. P-60, no. 157 (Washington, DC: U.S. Government Printing Office, August, 1987), table 18:30, in ibid.

10. William B. Johnson et al., *Workforce 2000*, p. 89, in ibid., p. 3.

11. Price M. Cobbs, "Valuing Diversity," p. 154.

12. National Alliance of Black School Educators, *Saving the African American Child* (Washington, DC: National Alliance of Black School Educators, 1984), p. 12.

13. George D. Kuh and Elizabeth J. Whitt, *The Invisible Tapestry: Culture in American Colleges and Universities*, ASHE-ERIC Higher Education Report no. 1. (Washington, DC: Association for the Study of Higher Education, 1988).

14. Ibid., p. 96.

15. Ibid., pp. 12–13.

16. Eric Lincoln, "The Uses of Black Culture" (Address delivered at Spelman College, Atlanta, GA, July 22, 1981).

17. George S. Counts, *Dare the School Build a New Social Order?* (New York: Arno Press, 1969). Originally published in 1932.

18. Mary Frances Berry and John W. Blassingame, *Long Memory: The Black Experience in America* (New York: Oxford University Press, 1982), p. 7.

19. Meyer Weinberg, *A Chance to Learn: A History of Race and Education in the United States* (Cambridge: Cambridge University Press, 1977), p. 11.

20. Berry and Blassingame, *Long Memory*, p. 3.

21. Weinberg, *Chance to Learn*, pp. 12–13.

22. Carter G. Woodson, *Mis-education of the Negro* (Washington, DC: Associated Publishers, 1933) p. xiii.

23. Janice E. Hale-Benson, *Black Children: Their Roots, Culture, and Learning Styles*, rev. ed. (Baltimore: Johns Hopkins University Press, 1986), p. 9.

24. See ibid., pp. 9–19; John W. Blassingame, *The Slave Community: Plantation Life in the Anti-Bellum South* (New York: Oxford University Press, 1972), pp. 1–76; Maulana Karenga, *Introduction to Black Studies* (Los Angeles: Kawaida Publications, 1982), pp. 36, 204–208; Sterling Stuckey, *Slave Culture: Nationalist*

Theory and the Foundations of Black America (New York: Oxford University Press, 1987), pp. 3–97; C. Eric Lincoln, "Black Studies and Cultural Continuity," *Black Scholar* 10 (October 1978: pp. 12–17; Robert Blauner, *Racial Oppression in America* (New York: Harper and Row, 1972), pp. 111–161; Lawrence W. Levine, *Black Culture and Black Consciousness: Afro-American Folk Thought from Slavery to Freedom* (New York: Oxford University Press, 1977); Lorenzo D. Turner, *Africanisms in the Gullah Dialect* (Chicago: University of Chicago Press, 1949); and Melville Herskovits, *The Myth of the Negro Past* (New York: Harper, 1941).

25. Blassingame, *Slave Community*, p. 41.

26. See Thomas L. Webber, *Deep Like the Rivers: Education in the Slave Quarter Community, 1831–1865* (New York: W. W. Norton, 1978).

27. Allen B. Ballard, *The Education of Black Folk: The Afro-American Struggle for Knowledge in White America* (New York: Harper and Row, 1973), p. 9.

28. Martin Carnoy, *Education as Cultural Imperialism* (New York: David McKay Company, 1974), p. 272.

29. Ibid., pp. 272–273.

30. W. E. B. DuBois, *The Souls of Black Folk* (Chicago: A. C. McClurg, 1903).

31. Horace Mann Bond, *Negro Education in Alabama: A Study in Cotton and Steel* (New York: Antheneum, 1969), p. 196.

32. Berry and Blassingame, *Long Memory*, pp. 285–286.

33. Ibid., pp. 286–287.

34. Ibid., p. 287.

35. Niara Sudarkasa, "Black Enrollment in Higher Education: The Unfulfilled Promise of Equality," in *The State of Black America, 1988*, National Urban League (New York: National Urban League, 1988), p. 19.

36. J. L. Greer, *Minority Access to Higher Education*, AAHE-ERIC Higher Education Research Report no. 1 (Washington, DC: American Association for Higher Education, 1982), in Sudarkasa, "Black Enrollment," p. 10.

37. Alan K. Colón, "A Critical Review of Black Studies Programs," (Ph.D. dissertation, Stanford University, March 1980), pp. 44–45. See also Harry Edwards, *Black Students* (New York: The Free Press, 1970); and James McEvoy and Abraham Miller, *Black Power and Student Rebellion* (Belmont, CA: Wadsworth, 1969).

38. Berry and Blassingame, *Long Memory*, p. 287.

39. St. Clair Drake, "Reflections on Black Studies." (Expanded version of a paper presented to the Danforth Workshop on Liberal Arts Education, Colorado College, Colorado Springs, CO, July 1970), p. 4.

40. Martin Weston, "Black Studies: Dead or Alive?" *Essence* 5 (August 1974): p. 57.

41. See E. J. Dionne, Jr., "Civil Rights Rulings Have Many Asking, Is the Second Reconstruction Coming to an End?", *New York Times,* July 13, 1989, p. 20.

42. Sudarkasa, "Black Enrollment," p. 20.

43. Reginald Wilson, "Black Higher Education: Crisis and Promise," in National Urban League, *State of Black America, 1989,* p. 20.

44. See ibid., pp. 128–129.

45. Ibid., p. 126.

46. Allan Bloom, *The Closing of the American Mind* (New York: Simon and Schuster, 1987); and E. D. Hirsch, Jr. *Cultural Literacy: What Every American Needs to Know* (New York: Houghton Mifflin, 1987).

47. James A. Anderson, "Reconstructuring the Intellectual Character of the College Experience Through the Infusion of Gender and Race" (Remarks delivered at a preconference workshop for the Conference on Opening the American Mind: Race, Ethnicity and Gender in Higher Education, Rutgers University–Camden, Camden, NJ, September 20, 1989).

48. Robert H. Atwell, "Minority Participation in Higher Education: We Need a New Momentum" (Remarks delivered at the ACE Annual Meeting, Washington, DC, January 19, 1988).

49. Ibid., p. 6.

50. Asa G. Hilliard, III, "The Rationale, Issues and Practice for Cultural Pluralism in the Curriculum" (Remarks delivered at a preconference workshop for the Conference on Opening the American Mind: Race, Ethnicity and Gender in Higher Education, Rutgers University–Camden, Camden, NJ, September 20, 1989).

51. Ibid.

LEON BOTSTEIN

Chapter Five

The Undergraduate Curriculum and the Issue of Race: Opportunities and Obligations

INTRODUCTION

During the past decade administrators have found themselves in a reactive position in dealing with issues of race and racism. Responding to incidents and external pressures has been the norm. In terms of long-range planning, often they are left to worry about the problem without much prospect of being able to do something about it. The ability to seize the initiative and create a climate on campus genuinely inhospitable to racism has proved elusive. The continuing presence of racism in our culture is visible on campus in overt and implicit ways. Actual hostility, avoidance and condescension—even if it is thoughtless liberal rhetoric—are all elements of the larger dilemma.

A promising but difficult arena for effective action is the college curriculum. Not only can racism be combated directly and profoundly, but the horizons of students can be broadened in a way that can retard the spread of prejudice. How can knowledge, tolerance, respect and affection be nurtured through the work done by students in the college classroom?

Chief administrators usually focus on dealing with racism in the governance of the campus. Admissions, student life and hiring practices are among the most common issues. This essay focuses on the heart of the university, the curriculum. Policy makers on campus must find a way to address the issue of race in the teaching function of the university without falling prey to strategies and techniques that provide little more than the appearance of efficacy.

The conventional approaches to the problem within the curriculum (e.g., special courses) may satisfy the immediate politics surrounding race issues. But these solutions can also disfigure the educational process, achieve little effect and even backfire. The calls for diversity and the attacks on traditional curricular practices seem to be effective slogans. But a more thoroughgoing reform of the undergraduate curriculum is necessary if the issue of race is really going to be grappled with.

The reform that is required may end up being more conservative in appearance and more radical in substance than any warring faction on today's campus may be willing to tolerate. Attacking racism in the curriculum requires attention to the aspirations and principles of liberal education to an extent that few institutions realize or may be prepared to give.

Historically, effective change within the university has required decisive leadership from above. In the matters of race, a commitment to widening access for students, diversifying the composition of the faculty and staff, and creating an atmosphere of respect and tolerance on the campus have clearly needed support from chief administrators and governing boards. With respect to the college curriculum, however, the patterns of change are more ambiguous. The protection of academic freedom and the traditions of faculty governance make intervention or leadership from above more problematic. Nevertheless, a commitment to a curricular vision and curricular principles and priorities on the part of the senior administration is indispensable.

This indispensability is not merely a function of the need to ensure that the proper resources are allocated. Substantive direction is required. Unfortunately, the recent pattern of administrative appointments has not demonstrated that intellectual leadership has been prized. Search committees have tended to select conciliators, mediators and managers. If the racial crisis within the university is going to be solved, principled intellectual leadership at the top will be necessary. Chief administrators can direct debate, eliminate uncertainty and combat inertia regarding the undergraduate curriculum, particularly where issues of race are at stake.

First, ten practical strategic suggestions are in order. They will be followed by a philosophical interlude which interprets the background behind the curricular debates now underway on many campuses. Last, some specific principles of curricular design will be discussed.

    1. Administrators should raise the curricular question of how the curriculum deals with the issue of race even in the absence of a crisis or an existing debate.

2. The issue must be raised for all students, no matter their majors. The issue then becomes one of general education.

3. The curricular question must be posed in terms of the larger goals of the curriculum, not as a reflection of the interests of any specific field or group. Proposals should be evaluated in the context of a consistent notion of how and why the curriculum is organized in a particular manner.

4. The issue of resources should be set aside so that the discussion cannot immediately be translated into potential losses and gains for particular parties. Change within existing constraints should be stressed.

5. The administration should tap faculty leadership on the basis of how respected they are, not how vocal they are on this issue. The most helpful faculty may be those who by autobiography or field have not dealt directly with the issue. Expertise and professional qualifications related to the study of an ethnic group or the phenomenon of racism may not be initially helpful.

6. Inflammatory, self-aggrandizing rhetoric and journalistic clichés on the issue should be avoided scrupulously. The administration should draft a written challenge, a statement which helps frame campus debate on the curricular dimension in the most powerful and principled manner without accusation or praise. Achieving popularity is not the goal. No one will be entirely satisfied.

7. Outside assistance, in the form of a visiting committee, for example, should be considered so that a larger national and cultural issue does not deteriorate into a local provincial battle in which participants lose perspective. The issue of race should at no time be segregated from the larger questions of overall goals, standards and practices in the curriculum.

8. Adding courses and faculty will not solve the issue.

9. The underlying assumptions of protagonists as the debate proceeds must be examined vigilantly. The administration should, in an even-handed manner, question the facile claims of all groups.

10. Addressing the issue of race in the curriculum means reaching students, not preaching to them or satisfying nonstudent constituencies. This means providing students with a serious and vital general education which has resonance far beyond the issue of race, since how we deal with race and racism reflects the essential character of our values, our concept of truth and our attitude towards democracy.

PHILOSOPHICAL INTERLUDE

It may be useful to step back from the practical concerns of the curriculum to reflect on some important underlying philosophical factors that have a fundamental although indirect relevance to our concern with the relationship between the undergraduate curriculum and racial and ethnic issues on campus.

> But I did not get my picture of the world by satisfying myself of its correctness; nor do I have it because I am satisfied of its correctness. No: it is the inherited background against which I distinguish between true and false . . . All testing, all confirmation and disconfirmation of a hypothesis takes place already within a system. And this system is not a more or less arbitrary and doubtful point of departure for all our arguments: no, it belongs to the essence of what we call an argument. The system is not so much the point of departure, as the element in which arguments have their life.[1]

Wittgenstein's reformulation of the dilemmas of certainty and objectivity point to how difficult it has become to talk about the central activities of the university: inquiry, teaching and learning. We have become uncomfortable with the assumption that convictions are subject to verification by evidence or that proof and argument can be marshaled and communicated satisfactorily.

Contemporary philosophical and methodological discourse has generated fundamental skepticism about ideas of commonality and coherence. It has made agreement regarding the purposes, practices and principles of the university harder to obtain than ever before. As scholars, teachers and learners, we have come to identify ourselves locally—by gender, race, religion and nationality. The idea of a larger category—humanity—of which we all are part has disintegrated politically, socially and intellectually. It remains understood as the residue of a particular cultural conceit and not as a timeless, universal aspect. The same might be said of the idea of reason.

No discussion of so crucial a matter as race and racism within the curriculum can avoid confronting the underlying debate concerning epistemology and interpretation. Without valid intercultural canons of reason and objectivity, universal standards (however modified) combating racism intellectually on a comprehensive basis become difficult.

On the issue of certainty—and therefore the matter of truth—Wittgenstein avoided a position of radical subjectivity. Knowing something for sure, accepting the validity of an argument, or acknowledging the results of some procedure of verification become contingent on an "inherited background," a "system." The inherited system must be accepted before the process of determining truth begins. It is the framework in which language functions. That framework has rules, which themselves, as Noam Chomsky's work suggests, are prior to experience and the use of rules of grammar. These rules secure the utility and comprehensibility of language among humans.[2] What appears as a concession to relativism is really a clarification of the rules of life.

Wittgenstein sought to contribute to the philosophical challenge of the early twentieth century, to reigning nineteenth century notions concerning truth, the scientific method, the relation of subject and object, the character of perception, the notion of the external world and the function of language as instrument of reason. These traditional verities frequently are condemned under the common heading of "positivism."

Despite the radical epistemological implications of his formulations, Wittgenstein was making a plea for identifying grounds of common truths. He was uncomfortable with either silence or the resigned acceptance of a jungle of diverse epistemologies, a Tower of Babel where there are no priorities, no legitimate questions of reliability or criteria of truth.[3] Wittgenstein's position is helpful. It stands in sharp contrast to those who, pleading the case of diversity, deny the validity of any construct of multicultural standards of judgment or normative intellectual coherence. The case *against* racism, after all, is based on universal and true propositions of science, ethics and politics.

The model for the university with which we still work in our public and private institutions is a nineteenth century construct. It is organized structurally along lines compatible with traditional ideals about what can be learned from one generation to another, how inquiry can be conducted, and the standards of verification ("testing, confirmation and disconfirmation," in Wittgenstein's terms) and communication. America's nineteenth century model was influenced by the German university. One consequence of this legacy is the continuing hegemony of graduate school objectives over competing efforts to delineate a circumscribed, autonomous arena for undergraduate study.

The relative homogeneity—in terms of race, ethnicity, religion and social class—particularly before 1945 (when African-Americans in higher education were educated, if at all, largely in segregated contexts), of the professoriate and student body in America and the undisturbed allegiance to nineteenth century epistemological foundations are connected historically. Complementary relationships existed among (1) a stable intellectual ideology of knowledge and inquiry; (2) the structure of the university; and (3) the elite population the university served. The symmetry and symbiosis among these three elements has broken down since the early 1960s. This may be, in retrospect, the most striking legacy of the turmoil of the 1960s within the university.

In higher education, the past quarter century has brought economic and social democratization in terms of access. Since the mid-1960s halting but yet somewhat successful efforts to destroy the barrier of racial discrimination have occurred. The policies of the Reagan-Bush years will not reverse the process, despite the enormous retarding influence they have exerted. As the university faces the coming decades, the facts of our national demography (not to speak of the political and ethical imperatives) will occasion an even more radical departure from the traditional social profile of students and unfortunately, to a lesser extent, faculty and other professionals.

It is ironic that the progress in democratization in terms of race in the area of student access coincided, historically, with the triumph of the several parallel critiques of traditional views of the nature of and approach to knowledge. The loss of coherence reflects itself in the character of faculty debates regarding priorities in the curriculum. The critiques have targeted the ideal of "objectivity"; a universal construct of "reason"; notions of "facts" and "certainties"; the legitimacy of the distinction between "fact" and "value;" and the validity of any particular system of hierarchy whether about an external world or truths within philosophical discourse, particularly in ethics and aesthetics.

Language itself has drifted from the status of a potentially objective instrument of discourse to a mechanism imprisoned in contextuality whose use as a neutral instrument, despite the insights of transformational grammar, is devalued as a cultural conceit. Phenomenological critiques have damaged the stability of meaning and therefore texts. The activities of speaking, writing and reading have undergone critical revision, the result of which is to enshrine the fundamental instability of any effort to derive or ascribe meaning from language generally, or to communicate through language over time and space, in print, beyond local niches of specific cultural coherences, ethnographically determined.[4]

The basic vehicle of learning, the written text, has been denied its historic and radical potential—to communicate over time and space with stable meaning, to carry identifiable meaning universally, irrespective of the identity of the reader. Complex modern theories of interpretation have damaged the idea of a fixed, shared object as the basis of discourse.

Since the 1970s, the American university has become a battleground of competing revisions of nineteenth century views of the enterprise of university education and research. This has been particularly acute for the humanities and social sciences, although the natural sciences have also been affected. The idea of "general education" is under a cloud, as a remnant of a particular social and intellectual tradition, as the residue of an historic and sustained domination by "others."

In the foreground of today's debate about methodologies of inquiry and expression is the intense struggle over content. Since the late 1970s, the attack on canons, the demand that heretofore forgotten dimensions of the past and present be reconstructed (e.g., the voices of women and minorities), the call for "globalization" in the curriculum, all have been hard. There is a sense that the inherited traditions cry out for revision and new interpretation. Behind these calls for change are voices representing women and the disadvantaged ethnic and racial minorities.[5]

The demand for access to the university, particularly with regard to race, which began in earnest during the civil rights movement in the 1960s, no longer can be described in ways analogous to the historic effort to gain access to the lunch counter, the voting booth and the purchase of housing—other objectives of the civil rights movement. No matter how uneven the achievements, the rights and services to which access has been gained (or still is being sought) other than the university remain quite fixed in their definition and social utility. With respect to higher education, however, the heretofore discriminated populations (whose equal access to the university is a political and ethical necessity) now encounter an institution once noted for its exclusivity whose character and purpose are in disarray. In other words, in terms of higher education, at the moment a new population is ready to sit down at the lunch counter, the counter is devalued. It is as if voting is suddenly deemed by its previous users as obsolete and fraudulent. The housing so eagerly sought is abandoned.[6]

The paradox is that at the moment access to an effective instrument seems at hand, the premises on which the existing system has wielded power (sometimes in an unabashed, arbitrary manner) are being undermined fundamentally. Those premises were considered the normative, universal rational methods and objectives now under attack. Therefore the university that functioned to provide power and confer status loses efficacy in the eyes of the elites that crated them just at the moment of serious social and ethnic democratization.

This process of theoretical undermining may look "liberal," even "radical," on the surface. Some of its advocates may be victims of discrimination. But the radical critique may actually be a form of delegitimization. Its impact may be reactionary and discriminatory, perhaps unconsciously designed to perpetuate the monopoly on power and authority of the traditional elite. In the case of the university one might say, following Wittgenstein: Yes, our institutions of learning are imperfect, conceited, and in some sense corrupt. But one might ask, are institutions in the world ever perfect? Might they really be different? Has there ever been a practical vehicle that did not break down, a bureaucracy without inefficiencies? Are not shortcomings really a matter of tolerable distances (within the complexities of modern society) between ideals and results rather than reflections of weaknesses in the ideals on which our institutions have been based historically?

If no utopian project has ever seen effective realization *in the world*, then perhaps the radical, skeptic attack on the epistemological traditions of discourse within the university is a highly masked but subversive project, particularly in terms of redressing racism. The fact that the rhetoric of critique is loaded with all sorts of claims regarding the possibility of achieving greater justice and equality in the future does not diminish the fact that the effect of the methodological internal strife is to weaken the university and its significance.[7]

Politically conservative theorists in recent years have contented themselves with attacks on relativism. They preach a nostalgic and tendentious allegiance to a mythical consensus about standards, methods and content of the past. The appropriation of the word "excellence" during the 1980s by educational policy makers associated with the Reagan years is one egregious example. There is, therefore, the prospect that after two centuries of hegemony, the ruling elites, radicals and conservatives alike, are undermining the American university and its working definitions while graciously inviting those who have been shut out to enter. What may be left are dismantled remnants. The elite seems content to muse that the enterprise and its intellectual foundations are without firm utility, epistemological security, or ethical or political priority.

If the university does not come to grips with the fundamental crisis of method, content and social function, a process of such serious devaluation of the enterprise of higher education for the decades ahead may take place. The once coveted groves of academe may become abandoned neighborhoods. In the name of modernity, methodological sophistication, deconstruction, the continuing crisis of philosophical and linguistic conscience—thinking that is neither naive nor merely idle careerist speculation—the highly prized enterprises of research and learning become trivialized as credentialling operations based on subjective conceits and illusions. Higher education is left without the philosophical foundation and the epistemological prestige that can give the university its importance in helping humanity attempt to progress from barbarism to civilization, from war to peace, from oppression, race and class discrimination to justice. Diversity itself is no answer.

This is not to diminish the significance of essential critical discourse, the profoundly ethical and tortured reflection of which Wittgenstein was uniquely capable. As we proceed rapidly on the task of eliminating racism and incorporating the African-American and other cultural traditions associated often with victims of injustice into the university, we must not impose an insupportable, false or artificial epistemological order on our institutions. However, in order to come to grips with the racial crisis, we must generate a common theoretical basis and clarify shared principles of action and belief, even if it means seriously changing the structure of how we conduct research and teach. The obligation to find a solid, valid basis for continuing the functions of the university may mean preserving and extending the inherited tradition of practice, particularly in the matter of curriculum.

The superficial claim that tradition has been ethnocentric and Eurocentric will not suffice. The proper integration of diverse methods, materials, perspectives and traditions is part of the dynamic of the old-fashioned project of the university. But the denial of the fundamentals of the old-fashioned enterprise without providing a resolution that creates an equivalent to the common-ground characteristic of the past is unacceptable.[8] The empowerment that higher education promised, if not delivered in the past, assumed that common ground.

In a democracy, the political project that underlies the racial integration of student-faculty populations in the traditional university and the legitimate demand for cultural diversification within the curriculum is the search for meanings for that which is common among humans. The project of universal literacy and the provision to all citizens a high level of education assumes the dissemination of a shared language and criteria for judging good and evil so that violence might be contained and peace and justice flourish.

Higher education as it exists today still depends on the assumption that the rhetoric of social contract theory has value; that ideas of human nature, reason and freedom can be developed in ways that hold beyond diversity; that universality in ethical terms is desirable. What might be common to all humans—notions of individuality, dignity, tolerance and respect—ought to be concrete and meaningful.

The failure to defend common-sensical truth, content and the *shared* political project with respect to higher education on the part of the committed opponents to racism unfortunately has given credence to simplistic fulminations from the political right about the triumph of relativism and radical subjectivism in the American university.[9] Our task within higher education (particularly in the curriculum) is to clarify and restore—in service of the ideals of racial justice and the death of prejudice and oppression—the validity of the "inherited background," the "system" in which we operate. That system serves to make the university an institution capable of sustaining freedom and truth against unpredictable but historically real enemies and odds.

Culture, knowledge, science, reason, and the search for and communication of truth—all the clichés reminiscent of tiresome, self-congratulatory university and liberal arts rhetoric—demand active reconstruction in ways that are compatible with institutional functioning as it is, not as it might be and never remotely was; with the university's central role in a society dependent on information and technology. We have an obligation to make the system and its rules work better than ever before.

THE UNDERGRADUATE CURRICULUM:
THE CASE OF GENERAL EDUCATION

Recent debates on curriculum, particularly those at Stanford University, reveal that the balance between general education and the major—

specialization—must be redressed. The legitimate demand for the inclusion of non-Western materials and the need to respond to traditions such as the African-American, Mexican-American and Native American within the general education framework cannot be addressed if the total amount of time devoted to general education remains fixed.

Too little time is allocated now to general education in American colleges. As a result, what emerges is a false and divisive debate between so-called traditionalists and radicals, between supporters of "Western" culture and those who argue diversity and deny canons, or any effort to sustain hierarchies of cultural judgment. All sides of the issue are fighting over a marginal amount of curricular time. As the legitimate agenda for general education grows, so must the time devoted to it. College might start earlier and become a six-year program of study, and high school be reduced to a two-year program.

The argument for maintaining current general education schemes or restoring past programs is often an example of false history masquerading as a plea for tradition. The programs of the past, focused as they were on the "Western Tradition", were neither so coherent nor so effective as to merit nostalgia. Living alumni often provide inadvertent evidence of the failure of past programs of general education to civilize students and instill the lifelong love of learning and critical thinking.

But an unnecessary struggle is provoked as requirements for completing the undergraduate major—which occupies up to 80 percent of a student's time in college—remain stable in terms of the numbers of courses. The demands now being made regarding content diversity are directed at an artificially determined block of time devoted in the curriculum to general education, particularly of a required sort. Apart from the growing extent of remediation required of all undergraduates (owing to the failure of high schools to educate adequately both the advantaged and the disadvantaged student) and the range of basic skills ideally deemed desirable at graduation from college, the demographic and cultural changes of the twentieth century have substantially enlarged the potential need for and agenda of general education. Therefore, leadership on the curriculum must involve guidance on the basic issue of how much time in the undergraduate calendar should be devoted to common study within a general education program for all undergraduates, notwithstanding the range or diversity of the future interests of students in terms of specialization.

The curriculum debate—the desire and call for cross-cultural comparisons and the extensive integration of non-European materials—mirrors a process of de-Europeanization in terms of world politics, culture and the character of the United States. The way out of the static debate regarding a canon and a core is not to concede that there are no canons, or that no valid core can be constructed for all students. Rather, we should recognize that canons—as canons, not mere preferences—have always changed and must change periodically.

Two hundred years ago, Roman history and Latin authors occupied a central place in education. The Roman tradition provided many of the models for the Founding Fathers in America and the leaders of the French Revolution. But today, not even the most conservative proponents of courses on a common Western heritage, or even the centrality of antiquity are calling for Horace, Vergil, Sallust, Cicero or Tacitus. Since the late nineteenth century, in England, Germany and the United States, arguments for the pedagogical centrality of antiquity have been centered on the heritage of Ancient Greece.

If required general education is given the proper place, then racism can be addressed in the curriculum in part through diversity. The inherited traditions will flourish precisely through the integration of wholly new materials and perspectives. A core and canon might both emerge, specific to each institution. Dropping items and including new ones and basic redesign need not involve radical compromises in coherence or integrity.

Furthermore, if general education as such is properly prized by an institution as part of a genuine commitment to liberal learning, then the issues debated cease to be ones of constituent representation and political symbolisms, but become ones of authentic curricular and pedagogical principles. One reduces the likelihood that the curriculum will become a surrogate arena for political conflicts within institutions that have little to do with what is taught and required.

What has enraged so many observers is that the debate on the curriculum seems to be managed by all sides—by protagonists of change and those who defend tradition—as if the issues at stake were comparable to those associated with affirmative action policies, where numerical analysis and proportionate measurement are used to evaluate the legitimacy of the result. The proper conceit in faculty discourse about curriculum development is that the criteria of educational need and quality in materials and design—seemingly substantive and autonomous issues—must prevail. Within the accepted rhetoric of curricular discussion, a simple plea for diversity and representation is properly deemed insufficient.

The argument for change on behalf of issues and materials reflecting racial diversity and the equality of races should not resist the traditional premises of curriculum design. Neither should it manipulate them by using the rhetoric of curriculum as a thinly veiled disguise for other agendas. The best bases on which to challenge—from the perspective of excluded cultures—so-called tradition, current practice or reactionary schemes for core programs are the classic assumptions, ideals and rhetoric of the liberal arts. These are the apparent premises embraced by the opposition.

Few existing programs actually honor the standards and normative claims asserted by those who think they are defending an historic curricular and intellectual tradition. Coherence and the transmission of the Western cultural heritage are difficult to document in existing programs of undergraduate study, least of all in distribution requirements or the definition of majors. The critics of pressures for curricular change have a hard time defending present or recent practice on the very grounds they invoke against reformers seeking to integrate new materials and points of view: effectiveness and coherence.

The call for cultural diversity in the curriculum coincides with the long overdue need to reconsider conventional undergraduate curricular design. The defense of changes which seek to deal with matters of race can, and should, be couched in terms of the overall validity of liberal learning. The virtues of the collection of courses and requirements outlined in most college catalogues, in terms of the ideal of the liberal arts, are rarely sufficient to frame a powerful argument for keeping curricular practice intact on the grounds of the traditional rhetoric of liberal learning.

However, if one takes the idea of general education seriously, then the matters of race and diversity come into play in a fundamental manner quite apart from efforts at visible racial representation in curricular materials.[10] The kind of so-called curricular affirmative action argument that seems so offensive to so many faculty does not need to be invoked.

The obstacles to change in the curriculum that face proponents of diversity are the same obstacles facing the creation of any effective program of general education per se. These obstacles include (1) the criteria of hiring and promotion, which place a low value on participation in general education; (2) the excessive disciplinary narrowness of graduate training, which renders the Ph.D. holder insufficiently trained to teach in well-designed general education programs; (3) the failure of institutions to redress these two shortcomings, particularly to curb the power of departments; (4) the reluctance of faculty to train to teach outside of their disciplines; (5) the absence of sufficient resources to ensure that a general education program can be designed and implemented in a way that accounts for legitimate scholarly specialization and eliminates the fear that general education curricula must be, by definition, intellectually invalid and suspect from the perspective of individual disciplines.

Taking two common alternative principles of undergraduate curricular design—(1) the focus on broad issues and problems, and (2) the concentration on the historical dimension—the possibilities for practical resolution become clear. If one asked the question, how does one develop among contemporary undergraduates the capacity to think, inquire and debate articulately about issues such as justice or the individual in society, then in proposing serious curricular solutions, the matter of race, nonwhite and non-Western cultures, as well as a reformulated construct of the Western tradition, all must come into play.

One must not forget that one is designing curricula for students born between 1970 and 1980. What will motivate them, in the first place, to serious thinking, reading and writing? In answering that question one must face the shared political and historical autobiography of the student body. Race and the development of African-American community, for example, cannot be avoided; neither can the cultural materials from that tradition. The history of slavery and the politics of race since 1860 until 1970 is essential history. By asking fundamental questions about what should be learned and how, the globalization and diversification process in terms of issues, materials and modes of interpretation can occur coherently. Serious attention to normative issues such as justice in the late twentieth century must include diverse and new materials and issues. Dusting off a curricular design from thirty years ago is clearly insufficient.

Alternatively, if one takes the historical as an essential, desirable sensibility to be encouraged by general education, the same conclusion will emerge. Clearly, one cannot teach traditional Western history, Chinese history and African history and account for new perspectives of historical research and inquiry in each arena all in two semesters. But if one devoted a reasonable block of time, then one could argue rationally and fashion a sequence of courses. For example, as part of a requirement to develop an understanding of history and the character of historical narratives and explanations, an undergraduate in California might read Herodotus for the interpretation of cultural difference; Thucydides for the relation of democracy to the pursuit of economic and military imperialism in a world power; and Bernal Diaz and Prescott on the conquest of Mexico. No American or Californian should be ignorant of Mexican history and culture, before Cortes and after.

Here the so-called classical tradition and the contemporary imperative to respond to matters of race and ethnicity merge easily. American history must also be taught. Cross-cultural comparison by the student then becomes ineluctable. The issues and correctives emerging from new social historical research can be integrated. When the motivation behind curricular decisions remains a vision of shared educational objectives and constructs of a common need, curricular coherence in terms of content and modes of interpretation is not hard to develop.

In the final analysis, it is the time-honored rhetoric of liberal learning that is the best strategy for widening the curricular frame of reference in terms of race. Students who graduate from our colleges, white and black, need to (and should want to) question, think about and understand the world they live in. That has always been the guiding assumption of liberal arts curricula. Tradition and intellectual continuity have therefore been essential virtues. But tradition need not be construed as restoration. Tradition is not a static concept, but a dynamic one.

The great innovations in core curricula of the past to which we are inclined to turn for inspiration were motivated by specific political agendas. The Columbia University general education program was an outgrowth of the first World War and America's decisive entrance into European affairs. Hutchins' programs and those of Barr and Buchanan at St. John's College (and those of the Deweyite progressive opposition to core programs in the 1930s) were responses to the crisis of confidence in American democracy in the face of the arrival at the university of diverse ethnic and religious groups after 1918, and the allure of fascism and communism in the 1930s. The Harvard "Redbook" program of the postwar era sought to address specific perceived needs, which derived from an interpretation of the challenges of the postwar era.

There never has been a general education curricular program free of a political agenda. The only question, therefore, in the context of the centrality of race, is not the mere representation of cultural diversity, but rather what the political project beneath a curriculum in our era should be. A disciplined answer to that question will force the creation of a modern, culturally diverse program of study that honors the cultural traditions of the West (as they are now understood) and offers a more compelling strategy for teaching essential intellectual skills of analysis.

The obligation of administrators in any given institution, therefore, is to get the faculty to confront fundamental issues of general education and liberal learning. The traditions of liberal learning offer a fixed and stable context from which to combat racism. Superficial, short-term self-interest and vulgar politics can be deflected. There is no normative curriculum. Specific curricular content in general education will necessarily differ from one institution to the next. But there will be common features if the definition of objectives is fundamental. We live, after all, in the same national context. We all live on the same planet and face comparable challenges as a result.

What might be common, shared, basic objectives, in fundamental political terms, of curriculum building on the undergraduate level as we face the end of the twentieth century? Among those objectives must be the fostering of racial understanding, tolerance and pride within diverse heritages. At the core must be convictions about the character and direction of those aspects of life that all individuals and distinct groups share in common. The celebration of diversity is legitimated by the support that celebration provides to the ethical priority of the sense of commonality and the recognition of the essential potential dignity and value of all human beings. The pursuit of the examined life by individuals in a democracy is the essential objective. Fulfilling the obligation of higher education demands that we assist all students in that confrontation.

Wittgenstein's "element in which arguments have their life" with respect to race, diversity and the curriculum is the traditional ideology of the liberal arts. The inclusion of cultural voices and heritages from within the United States and the global community is validated as an imperative consistent with tradition. The classic materials, primarily from Western history and literature, will continue to frame the enterprise, since the objectives—a critical, literate and politically active citizenry (not to speak of a productive one)—are themselves culturally derived and integral to the theory of democracy in the West.

The concept of rational discourse (no matter how refined and subtle), the encouragement of participation in decision-making within the public sphere, constructs of ethical responsibility, and individual autonomy gain their contemporary meaning within a stable historical framework. The result of vigilant criticism and review is a useful notion of freedom. Within the political project of linking education to democracy, the university can continue to function quite traditionally and effectively for all groups.

The expansion of programs of general education and the diversification of their content are crucial components in the service of this quite conservative definition of the goals of a college education. The radical epistemological critique that seeks to question the validity of the intellectual assumptions behind the university and its political significance ironically will serve the cause of combating racism only insofar as it helps to redefine the common human project, and does not subvert it.

The ultimate irony of the heated debate currently underway at many institutions is that the historic function of the undergraduate years in terms of traditional liberal learning has been honored for the most part only in rhetoric. The most radical avenue to combat racism in the undergraduate curriculum is therefore the most truly conservative: a genuine, if not revolutionary, effort to create serious programs of general education. Before the century comes to a close, we must realize the potential, in curricular practice, of the liberal arts. If we succeed, the promise of democracy for all citizens and the protection of freedom—not to speak of the potential of the United States culturally, politically and economically—might finally be realized.

NOTES

1. Ludwig Wittgenstein, *On Certainty* (New York: Harper and Row, 1969), pp. 15–16.

2. See the essays, including one by Chomsky, in John Searle, *The Philosophy of Language* (Oxford: Oxford University Press, 1971).

3. For a general and accessible view of these issues, see A. J. Ayer's *Philosophy in the Twentieth Century* (New York: Random House, 1982).

4. On the matter of reading, see for example "Reading: Old and New," in *Daedalus* 112, no. 1 (1983).

5. On the conservative side, a comparable call for radical revision of instructional practice (a variant on the general critique of the reigning intellectual foundations) has been reflected in the reintroduction of sacred premiums, the restoration of the regard for divine truth and Christian ethics, and the rejection of secular traditions of science and the nonsectarian claims to universal humanism. The flowering of new Christian colleges and universities and their struggle to integrate somehow modern science and the tradition of "neutrality" in scholarship with normative Christian ideals is the politically reactionary dimension of the general plight of the late twentieth century American university.

6. The closest analogy to this process as it regards the university is the contemporary critique of the legal system. The arguments of recent critical legal theory have deepened the skepticism regarding legal reasoning and assumptions about the traditions of the rule of law, including the autonomy of the legal dimension. The aura of neutrality—the law as blind to racial and class differences and as a vehicle through which justice might be achieved—has been cast into greatest doubt, ironically, within the university law schools.

7. This possibility is especially poignant given the general cultural climate that militates against the influence of the university and its curriculum on students. Confidence in the university needs to be higher, particularly because of the growing number of so-called nontraditional constituents. See Leon Botstein, "American Letters: An Absent Rigour," *Times Literary Supplement*, September 15–21, 1989.

8. It would be well to look for a moment at the political roots of much of modern theoretical skepticism in literary criticism, social science and philosophy. Beneath claims regarding the nature of inquiry and theories of language are often political projects. The cases of Paul de Man and Martin Heidegger are instructive. The arguable connections between their intellectual work and their association with radically evil political movements should inspire us to look carefully at the political overtones and linkages of contemporary, fashionable theories of perception, criticism and knowledge; at the connection between a philosophical psychology and methodology of interpretation and the inherent and potential political consequences. On Heidegger, see Victor Farias, *Heidegger und der Nationalsozialismus* (Frankfurt: S. Fischer, 1989), particularly the introduction by Juergen Habermas.

9. We currently focus on Allan Bloom's *The Closing of the American Mind* (Simon and Schuster, New York: 1987). For a serious example of the conservative critique, directed at the development of modern social science, see Leo Strauss, *Natural Right and History* (Chicago: University of Chicago Press, 1956).

10. Among the institutional and curricular solutions to be avoided is the creation of ghettolike enclaves such as area studies programs, which not only permit courses reflecting diverse cultures to be taken by students—in isolation—but also to be ignored.

WILLIAM T. TRENT

Chapter Six

Student Affirmative Action in
Higher Education:
Addressing Underrepresentation

The program of the 1969 Annual Meeting of the American Council on Education has as its theme "The Campus and the Racial Crisis." Events of the past academic year clearly indicate the need to examine and discuss this problem. Until the racial conflict can be mitigated, the academic community will lack the unity of coherence and endeavor it needs to move ahead.[1]

Disturbed by the faltering pace of minority advancement in American life and by the discouraging decline of participation of minority individuals in higher education, the American Council on Education (ACE) Board of Directors convened a special meeting in February 1987 to consider how higher education could take a leadership role in rekindling the nations commitment to the full participation of minority citizens.[2]

The above quotes were published twenty years apart and yet they could be interchanged between their respective documents with minor editing and almost no one would note a difference. This compatibility however must not be taken to mean that nothing has changed. Indeed, virtually the opposite—everything has changed—is perhaps a more accurate characterization of the legal, social and political climate surrounding minority advancement in 1989.

Twenty years ago:

- The racial crisis on campus focused solely on the demands and needs of blacks. Today the focus is on the needs of blacks, Hispanics, Native Americans and women in higher education.

- The proportion of entering black freshmen in white colleges was about 50 percent of total black enrollment. Today that figure is about 70 percent.
- The debate regarding higher education and race was occurring in an atmosphere of heightened expectations for equal opportunity and social justice. Today we monitor urban infant mortality rates that exceed those of third world countries.
- The Supreme Court was viewed as an ally in the struggle for civil rights. Today the conservative tone of the court has rendered decisions deemed detrimental to those earlier accomplishments.
- The nation seemed secure in its economic hegemony, confident in its ability to maintain and improve the quality of life for its citizens. Today the nation approaches the status of a debtor nation, with the budget deficit, declining competitive strength and a severe education crisis.

Along with these changes and many others, there has been progress for minorities and women in higher education. Women now constitute about 51 percent of undergraduate enrollment;[3] the black-white gap in high school graduation has narrowed;[4] total black enrollment in higher education was about 150,000 in 1960, but by 1975 had increased to over one million.[5] There has also been stagnation and decline as the momentum and optimism of the 1960s and early 1970s has been lost. As a result of this history of inconsistent progress, decline and stagnation, considerable inequality persists and in some ways has worsened. Education, especially higher education, is a fundamental component of social equality. Our dilemma remains one of deciding what equality means and what steps are legally and morally justifiable in achieving it.

This essay examines the problem of underrepresentation of blacks, Hispanics, Native Americans and women in higher education by focusing first on the characteristics of programs and practices implemented at the postsecondary level to address this issue, and next on two legal strategies—desegregation and affirmative action—that have been the primary basis for sustaining these efforts. The examination of the desegregation strategy is based on secondary analysis of national enrollment data while the affirmative action discussion is based on a brief discussion of the results of a post-*Bakke* study conducted in 1979. The chapter concludes with a limited discussion of policy recommendations and strategies.

THE AFFIRMATIVE ACTION CONCEPT AND PROGRAM COMPONENTS

Variously composed, strategies to increase representation are conventionally labeled student affirmative action activities due to their legal and conceptual evolution out of Executive Order 10925 issued by John F. Kennedy in 1961[6] and Executive Order 11246 issued by President Lyndon Baines Johnson in 1965.[7] In 1967 President Johnson issued Executive Order 11375 which included sex along with race as an illegitimate basis of discrimination.[8] The core principle of affirmative action is that of requiring "something more" of employers in order to overcome prior discrimination. It was this principle that President Johnson viewed as giving teeth to Title VI of the 1964 Civil Rights Act.

Student affirmative action references those programs and strategies, usually directed at blacks, Mexican-Americans, Native Americans, Puerto Ricans and women, employed by colleges and universities that are intended to increase the pool of applicants to, and enrollees in, the respective colleges and universities. Typically these programs entail special efforts over and above those aimed at the so-called "traditional" student, since there is evidence that the history of past discrimination and its continuing vestiges serve as barriers to the elimination of persisting inequalities. Such efforts may be required as a result of a finding of discrimination or they may be voluntary. To the extent that the concept references efforts that assure equal competition, it has enjoyed a fairly broad base of public support. When such efforts have appeared to entail preferential treatment due to race, ethnicity or sex, as has been contended since the 1970s, their legal and moral basis have been challenged.[9]

The special efforts to recruit, admit, enroll, retain and graduate underrepresented groups in higher education at both the undergraduate and graduate levels usually consist of some combination, or all, of the following components: broadened information dissemination regarding the college-going process—increasingly directed at students early in the education pipeline; assistance in securing and completing the various forms and applications associated with entry tests, admissions and financial assistance; a precollege visitation and/or summer enrichment experience; broadened and more sensitive admission criteria; targeted financial aid packages; social and academic counseling and advising; cultural centers and services designed to foster a more pluralistic and receptive environment; and, more recently, undergraduate internships intended to foster further educational endeavors. At the graduate level attention has turned to strategies that foster mentoring and promote professional socialization.[10] While the above strategies concentrate primarily on service delivery with an intended clientele, a broader strategy being fashioned at many colleges and universities entails introducing curricular reforms that shape a core undergraduate learning experience requiring coursework that embraces the sociocultural experiences of minorities and women in American society.

The origin and impetus for these programmatic responses to underrepresentation vary from one institution to the next and over time.

Some colleges began their efforts in the early 1960s in response to the moral fervor of the civil rights movement or to the urban unrest that expressed the frustrations of minorities with blocked opportunities. Still others evolved following the assassination of Dr. Martin Luther King in 1968. Especially in the South, where the black population was greatest and where the majority of the historically black colleges and universities are located, the response of public higher education to the need for increased access received its impetus from *Adams*, which is discussed below.[11]

Inexplicably, the set of programs known as "TRIO" programs—funded under Title IV, subpart 4, of the Higher Education Act of 1965—are rarely cited in the literature as having been of direct benefit to these early (and current) efforts. TRIO programs were often housed on college campuses and provided direct access to students, or in the case of Talent Search, supplemented and relieved high school and college counselors in the tasks associated with getting poor and minority students through the college identification, application and admissions process. Even with these early and more recent efforts, a crisis remains.

The crisis in American higher education reflected in the declining or low levels of enrollment and persistence (retention) for blacks, Hispanics and Native Americans and in the uneven distribution of women and Asian-Americans in selected fields of study is a threat to our core values of economic and social justice. Moreover, this crisis has, in the past ten years, demonstrated its challenge to the economic and social viability of this society. As we approach the twenty-first century, as many as one-third of the nation's work force will be members of an underrepresented minority group, and the failure to prepare them well has obvious and known implications. While the complexity of the problem of underrepresentation in higher education requires local, state and national efforts that exceed the scope of higher education, the efforts of the universities and colleges are crucial if not central. Effective student affirmative action policies and practices will be the cornerstone of the efforts of higher education in addressing the crisis of underrepresentation. These strategies and practices will be based on a combination of enforced legal mandates and good-faith efforts to eliminate racial inequalities in higher education. Both *Adams* and *Bakke* give clarity to the legal mandates and offer insight to enforcement. These two cases and their impact will be discussed, following a brief overview of key prior cases.

ACHIEVING EQUAL ACCESS

Depending upon one's choice of critical legal precedent, the undergirding justifications for and purposes of fair and equitable access to higher education have a twenty-five to forty year history. In *Sipuel* v. *Board of Regents of the University of Oklahoma* (1948) the Supreme Court ruled that a state could not deny a student admission to a public institution solely on the basis of race.[12] The enactment of the 1964 Civil Rights Act, just twenty-five years ago, further extended the legal basis of support for ensuring fair and equal access to higher education. The past two decades commencing with the original filing of *Bakke* in 1973, have witnessed protracted and heated debate over the limits and conditions of use of criteria to assure fair and equitable representation in higher education. Desegregation in education has been the primary way in which blacks and other minorities have contested for expanded opportunity in education at all levels. Affirmative action growing out of Title VI of the 1964 Civil Rights Act and the aforementioned executive orders have been the basis for securing more equitable representation.

DESEGREGATING HIGHER EDUCATION

Prior to the landmark Supreme Court decision, *Brown* v. *Board of Education*, 347 U.S. 483(1954),[13], there were four cases regularly cited as providing critical clarification of the responsibilities of colleges and universities to provide full and fair access. The first, *Missouri ex rel. Gaines* v. *Canada*, 305 U.S. 337(1938) centered on the denial of admission to law school of Lloyd Gaines, a black college student.[14] The state of Missouri argued that separate facilities could be provided for Gaines but the Court, finding that such facilities did not exist, ordered him admitted to the "white" University of Missouri Law School,[15] arguing that the student could not be denied admission solely on the basis of race.[15] In *Sipuel*, mentioned above, the Supreme Court ruled that the state of Oklahoma could not deny Ada Sipuel admission to law school solely on the basis of race and that the state must provide her education in conformity with the United States Constitution, as it did for white students.

In neither of these cases had the courts addressed the issue of segregation in education directly. This issue was, however, at the core of two subsequent cases: *Sweatt* v. *Painter*, U.S. 629(1950)[16] and *McLauri* v. *Oklahoma State Regents for Higher Education,* 339 U.S. 637 (1950).[17] In *Sweatt*, Texas attempted to circumvent the rulings of *Gaines* and *Sipuel* by arguing that separate but equal facilities existed and hence the black students suffered no loss of access. The Court ruled however that those separate facilities were inadequate and ordered that Sweatt be admitted to the University of Texas Law School.

George W. McLaurin, a retired professor from the faculty of Langston

University, was admitted to the University of Oklahoma in 1948 following a ruling in his favor by a three-judge panel finding that he had been denied access solely on the basis of race. The Oklahoma Board of Regents ruled however that he could be segregated within the university, giving rise to his subsequent suit protesting the harmful and detrimental effects of segregation from his fellow students. The court ruled in his favor (339 U.S. 641 [1950]), arguing that for educational reasons, the University of Oklahoma could not continue that practice.

The above cases precede *Brown* but provide important legal precedent and, according to Preer, provide an even richer and more telling discussion of the educational policy dilemma that has and continues to encompass the efforts of blacks to secure greater access to higher education.[18] At the heart of that dilemma is the role of historically black colleges and universities in the effort to expand opportunities. Preer argues that the legal strategies pursued in these cases necessitated challenging the quality of historically black institutions, thereby damaging their credibility and achievements, or pursuing strategies that would reinforce segregation. This conflict continues to challenge the role of those colleges and universities that have historically sought to meet the higher education needs of blacks, Hispanics and Native Americans.

In *Brown* v. *Board of Education*, 347 U.S. 483 (1954), the Court found that state policies to segregate students on the basis of race were unconstitutional and required all school systems to take affirmative steps to remove the vestiges of past discrimination "with all deliberate speed." Following on the heels of *Brown,* the Court ruled in *Florida ex rel. Hawkins* v. *Board of Control,* 350 U.S. 413 (1956) that *Brown* also held for higher education. Despite these rulings, progress in desegregating higher education in those states where de jure segregation persisted, was not forthcoming.[19] Title VI of the 1964 Civil Rights Act provided for federal regulation of higher education by prohibiting the distribution of federal funds to colleges and universities that discriminate on the basis of race, color or national origin.[20] Federal legislators intended it to enhance implementation of *Brown*. The *Adams* litigation resulted from the unsuccessful efforts of the then Department of Health, Education and Welfare (DHEW) to secure compliance from those colleges and universities that were found to be out of compliance with desegregation following DHEW reviews conducted in 1968 and 1969.[21]

Initially ten states were cited, but in 1970 DHEW did little to extract compliance partly because President Nixon, following the election, adopted a new policy of nonenforcement of desegregation laws and policies[22] (a presidential strategy revisited with much greater vigor under President Reagan following his election in 1980). The initial suit, *Adams* v. *Richardson*, was filed in U.S. District Court for the District of Columbia,

Judge John H. Pratt presiding. It has remained there throughout its complex history. The suit sought to change President Nixon's policy by requiring DHEW to (1) respond to the plans that had been received two to three years earlier; (2) institute enforcement proceedings where necessary; (3) monitor progress; and (4) conduct additional reviews in other states. Judge Pratt ruled in 1973 that DHEW had failed to execute its responsibilities under Title VI and that time permitted for voluntary compliance had long since passed. Initial criteria for the states to follow in constructing their plans were provided in 1973 and amended in 1977. In 1987 Judge Pratt ruled that the plaintiffs in *Adams* no longer had legal standing and dismissed the case.[23] This ruling was overturned in July of 1989, when the case was reinstated, but several questions were left unanswered.[24] Nonetheless the reinstatement of the case does restore the potential for securing greater access for blacks through mandated compliance. The history of this case also demonstrates the precarious and tenuous nature of even legally mandated compliance. The political climate of the past decade, nurtured by the deliberate efforts of the Reagan Justice Department to eliminate enforcement of, and to overturn, civil rights and affirmative action rulings, has not been friendly to the educational aspirations of underrepresented minorities. Evidence of the deterioration of educational opportunity is presented below.

The amended criteria for Title VI compliance resulting from *Adams* contained five broad categories: (1) disestablishment of the dual system; (2) desegregation of student enrollment; (3) desegregation of faculty, administrative staffs, nonacademic personnel and governing boards; (4) submission of plans and monitoring; and (5) definitions.[25] For purposes of this essay, only parts 1 and 2 are briefly mentioned. Part 1B required specification of the role of the traditionally black colleges in the state system, stating in particular that plans identify how they would be strengthened. In part 1C the states were required to identify the procedures they would follow in eliminating unnecessary program duplication among the formerly segregated colleges. These two issues are mentioned here because they are currently central to ongoing deliberations in several of the affected states, continuing to reflect the conflict between equality and opportunity discussed earlier.

Part 2 addressed the problem of student enrollments throughout the respective state systems and articulated specific targets based on proportional comparisons in enrollment. At the graduate level, these goals were to be articulated with respect to particular fields, recognizing that minorities and women have had differential success in fields like education as compared to the sciences and technical fields. While the ongoing debates over the issues in part 1 regarding the role of traditionally black colleges offer some evidence, the evidence for part 2 issues regarding desegregation and enrollment is somewhat clearer, with the availability of enrollment and degree attainment data from the Higher Education General Information Surveys (HEGIS — now the Integrated Postsecondary Education Data System, IPEDS).

This section presents data exploring two issues central but not limited to *Adams*: desegregation in student enrollment in the nation's public colleges; and the extent to which such desegregation has increased enrollment. The data presented are for the years 1976 and 1984 covering full-time undergraduate enrollment and full-time graduate enrollment. The desegregation index for undergraduate enrollment is presented for public and private, two-year and four-year colleges by region.[26] Black enrollments are also presented by college-type for each year for undergraduates and graduates. The latter are helpful in examining the impact of desegregation on black enrollment.

Thomas et al. reasoned that the central concern of desegregation proponents was the matter of access.[27] In short, the benefit of desegregation is as a strategy for increasing the number of slots held by blacks in higher education or greater black enrollment. Indeed the criteria of *Adams* explicitly calls for the enhancement of historically black colleges while at the same time increasing black enrollment in historically white colleges. In research focusing on the production of black doctorates in five *Adams* states, Trent and Copeland report minimal change in graduate enrollment and declines in some states, apparently due to the absence of graduate programs at the historically black campuses.[28] Desegregation without increased overall numbers of black students — increased access — is not a sufficient measure of progress.

The Coleman segregation index is employed in this study as it has an easily interpretable 0 (low) to 1 (high) range. The index represents the proportional underrepresentation of one group in the environment to the average number of members of another group. For these two years the percent of reporting institutions averages 96 percent. For these analyses only those institutions reporting nonzero black enrollment are included. As a result those colleges reporting no enrolled blacks during the 1976 or 1984 period are excluded. This has the effect of producing conservative estimates of college segregation.

The results are presented in tables 1 through 5. Table 1 presents the black enrollment figures by category for full-time undergraduates for all institutions included in the analyses and for only the traditionally white institutions included in the study. This table allows us to examine the 1976 to 1984 changes in black enrollment for all institutions compared to changes over the same time period for traditionally white institutions. Table 4 presents the same comparisons for black graduate enrollment. Tables 2 and 3 present the segregation indices for full-time undergraduates for all institutions

TABLE 1

Black Full-Time Undergraduate Enrollment

Region, Level and Control[1]	All Institutions[2]		Traditionally White Institutions[3]	
	1976	1984	1976	1984
Nation	604517	551442	454083	424556
North	102681	86983	99963	84732
Two-Year	36172	28056	36172	28056
Public	36617	18515	31617	18515
Private	4555	9514	4555	9514
Four-Year	66509	58927	63791	56676
Public	39690	27757	36927	26506
Private	26819	30170	26819	30170
Midwest	126025	110226	122722	108485
Two-Year	45470	39275	45470	39275
Public	41474	33159	41474	33159
Private	3996	6116	3996	6116
Four-Year	80555	70951	77252	69210
Public	55362	47511	53128	46662
Private	25193	23440	24124	22548
South	309527	303945	165114	181071
Two-Year	89343	83003	81760	76979
Public	81930	67104	76598	62586
Private	7413	15899	5162	14393
Four-Year	220184	220942	83354	104092
Public	156944	160598	68473	85775
Private	63240	60344	14881	18317
West	66284	50268	66284	50268
Two-Year	39442	24497	39442	24497
Public	39179	23634	39179	23634
Private	263	863	263	863
Four-Year	26842	25771	26842	25771
Public	21128	19784	21128	19874
Private	5714	5987	5714	5987

SOURCE: The data reported in these analyses are from the Higher Education General Information Surveys (HEGIS) of fall enrollment for 1976 (HEGIS XI) and 1984 (HEGIS XIX) public-use data tapes.

[1] The regions are defined as follows: North: ME, NH, VT, MA, RI, NJ, NY, PA, CT
Midwest: IL, IN, IA, KS, MI, MN, MO, NE, ND, OH, SD, WI
South: AL, AR, DE, DC, FL, GA, KY, LA, MD, MS, NC, OK, SC, TN, TX, VA, WV
West: AK, AZ, CA, CO, HI, ID, MT, NV, NM, OR, WA, WY

[2] The number and percent of colleges included in these calculations for 1976 and 1984 respectively were 2623 (91.9%) and 2784 (91.5%).

[2] The number and percent of colleges included in these calculations for 1976 and 1984 respectively were 2316 (86.4%) and 2698 (91.2%).

and for traditionally white institutions respectively. Tables 5 and 6 provide the indices for graduate enrollment.

Turning first to table 1, we see that black enrollment declined by 53,075 students nationally for these data. That pattern is consistent across all levels of enrollment for each region except the South. In the South, while overall enrollment declined, it was primarily among the two-year colleges and private four-year colleges. For four-year public colleges, those most central to the desegregation-access issue, black enrollment increased between 1976 and 1984 from 220,184 to 220,942 or 758 students.

The next panel of enrollment figures is for traditionally white institutions only. Again, for the nation, black enrollment declined from 454,083 to 424,556 in 1984, a drop of 29,527. This pattern again holds true for all regions except the South. Also, it is important to note that increases are apparent in the North and West for private two-year and four-year colleges and in the Midwest for private two-year colleges. In the South, black enrollment overall increased from 165,114 to 181,071, a gain of 15,957.

These figures suggest the following patterns. First, the decline in black undergraduate enrollment reported for all institutions, 53,075, is nearly twice as great as the decline reported for just traditionally white institutions, 29,527. That suggests that traditionally and predominantly black colleges and universities suffered a decline of nearly 24,000 students nationally. Clearer evidence for this is gained by examining the change in black enrollment for the South in these panels. Note that while black enrollment in the South showed an overall decrease when all institutions are included, the opposite is true for traditionally white institutions only. Here there is an overall gain of approximately 16,000 students, largely attributable to the four-year enrollment change. Even more clearly traditionally white four-year colleges enrolled a 38 percent share of full-time black enrollment in 1976 compared to a 47 percent share in 1984. The comparable figures for the public four-year colleges are 44 percent (68473/156944) in 1976 and 53 percent (85775/160598) in 1984. What distinguishes the South from other regions during this period is *Adams*. These figure suggest that the *Adams* effort was effective in increasing the enrollment of black students in traditionally white colleges, but probably at the expense of the traditionally black colleges. These are patterns indicating that shifts in enrollment, rather than actual increases in black enrollment, are what would account for any apparent gains on the part of traditionally white institutions. This addresses part of our question regarding the benefits of desegregation. It seems clear that whatever change in desegregation has occurred in higher education it has not resulted in increased access.

Turning next to tables 2 and 3, we can examine the change in

TABLE 2

Enrollment of Full-time Undergraduate Students in Higher Education

All Institutions[1]

Region,[2] Level and Control	1976					1984				
	Total Full-time Under-graduate Enrollment	Percent Black	Percent White	Ratio of White to Black Enrollment	Segre-gation Index	Total Full-time Under-graduate Enrollment	Percent Black	Percent White	Ratio of White to Black Enrollment	Segre-gation Index
Nation	5856640	10.3	82.3	8.0:1	38.4	5927023	9.3	80.6	8.7:1	34.0
North	1341310	7.7	86.5	11.2:1	25.5	1313305	6.6	86.0	13.1:1	21.4
Two-Year	316905	11.4	82.1	7.2:1	39.5	298787	9.4	84.0	8.9:1	29.9
Public	275399	11.5	82.0	7.1:1	41.2	236972	7.8	86.1	11.0:1	25.9
Private	41506	10.9	82.5	7.6:1	27.3	61815	15.4	76.3	5.0:1	35.3
Four-Year	1024405	6.5	87.9	13.5:1	17.7	1014518	5.8	86.5	14.9:1	16.9
Public	517391	7.7	86.3	11.2:1	24.8	464370	6.0	88.0	14.7:1	15.2
Private	507014	5.3	89.6	16.9:1	7.0	550148	5.5	85.3	15.6:1	15.9
Midwest	1544849	8.2	88.4	10.8:1	28.3	1606092	6.9	87.8	12.7:1	23.0
Two-Year	336934	13.5	83.1	6.2:1	49.9	352047	11.2	84.0	7.5:1	37.0
Public	316809	13.1	83.7	6.4:1	49.5	317694	10.4	85.1	8.2:1	38.1
Private	20125	19.9	73.2	3.7:1	53.3	34353	17.8	74.1	4.2:1	26.2
Four-Year	1207915	6.7	89.9	13.5:1	15.9	1254045	5.7	88.8	15.6:1	14.8
Public	866795	6.4	90.5	14.2:1	13.3	912845	5.2	89.6	17.2:1	12.5
Private	341120	7.4	88.5	12.0:1	21.6	341200	6.9	86.7	12.6:1	19.2
South	1787667	17.3	76.6	4.4:1	49.1	1867792	16.3	74.9	4.6:1	42.5
Two-Year	456558	19.6	71.5	3.7:1	20.8	454162	18.3	70.7	3.9:1	20.6
Public	425801	19.2	71.5	3.7:1	18.2	404128	16.6	71.6	4.3:1	16.7
Private	30757	24.1	70.7	2.9:1	49.9	50034	31.8	63.8	2.0:1	35.2
Four-Year	1331109	16.5	78.4	4.8:1	59.4	1413630	15.6	76.2	4.9:1	49.9
Public	1010926	15.5	79.6	5.1:1	53.6	1087281	14.8	77.3	5.2:1	43.2
Private	320183	19.8	74.6	3.8:1	74.3	326349	18.5	72.4	3.9:1	68.6

(Continued)

TABLE 2

(Continued)

All Institutions[1]

Region,[2] Level and Control	1976					1984				
	Total Full-time Undergraduate Enrollment	Percent Black	Percent White	Ratio of White to Black Enrollment	Segregation Index	Total Full-time Undergraduate Enrollment	Percent Black	Percent White	Ratio of White to Black Enrollment	Segregation Index
West	1182814	5.6	77.9	13.9:1	23.1	1139834	4.4	73.7	16.8:1	21.5
Two-Year	463923	8.5	72.8	8.6:1	29.7	379572	6.5	68.3	10.5:1	28.7
Public	456093	8.6	72.6	8.4:1	29.3	362112	6.5	68.0	10.5:1	29.2
Private	7830	3.4	82.7	24.3:1	59.3	17460	4.9	74.5	15.2:1	13.6
Four-Year	718891	3.7	81.2	21.9:1	10.5	760262	3.4	76.4	22.5:1	12.9
Public	575877	3.7	81.3	22.0:1	10.7	600078	3.3	76.5	23.2:1	13.2
Private	143014	4.0	80.6	20.1:1	9.3	160184	3.7	76.1	20.6:1	12.0

SOURCE: The data reported in these analyses are from the Higher Education General Information Surveys (HEGIS) of fall enrollment for 1976 (HEGIS XI) and 1984 (HEGIS XIX) public-use data tapes.

[1] The number and percent of colleges included in these calculations were 2623 (91.9%) and 2784 (91.5%).

[2] The regions are defined as follows: North: ME, NH, VT, MA, RI, NJ, NY, PA, CT

Midwest: IL, IN, IA, KS, MI, MN, MO, NE, ND, OH, SD, WI

South: AL, AR, DE, DC, FL, GA, KY, LA, MD, MS, NC, OK, SC, TN, TX, VA, WV

West: AK, AZ, CA, CO, HI, ID, MT, NV, NM, OR, WA, WY

TABLE 3

Enrollment of Full-time Undergraduate Students in Higher Education

Traditionally White Institutions Only[1]

Region, Level and Control[2]	1976					1984				
	Total Full-time Undergraduate Enrollment	Percent Black	Percent White	Ratio of White to Black Enrollment	Segregation Index	Total Undergraduate Enrollment	Percent Black	Percent White	Ratio of White to Black Enrollment	Segregation Index
Nation	5693483	8.0	84.5	10.6:1	21.4	5783083	7.3	82.5	11.3:1	17.5
North	1338115	7.5	86.7	11.6:1	24.1	1310857	6.7	86.1	12.9:1	19.4
Two-Year	316905	11.4	82.1	7.2:1	39.5	298787	9.4	84.0	8.9:1	29.9
Public	275399	11.5	82.0	7.1:1	41.2	236972	7.8	86.1	11.0:1	25.9
Private	41506	10.9	82.5	7.6:1	27.3	61815	15.4	76.3	5.0:1	35.4
Four-Year	1021210	6.2	88.2	14.2:1	15.1	1012070	5.6	86.7	15.5:1	13.8
Public	514196	7.2	86.8	12.1:1	20.9	461922	5.7	88.4	15.5:1	11.8
Private	507014	5.3	89.6	16.9:1	7.0	550148	5.5	85.3	15.5:1	15.9
Midwest	1540619	8.0	88.6	11.1:1	26.9	1603491	6.8	87.8	12.9:1	22.2
Two-Year	336934	13.5	83.1	6.2:1	49.9	352047	11.2	84.0	7.5:1	36.9
Public	316809	13.1	83.7	6.4:1	49.5	317694	10.4	85.1	8.2:1	36.7
Private	20125	19.9	73.2	3.7:1	53.3	34353	17.8	74.1	4.2:1	26.2
Four-Year	1203685	6.4	90.2	14.1:1	13.0	1251444	5.5	88.9	16.2:1	13.4
Public	863674	6.2	90.7	14.6:1	10.5	911150	5.1	89.7	17.6:1	11.8
Private	340011	7.1	88.8	12.5:1	18.4	340294	6.6	86.9	13.2:1	16.2
South	1631935	10.1	83.5	8.3:1	15.6	1728901	10.5	80.5	7.7:1	12.9
Two-Year	448660	18.2	72.7	4.0:1	15.3	447948	17.2	71.7	4.2:1	15.8
Public	420239	18.2	72.4	4.0:1	14.2	399481	15.7	72.4	4.6:1	11.9
Private	28421	18.2	76.4	4.2:1	34.0	48467	29.7	65.8	2.2:1	30.5
Four-Year	1183275	7.0	87.7	12.5:1	9.7	1280953	8.1	83.6	10.13:1	7.5
Public	914259	7.5	87.4	11.7:1	9.4	1001015	8.6	89.3	9.7:1	6.4
Private	269016	5.5	88.6	16.1:1	11.1	279938	6.5	84.3	13.0:1	12.1

(*Continued*)

TABLE 3

(Continued)

Traditionally White Institutions Only[1]

Region, Level and Control[2]	1976					1984				
	Total Full-time Undergraduate Enrollment	Percent Black	Percent White	Ratio of White to Black Enrollment	Segregation Index	Total Full-time Undergraduate Enrollment	Percent Black	Percent White	Ratio of White to Black Enrollment	Segregation Index
West	1182814	5.6	77.9	13.9:1	23.1	1139834	4.4	73.7	16.8:1	21.6
Two-Year	463923	8.5	72.8	8.6:1	29.7	379572	6.5	68.3	10.5:1	28.7
Public	456093	8.6	72.6	8.4:1	29.3	362112	6.5	68.0	10.5:1	29.3
Private	7830	3.4	82.7	24.3:1	59.3	17460	4.9	74.5	15.2:1	13.6
Four-Year	718891	3.7	81.2	21.9:1	10.5	760262	3.4	76.4	22.5:1	11.5
Public	575877	3.7	81.3	22.0:1	10.7	600078	3.3	76.5	23.2:1	13.2
Private	143014	4.0	80.6	20.1:1	9.3	160184	3.7	76.1	20.6:1	12.0

SOURCE: The data reported in these analyses are from the Higher Education General Information Surveys (HEGIS) of fall enrollment for 1976 (HEGIS XI) and 1984 (HEGIS XIX) public-use data tapes.

[1] The number and percent of colleges included in these calculations for 1976 and 1984 respectively were 2316 (86.4%) and 2698 (91.2%).

[2] The regions are defined as follows: North: ME, NH, VT, MA, RI, NJ, NY, PA, CT

  Midwest: IL, IN, IA, KS, MI, MN, MO, NE, ND, OH, SD, WI

  South: AL, AR, DE, DC, FL, GA, KY, LA, MD, MS, NC, OK, SC, TN, TX, VA, WV

  West: AK, AZ, CA, CO, HI, ID, MT, NV, NM, OR, WA, WY

desegregation over the two time periods. The patterns here are as clear as were the enrollment patterns: Based on these indices, segregation has decreased in virtually every category included. The exceptions, those instances where segregation increased, are in those private college categories where enrollment increases were noted. As was stated earlier, it is one of the properties of this measure that it is useful for assessing the lack of uniform distribution across establishments within certain aggregates. In this instance, the increases in segregation in the private college aggregates suggests that the distribution of blacks across the schools within the respective categories was very uneven.

In the South segregation decreased considerably over the two time points, but remained at 49.9 for four-year colleges overall and 68.6 for private four-year colleges in 1984. In both instances the segregation indices seem likely even if for different reasons. Private colleges are a varied collection including both religious and independently controlled members, are usually affected by different economic and philosophical pressures and are not subject to the same constraints as their public counterparts. As a result there is less reason to expect more uniformity in the distribution of blacks among them.

A similar pattern emerges from the examination of table 3 for changes in segregation for the traditionally white institutions. Generally, segregation declined across all categories except private colleges. Note also that for four-year colleges in the South, blacks were a higher percentage of a higher overall enrollment in these schools, both public and private.

Segregation, however, decreased in the public category while it increased in the private category, suggesting again that the uniformity of distribution was greater for the public colleges. Finally it is also apparent that traditionally white college categories in all other regions are more segregated than in the South at either time point.

These findings regarding desegregation at the undergraduate level provide some evidence that whatever amount of desegregation has occurred, it has not been accompanied by net gains in enrollment. Inasmuch as this remains the case, the mandate of *Adams* remains crucial, especially in those states most heavily populated by blacks. The successes of *Adams* can be inferred in that the traditionally white public colleges in the South have both increased their enrollment and as a group appear less segregated. There were no other public college categories in any region in which both changes are apparent.

The graduate enrollment figures presented in table 4 show a uniformly distressing picture of declining black graduate enrollment across every category in every region. For purposes of examining the impact of *Adams*, these data reveal none of the potential benefits in the South that were

TABLE 4

Black Full-Time Graduate Enrollment

Region, Level and Control[1]	All Institutions[2]		Traditionally White Institutions[3]	
	1976	1984	1976	1984
Nation	22058	18077	18674	14674
North	4143	3464	4129	3363
Four-Year	4143	3464	4129	3363
Public	1443	1227	1427	1126
Private	2700	2237	2702	2237
Midwest	5917	3684	5908	3668
Four-Year	5917	3684	5908	3668
Public	4099	2533	4090	2517
Private	1818	1151	1818	1151
South	9322	8729	5961	5443
Four-Year	9322	8792	5961	5443
Public	5999	5882	4066	3956
Private	3323	2847	1895	1487
West	2676	2200	2676	2200
Four-Year	2676	2200	2676	2200
Public	1694	1219	1694	1219
Private	982	981	982	981

SOURCE: The data reported in these analyses are from the Higher Education General Information Surveys (HEGIS) of fall enrollment for 1976 (HEGIS XI) and 1984 (HEGIS XIX) public-use data tapes.

[1] The regions are defined as follows: North: ME, NH, VT, MA, RI, NJ, NY, PA, CT

                Midwest: IL, IN, IA, KS, MI, MN, MO, NE, ND, OH, SD, WI

                South: AL, AR, DE, DC, FL, GA, KY, LA, MD, MS, NC, OK, SC, TN, TX, VA, WV

                West: AK, AZ, CA, CO, HI, ID, MT, NV, NM, OR, WA, WY

[2] The number and percent of colleges included in these calculations for 1976 and 1984 respectively were 657 (67.3%) and 733 (63.8%).

[3] The number and percent of colleges included in these calculations for 1976 and 1984 respectively were 626 (66.3%) and 698 (64.7%).

observed for the undergraduate level. For example, where traditionally white institutions (TWIs) in the South enrolled a larger percentage of blacks at the undergraduate level in 1984 compared to 1976, the reverse is true or the graduate level—from 64 percent in 1976 to 62 percent in 1984. Public TWIs showed virtually the same pattern: 68 percent in 1976 and 67 percent in 1984. While the overall share of black graduate enrollment the TWIs enjoy is greater than their undergraduate share, it does not necessarily infer success, since *Adams* clearly called for the enhancement of graduate programs at the traditionally black institutions (TBIs). These data cannot answer the question of whether increases in the availability of graduate programs at TBIs would reduce the TWI share of black graduate enrollment.

Turning next to the question of whether black graduate students are more or less segregated across all institutions and among traditionally white institutions, the data show a mixed pattern of declines and increases in segregation.

For the nation as a whole, segregation declined from 19.8 to 17.8. In all regions except the South segregation appears to have been reduced by more than half. Combined with the enrollment declines, this suggests that a smaller number of black graduate students were more broadly and evenly distributed across the enrolling institutions. This interpretation lends credence to the lament of black graduate students that there "just aren't enough of us." In the South the picture is different. Although the actual rates are virtually unchanged from 1976 to 1984, the direction of the change indicates increasing segregation. This is problematic for at least two reasons. First, it suggests that the increased numbers of black undergraduates in southern TWIs are not converting that experience into increased graduate enrollment across the same institutions. Second, it suggests that *Adams* successes at the undergraduate level are not being duplicated at the graduate level.

The segregation indices in table 6 for TWIs help to clarify these patterns somewhat. With the removal of the TBIs, segregation in the South also decreased by almost half in all but the public sector. Here again the implication is that a smaller number of black graduate students are more broadly and evenly distributed across the enrolling schools.

The purpose of this analysis was to assess the progress made in reducing segregation and increasing access across the nation, and particularly in the South where de jure segregation had been ruled unconstitutional. By inference, the effectiveness of *Adams* could be examined given the years covered in these data. The results show support for progress in reducing segregation, but that progress does not appear to translate into increased access. It is especially important that the increased enrollment of blacks in TWIs at the undergraduate level is not generating greater graduate enrollment. It has often been reasoned that low levels of black graduate enrollment was a reflection of matriculation from undergraduate environments that were not conducive to nurturing graduate aspirations. If the increased enrollment of black undergraduates in TWIs reflects some increase in matriculation from academic environments that are more nurturing of graduate aspirations, then we must explore those factors that are mitigating this expected benefit. Several of these issues are explored in other essays in this volume.

The black enrollment rates reported above however may also be a reflection, in part, of a post-*Bakke* effect. The *Regents of the University of*

TABLE 5

Enrollment of Full-time Graduate Students in Higher Education

All Institutions[1]

Region, Level and Control[2]	1976					1984				
	Total Full-time Graduate Enrollment	Percent Black	Percent White	Ratio of White to Black Enrollment	Segregation Index	Total Full-time Graduate Enrollment	Percent Black	Percent White	Ratio of White to Black Enrollment	Segregation Index
Nation	428105	9.2	82.5	9.0:1	19.8	447654	4.0	72.9	18.2:1	17.8
North	102838	6.3	85.9	13.6:1	9.9	110039	3.1	74.1	23.9:1	4.6
Four-Year	102838	6.3	85.9	13.6:1	9.9	110039	3.1	74.1	23.9:1	4.6
Public	36490	6.7	86.2	12.9:1	6.8	34397	3.6	74.2	20.6:1	6.9
Private	66348	6.1	83.8	14.1:1	11.8	75642	3.0	74.0	24.7:1	3.2
Midwest	117041	6.6	85.1	12.9:1	11.1	111539	3.3	73.5	22.3:1	2.3
Four-Year	116997	6.6	84.3	12.8:1	10.2	111539	3.3	73.5	22.3:1	2.3
Public	91082	5.4	84.3	15.6:1	8.9	86575	2.9	72.6	25.0:1	2.6
Private	25915	8.3	84.3	10.2:1	13.2	24694	4.7	77.1	16.4:1	3.6
South	116805	15.8	78.5	5.0:1	32.7	128260	6.8	71.4	10.5:1	32.9
Four-Year	116805	15.8	78.5	5.0:1	32.7	128260	6.8	71.4	10.5:1	32.9
Public	87110	16.1	78.3	4.9:1	26.4	94272	6.2	71.4	11.5:1	27.3
Private	29695	15.4	78.8	5.1:1	44.2	33988	8.4	71.4	8.5:1	44.5
West	91421	3.6	80.4	22.3:1	7.3	97816	2.2	72.9	33.1:1	3.0
Four-Year	91421	3.6	80.4	22.3:1	7.3	97816	2.2	72.9	33.1:1	3.0
Public	67703	3.0	81.3	27.1:1	7.3	68320	1.8	73.2	40.7:1	4.6
Private	23718	4.4	79.6	18.1:1	8.4	29496	3.3	72.3	21.9:1	0.6

SOURCE: The data reported in these analyses are from the Higher Education General Information Surveys (HEGIS) of fall enrollment for 1976 (HEGIS XI) and 1984 (HEGIS XIX) public-use data tapes.

[1] The number and percent of colleges included in these calculations for 1976 and 1984 respectively were 657 (67.3%) and 733 (63.8%).

[2] The regions are defined as follows: North: ME, NH, VT, MA, RI, NJ, NY, PA, CT
Midwest: IL, IN, IA, KS, MI, MN, MO, NE, ND, OH, SD, WI
South: AL, AR, DE, DC, FL, GA, KY, LA, MD, MS, NC, OK, SC, TN, TX, VA, WV
West: AK, AZ, CA, CO, HI, ID, MT, NV, NM, OR, WA, WY

TABLE 6

Enrollment of Full-time Graduate Students in Higher Education

Traditionally White Institutions[1]

Region, Level and Control[2]	1976					1984				
	Total Full-time Graduate Enrollment	Percent Black	Percent White	Ratio of White to Black Enrollment	Segregation Index	Total Full-time Graduate Enrollment	Percent Black	Percent White	Ratio of White to Black Enrollment	Segregation Index
Nation	423161	4.4	80.4	18.3:1	4.1	441959	3.3	73.7	22.3:1	2.4
North	102809	4.0	80.9	20.2:1	4.3	109895	3.1	74.1	23.9:1	2.7
Four-Year	102809	4.0	80.9	20.2:1	4.3	109895	3.1	74.1	23.9:1	2.7
Public	36461	3.9	83.3	21.4:1	3.1	34253	3.3	74.4	22.5:1	1.6
Private	66348	4.1	79.5	19.4:1	5.5	75642	3.0	74.0	24.7:1	3.2
Midwest	117009	5.1	80.4	15.8:1	5.7	111496	3.3	73.5	22.3:1	2.0
Four-Year	116965	5.1	80.4	15.8:1	5.7	111496	3.3	73.5	22.3:1	2.0
Public	91050	4.5	81.0	18.0:1	5.1	86532	2.9	72.7	25.1:1	2.3
Private	25915	7.0	78.5	11.2:1	6.8	24964	4.6	76.3	16.6:1	2.6
South	111922	5.3	82.6	15.6:1	5.0	122752	4.4	74.2	16.9:1	2.7
Four-Year	111922	5.3	82.6	15.6:1	5.0	122752	4.4	74.2	16.9:1	2.7
Public	84625	4.8	82.9	14.3:1	2.9	90865	4.4	73.6	16.7:1	2.9
Private	27297	6.9	80.4	11.7:1	7.7	31887	4.7	76.0	16.2:1	2.5
West	91421	3.6	80.4	22.3:1	7.3	97016	2.2	72.9	33.1:1	3.0
Four-Year	91421	3.6	80.4	22.3:1	7.3	97816	2.2	72.9	33.1:1	3.0
Public	67703	3.0	81.3	27.1:1	7.3	68320	1.8	73.2	40.7:1	4.6
Private	23718	4.4	79.6	18.1:1	8.4	29496	3.3	72.3	21.9:1	0.6

SOURCE: The data reported in these analyses are from the Higher Education General Information Surveys (HEGIS) of fall enrollment for 1976 (HEGIS XI) and 1984 (HEGIS XIX) public-use data tapes.

[1] The number and percent of colleges included in these calculations for 1976 and 1984 respectively were 626 (66.3%) and 698 (64.7%).

[2] The regions are defined as follows: North: ME, NH, VT, MA, RI, NJ, NY, PA, CT
Midwest: IL, IN, IA, KS, MI, MN, MO, NE, ND, OH, SD, WI
South: AL, AR, DE, DC, FL, GA, KY, LA, MD, MS, NC, OK, SC, TN, TX, VA, WV
West: AK, AZ, CA, CO, HI, ID, MT, NV, NM, OR, WA, WY

California v. *Bakke* generated public debate, scholarly research and political discourse which laid bare the range of issues embedded in affirmative action.[29] Allan Bakke, a white male, brought suit seeking relief under the equal protection clause of Title VI of the Civil Rights Act of 1964. He contended that the UC Medical School at Davis, having voluntarily established admissions procedures setting aside sixteen places for underrepresented minorities, having employed lower standards for admission to those places and having restricted white access to those places, had denied him access solely on the basis of race. A badly divided Supreme Court, in deciding in Bakke's favor, rendered a narrow ruling based on the reasoning supplied by Justice Powell. The ruling in the case decided three issues: (1) in the absence of a finding of specific discrimination traceable to a particular institution, race could not be used as a criterion for remedial benefits: (2) a person's race or ethic background could not be used as a sole criterion for admissions decisions: and (3) race or national origin, along with other criteria, could be a factor in admissions where those criteria are intended to meet certain institutional needs or priorities.

The charge of reverse discrimination and the subsequent debates have produced volumes, but little consensus has resulted. One key issue in these debates is the matter of how far we as a society are committed to go in the pursuit of equality, and what criteria we will use in establishing equality. In education, that debate has focused on defining parity as a standard but agreement on a baseline has not been achieved. For example, in *Adams* one criterion for undergraduate enrollment is that black and white high school graduates will enroll in college at equal percentages. The dilemma here is that while the gap in black and white high school graduation rates is closing, a disparity continues. Under these circumstances, even achieving equal rates of college entry delays social equality. Currently, high school graduation rates for blacks is increasing, but the rate of college entry is decreasing.

Some scholars have argued instead that equality should be based on parity defined in overall population terms,[30] feeling that this would necessitate far greater efforts than are currently being expended.[30] Moreover, to implement such efforts would entail remedies that would necessitate practices that are retributional in intent. Instead, some *Bakke* advocates take a position that argues mainly for racial neutrality or a "color blind" approach.[31] Most research in education clearly suggests that we are not now, nor have we ever been, color blind in our approach.[32] It is still the case, as President Johnson framed it, that the previously shackled runner merits something extra.

The debate surrounding *Bakke* prompted researchers who examined graduate and professional school admissions practices and enrollment following *Bakke* to conclude that there would likely be a "chilling effect"[33] on minority access, but not the dramatic declines that opponents of *Bakke* feared nor the no-change or stable growth that his advocates projected.[33] Whether or not the trends in enrollment, retention and graduation for minorities since *Bakke* fit our respective definitions of a "chilling effect," the findings of the Rockefeller Foundation's work are important because it is one of the few research-based discussions contributing to the debate.

Bakke, Weber, and Affirmative Action, published one year following the *Bakke* decision and sponsored by the Rockefeller Foundation, yielded several findings that informed the "chilling effect" summation. The three main findings of their survey were that: (1) affirmative action efforts to enroll minority students are not as extensive as their opponents fear and their proponents wish. They are more numerous in elite programs and in law and medical schools, least in nonelite undergraduate, business and education programs; (2) admissions requirements have not been lowered by affirmative action activities; and (3) a program's special recruitment efforts to attract minority students do appear to lead to increased minority acceptances.

Among the tentative conclusions drawn from the analysis were the following:

> A perception that *Bakke* has negatively altered the national attitude climate for affirmative action in enrollment policies is held by many admissions officers, particularly those in elite programs. Yet these same officers deny any such change affecting their own admissions policies . . . Suits and threats of suits from [the] majority on the grounds of "reverse discrimination" have become more common in recent years. . . . Alleged discrimination suits act as mediators of *Bakke* effects in that they cause admissions officers to regard the ruling more seriously and as making their minority admissions more difficult. . . .[34]

Pettigrew also challenged the assumption that there was any substantial commitment to affirmative action and minority admissions, suggesting that such an assumption "is at best suspect and, more likely, erroneous."[35] Pettigrew reasons then that *Bakke* may more profitably be viewed as an excuse that institutions and their officials can use to avoid, resist or stop doing what they did not wish to do.

The three principal findings are critically important because they attack prevailing myths about affirmative action in higher education. Such efforts are neither as plentiful nor as "accessible" as media might have it appear. It does not follow that because a few highly publicized elite schools have programs, less elite places do also, even though "conventional wisdom" would have us think so. The admissions standards have not been lowered to any substantial degree to bring in more minorities and every faculty member should receive a memorandum on this point. One interpretation of the basis for this widely held perception is that the conceptions held by members of the academic community regarding the intellectual capabilities of minorities leads to the association of increased minority student visibility with lowered standards. The third finding, that increased recruitment effort is effective in increasing minority acceptances is important for faculty and university officers. Some inertia in joining the effort to increase minority enrollment is due to perceptions of the difficulty of getting a good student yield from the investment of time, money and effort in recruitment efforts.

The conclusions cited above pointing to the mediating effects of *Bakke*, threats of similar suits, alleged suits and, more recently, the rulings of a more conservative Court in cases with direct bearing on affirmative action, cannot be underestimated. These have both a practical effect of delimiting what is in fact allowable as remedy and they have social effects. The latter impact the institution, and current and potential students. It is likely that, as Pettigrew reasons, these have the consequence of retarding institutional effort and dissuading potential applicants. They can also poison the climate or social atmosphere of the campus and the larger community. Together these factors can work to limit and reduce minority access by constraining affirmative action efforts.

THE CRISIS, CHALLENGE AND COMMITMENT

This essay has sought to show that progress on one goal, desegregation, has been made and that the legal justifications or basis for continued and expanded efforts is intact, even if it's more tenuous at this date. Equally important, the findings from the post-*Bakke* research provide what I think are important insights into our potential for considerably more progress. I focus first on the spread of affirmative action efforts.

Finding that student affirmative action activities are not as widespread as they are either desired to be or feared to be, should be viewed as good news if we can generate new effort on the part of a broader spectrum of higher education. Colleges and universities seeking guidance in initiating new or expanding existing efforts can draw upon a growing body of published experience. One such volume is the recently published *Minorities on Campus: A Handbook for Enhancing Diversity*.[36] In addition to providing a full discussion of program components and their character, the book emphasizes the importance of information management, a second implication of the post-*Bakke* study cited above.

Myths regarding the constraints on allowable strategies, the range of programs available or the status of university standards are clear impediments to the potential successes of student affirmative action programs. University officials can combat this problem with effective communications and monitoring. Much of the apparatus for this effort is already in place but must be better organized. In the aforementioned study of five *Adams* states[37] one of the core problems differentiating the affirmative action efforts was the administrative communications channels. Where well-articulated duties and responsibilities were present, there was generally a more successful set of services.

It is important to emphasize the findings regarding admissions. The research suggests that admissions criteria have not been compromised on quality and that at many nonelite institutions there is little or no change.[38] The number of such institutions suggests that the potential for considerable expansion of opportunities is great. This has the added benefit of broadening the geographic options available to minority students. It may be the case that many proximate institutions are not attracting their available minority candidates. An expanded and enhanced admissions process which treats race, sex and national origin as important but not sole criteria is permissible and is in the interest of the institution.

A related concern is the status of traditionally minority institutions. These institutions continue to be a primary source of opportunity for these students. The overrepresentation of traditionally black institutions in degree attainment for black students underscores their importance. Rather than question or threaten their quality, it is important to seek their cooperation and assistance and to find additional ways of enhancing their growth and vitality. Vigorous support of *Adams* is one way, but establishing formal mechanisms for cooperation and exchange between traditionally minority and traditionally white institutions is a more immediate means of improving opportunities for minority students.

Finally, it is important that recent efforts to encourage the development of a more pluralistic scholarship be supported. Through the active involvement of the professional associations for the different disciplines, and with the support of faculty for campus level core curricular reforms, the academic environment that students encounter on campus can be made both more hospitable and more reflective of the contributions of members of currently underrepresented groups.[39] These efforts will go a long way in improving the retention of minorities at both the undergraduate and graduate level.

Failing to pursue these and other strategies will likely result in a return to this topic in another twenty years just as the opening passages to this essay convey. We have learned that simple compliance or mere race- and sex-neutral practices will not achieve the desired results. Effective student affirmative action strategies will require our full commitment.

NOTES

1. American Council on Education, "The Campus and the Racial Crisis: Background Papers for Participants at the 52nd Annual Meeting of the American Council on Education" (Washington: American Council on Education, 1969), p. i.

2. Judith S. Eaton, "Foreword," in *Minorities on Campus: A Handbook for Enhancing Diversity,* ed. Madeleine F. Green (Washington: American Council on Education, 1989), p. vii.

3. Francis Keppel, "The Higher Education Acts Contrasted, 1965–1986: Has Federal Policy Come of Age?," *Harvard Education Review* 1 (February 1987):57.

4. Green, *Minorities on Campus,* p. 29.

5. Ibid., p. 1.

6. Mary C. Thornberry, "Affirmative Action: History of an Attempt to Realize Greater Equality," in *Elusive Equality: Liberalism, Affirmative Action, and Social Change in America,* eds. James C. Foster and Mary C. Segers (Port Washington: Associated Faculty Press, 1983), p. 49.

7. Ibid.

8. Ibid.

9. There was a virtual explosion of books and articles on affirmative action following the *Bakke* decision. Readers may wish to consult the following sources as representative of the legal and moral arguments surrounding affirmative action. Frank Williams et al., "Admissions Criteria and the Minority Student," *Journal of Non-White Concerns in Personnel and Guidance,* 11 (October 1983): 19–32; Nathan Glazer, *Affirmative Discrimination* (New York: Basic Books, 1975); Carnegie Council on Policy Studies in Higher Education, *Making Affirmative Action Work in Higher Education: An Analysis of Institutional and Federal Policies with Recommendations,* (San Francisco: Jossey-Bass, 1975); Barry R. Gross, ed., *Reverse Discrimination* (Buffalo: Prometheus Books, 1977); Nijole V. Benokraitis and Joe R. Feagin, *Affirmative Action and Equal Opportunity: Action, Inaction, Reaction* (Boulder: Westview Press, 1978); Allan P. Sindler, *Bakke, DeFunis, and Minority Admissions* (New York: Longman, 1978).

10. James Blackwell, "Mentoring and Networking Among Blacks," in *In Pursuit of Equality in Higher Education,* ed. Ann S. Pruit (Dix Hills: General Hall, 1987), pp. 146–162.

11. Adams v. Richardson, 356 F. Supp. 92 (D.C. 1973), modified, 480 F. 2d 1159 (D.C. Cir. 1973).

12. Albert P. Blaustein and Robert L. Zangrando, eds. *Civil Rights and the American Negro* (New York: Trident Press, 1968), p. 407.

13. Ibid., pp. 433–447.

14. Ibid., pp. 407–410.

15. Ibid., pp. 409–410.

16. Jean L. Preer, *Lawyers v. Educators: Black Colleges and Desegregation in Public Higher Education* (Westport: Greenwood Press, 1982), pp. 31–62.

17. Ibid., pp;. 95–126.

18. Ibid.

19. Ibid., pp. 137–144.

20. Blaustein, p. 524–550.

21. Leonard Haynes, III, *A Critical Examination of the Adams Case: A Source Book* (Washington: Institute for Services to Education, 1978).

22. John B. Williams, III, ed., *Desegregating America's Colleges and Universities: Title VI Regulation of Higher Education* (New York: Teachers College Press, 1988), p. 8.

23. Eileen M. O'Brien, "Judge Pratt Dismisses Adams Desegregation Case," *Black Issues in Higher Education* 4 (January 1988). 1–3.

24. Conciatore, "Appeals Court Breathes Life into Adams Desegregation Suit," *Black Issues in Higher Education* 11 (August 1989). 4–5.

25. Haynes, K 1–24.

26. Henry Jay Becker, "The Measurement of Segregation: The Dissimilarity Index and Coleman's Segregation Index Compared" (Baltimore, MD: Johns Hopkins University, Center for Social Organization of Schools, 1978).

27. Gail Thomas, Denise C. Daiger and James McPartland, "Desegregation and Enrollment: Access in Higher Education" (Baltimore, MD: Johns Hopkins University, Center for Social Organization of Schools, 1978).

28. William T. Trent and Elaine J. Copeland, *Effectiveness of State Financial Aid in the Production of Black Doctoral Recipients* (Atlanta: Southern Education Foundation, 1987).

29. Regents of the University of California v. Bakke, 438 U.S. 265 (1978).

30. Kenneth S. Tollett, "Foreword," in *Equal Educational Opportunity Scoreboard: The Status of Black Americans in Higher Education, 1970–1979,* ed. Lorenzo Morris (Washington: Howard University, 1981), pp. v–vii.

31. Thornberry, pp. 57–58.

32. *Harvard Education Review* 58, no. 3 (August, 1988). This special volume is devoted specifically to the discussion of race and education.

33. Thomas F. Pettigrew, "The Effects of the *Bakke* Decision: An Initial Look"

in *Working Papers:* Bakke, Weber, *and Affirmative Action* (New York: The Rockefeller Foundation, 1979), pp. 2–3.

34. Ibid., pp. 1–37.

35. Ibid., pp. 34–35.

36. Green, *Minorities on Campus.*

37. Trent and Copeland, *Effectiveness of State Financial Aid.*

38. Williams et al., 1983, "Admissions Criteria," pp. 19–32.

39. See especially chapter 8 in Green, *Minorities on Campus.* See also the report, "Meeting the National Need for Minority Scholars and Scholarship: Policies and Actions", available from the Office of the Assistant Vice Provost for Graduate Studies, SUNY at Stony Brook, N.Y.

Part 2

Faculty Issues

KENNETH W. JACKSON

Chapter 7

Black Faculty in Academia

INTRODUCTION

By almost any standard employed, it is without question that blacks are seriously underrepresented in terms of their participation in the scholarly community. However, in contrast to historical explanations of underrepresentation, the contemporary explanation of the genesis of this situation is not so readily accepted.

That is, the relatively small number of blacks in academia in the years preceding the 1960s can undeniably be attributed to deliberate exclusionary practices on the part of higher education. Such a contention is not only an accepted reality among a significant majority of the scholarly community, but is also supported by an abundance of empirical evidence. For instance, it is a well-documented fact that blacks were denied the opportunity to even acquire an education prior to emancipation, much less the advanced training necessary to become a participant in academia.[1] Similarly, it is also a well-documented fact that blacks who did manage to acquire the training necessary to become participants in higher education after emancipation were denied the opportunity of employment as faculty members in white institutions up until the late 1950s.[2] Even though there were notable exceptions in both cases, blacks for the most part were systematically and intentionally excluded from the mainstream of the academic world in any meaningful sense up until the beginning of the 1960s.

On the other hand, one finds that in the 1980s the representation of black faculty is considerably more complex than the outright exclusionary practices that existed prior to the early 1960s. Following several decades of increases in the representation of blacks among the general faculty pool, as well as among those employed in white institutions, the pool of black faculty has recently begun to show signs of stagnation and decline. This present situation has resulted in a serious debate over causal explanations that have as their base either past discriminatory policies or demographic realities that are directly devoid of any racial intent.

More specifically, the contemporary circumstances seem to imply a fairly stable consensus among academicians and lay individuals alike that the representation of black faculty in higher education is still less than it should be. On the other hand, the battle lines are clearly drawn in terms of explanations as to why. On one side of the debate are those who argue that the low representation is a function of supply—a function of supply in the sense that there is a lack of qualified black candidates with the necessary training and skills to fill the available positions. On the other side are those who argue that this inappropriateness of representation is a continuation of racial practices of exclusion and privilege that maintain advantages for those already entrenched in the system.

Because there tends to be supporting evidence for each of these conflicting positions, it appears that a more comprehensive interpretation of the present status of black faculty is in order if one is to legitimately understand the issues as they exist today. It may very well be that the data and their subsequent interpretations are really not at odds, but rather are merely two different sides of the same coin.

Thus, this essay attempts to examine these issues in greater detail. Specifically, an attempt is made to examine the relatively low representation of black faculty in the world of academia in light of the two dominant causal explanations given above. It is anticipated that the result of such a examination will be a more meaningful understanding of the situations that give rise to the relatively small number of blacks presently found in the scholarly community.

The discussion begins by first examining the demographics of historical circumstances that have lead to the contemporary state. This is then followed by discussions relating to the dominant perspectives and their implications as possible explanations of the present circumstances.

HISTORICAL CIRCUMSTANCES

In 1938 there were approximately 200 full-time black faculty members in America.[3] These faculty were employed almost exclusively within the traditionally black institutions (TBIs). In fact, prior to 1900 only three blacks are known to ever have taught in white institutions, and that number had only increased to six by 1938.[4]

In the twenty years or so following 1938 the number of black faculty increased tremendously; however, the exclusiveness of their employment in TBIs did not alter. By 1961 the total number had increased to 8,445. On the other hand, only 300, or approximately 3.5 percent, were employed as full-time faculty in white institutions.

Based on these observations it is fairly obvious that during the first sixty years of this century blacks made relatively tremendous gains in terms of their absolute numbers. What was significantly less dramatic was their representation among the general faculty pool. By 1961 that percentage had only reached about 3 percent. Even more dramatic was their representation on the faculties of white institutions. During this same year (i.e., 1961) it was a negligible figure that was considerably less than 1 percent. Thus, it appears that even though in the early 1960s significantly more black faculty existed in the entire faculty pool than had ever existed before, higher education still maintained a policy of racial exclusion and privilege that was fundamentally in conflict with its basic values and principles.

Due to some very aggressive affirmative action campaigns initiated during the mid-1960s, the trends observed earlier began to take on a somewhat different flavor in the 1970s. The evidence indicates that while the percentage of black faculty in academia continued to increase at a tremendous pace, they were no longer mostly employed in TBIs. Responding to pressures from the black community, students, and perhaps more significantly the federal government, white institutions began to aggressively seek the services of black faculty. In 1976 black faculty had increased their representation among the total full-time faculty pool to a level of 4.4 percent, with their absolute numbers increasing to 19,096. What was perhaps more significant about this increase was that of this 19,096, over 7,000 were now employed in white institutions.

The changes that began in the 1970s accelerated even more by the mid-1980s. The distribution of black faculty between TBIs and white institutions had completely reversed by 1985. During this year over 57 percent of all black faculty were employed in white institutions. Thus, in little over a twenty year period, the almost exclusive concentration of black faculty in TBIs was no longer a reality.

What is most unfortunate about this period, however, is that the rather substantial increases in the absolute number of black faculty, as well as their representation among the total faculty pool, had decreased to a snail's pace. For instance, between the years 1961 and 1976, the number of black faculty had increased by 10,651 or 126 percent. On the other hand, between the years 1976 and 1985, they only increased their numbers by 355 or 1.9

percent. This, again by any standard, is quite a significant decrease that surely requires some type of explanation.

Thus, changes evident in the late 1970s and early 1980s represent the nature of the contemporary conditions that surround the status of black faculty today. It appears that no longer are we discussing problems that deal with direct exclusionary practices or wholesale restrictions on access to the mainstream of academia; rather, the issues today center around problems of growth—growth in terms of steady and consistent increases in the size of the pool of black faculty, as well as growth in terms of the equity of professional status among those already in the pool.

These latter issues are at the heart of the contemporary debate. Those who espouse the view that there are too few blacks to fill the available positions focus on the size of the black faculty pool, while those who espouse the continued exclusionary view focus on the equity issue. Let's consider first the problem of growth in the size of the black faculty pool.

THE PRODUCTION OF BLACK FACULTY

Although blacks have made significant gains in terms of their representation in the overall faculty pool, it still goes without question that the present level of representation does not approach a situation of racial parity. As implied above, one of the principle explanations for this relatively low representation is that there are too few black graduates in the "pipeline" to fill the available positions.

In examining the available date, there does seem to be some validity to this argument. That is, there are indeed fewer potential black candidates for faculty positions today than there have been in the recent past. From 1968 to 1985 black enrollments at all levels of postsecondary education decreased by over 19 percent. However, what is more significant is that between 1976 and 1984 black graduate school enrollment declined by over 22 percent.

What makes this decline more complex than a simple decrease in numbers is that there does not seem to be any demographic explanation for its occurrence. In fact, the absolute number of blacks ages 18 to 24 actually increased, as did the number of high school graduates. Thus, it appears that the decrease in the number of black students going on to college and subsequently to graduate school is more a function of the educational institution itself, thereby implying a racial connotation that has no real basis in uncontrollable demographic patterns.

To highlight the racially specific nature of this problem, it is interesting to note that no similar enrollment declines can be observed for other minority groups. In fact, other groups have actually exhibited increases. Asians have increased their graduate school enrollment by a phenomenal 48.1 percent between the years of 1976 and 1984, while Hispanic enrollment in graduate school has increased by 14.4 percent during the same time period.

Given these rather contrasting enrollment patterns, it would seem instructive, then, to take a more direct look at the situations surrounding the declines for black students. In 1987 black students were more likely to graduate from predominately white colleges than from TBIs, a situation that is unprecedented in United States history.[5] However, what is most disconcerting about this relatively new black educational pattern is that the problems that many of these students experience on these white campuses are of such a nature as to make them (i.e., black students) less prone to pursue a career in the academic world.[6]

Survey data has indicated that black students enrolled in white institutions average higher attrition rates, greater states of alienation, and perhaps most significantly, less satisfactory relationships with faculty. On the other hand, students from TBIs evidence more positive psychosocial adjustments, greater relative academic gains during the college years, and higher attainment aspirations.[7]

Such occurrences may very well provide us with some insight into the problem of supply. As indicated above, fewer and fewer black students are now graduating from TBIs. In 1976 these institutions awarded 37.6 percent of all bachelor's degrees received by black students. By 1984 that rate was down to 32 percent. If the differences in characteristics for black students enrolled in white institutions as opposed to TBIs is accurate, and more black students are now attending and graduating from white institutions, then one would necessarily expect enrollment in postbaccalaureate programs to decrease. In fact, there is evidence that supports just such a conclusion. Not only is black graduate school enrollment down by over 22 percent, but in 1984 the top ten schools in baccalaureate origins of doctorates, except for one, were still TBIs, not white institutions where a significant proportion of black students are now enrolled.[8]

Additionally, the success of black students graduating from TBIs is also evident from surveys of TBI alumni. One such survey of approximately two hundred found that just under 90 percent were professionals in medicine, dentistry, teaching and law; 8 percent held white-collar jobs (secretaries, salesmen, office managers, etc.); and 3 present were blue-collar workers (waitresses, taxi drivers, cooks, etc.). In addition to this, approximately 50 percent of these graduates had earned a master's or doctorate degree and had an average income of $32,000.[9]

On the other hand, there is a general conception within the overall black community, primarily the middle-class black community, that these TBIs are not overly effective in terms of academic and professional success. In fact, a pool of subscribers to *Black Enterprise* magazine found that over 82 percent of the respondents thought that TBIs were serving a purpose that could not be met by other colleges. However, only half hoped that their children would attend a TBI.

These perceptions, buttressed by the general movement of black students away from TBIs into white institutions, as well as the experiences of black students once enrolled in these white institutions, have seemed to manifest themselves in decreases in postbaccalaureate enrollment rates and lower academic and professional aspirations. The result, from the point of view of the status of black faculty in academia, is indeed a smaller pool of potential candidates for employment.

It must be emphasized, however, that the genesis of this small pool is more complex than a mere decision on the part of individual undergraduates to not continue their education beyond this level. The available evidence seems to indicate that the actual size of the pool has racial connotations that are associated with the experiences of black students in white institutions and, if the success of TBIs can legitimately be used as an indicator of the importance of sensitive mentors, is inextricable tied to the overwhelming small number of black faculty found on these white campuses. In other words, the white institutions are simply not providing the type of experiences that would inspire black undergraduates to pursue a graduate education in the same sense as TBIs have done for so many years—a situation, no doubt, that is related to the inability or unwillingness of those most directly involved with students (i.e., the faculty) to be sensitive to the needs, desires and aspirations of black students on their campuses.

THE PROBLEMS OF EQUITY IN PROFESSIONAL GROWTH

Although the above discussion would seem to indicate that one of the major problems associated with the contemporary status of black faculty is indeed the decline in the number of potential candidates, the evidence also seems to indicate that there are additional concerns for those who are presently in the world of academia that significantly impact their representativeness. These concerns are related to hiring, tenure and promotion, and may be generally referred to as problems associated with equity in professional growth.

As of 1985 there was a total of 19,451 full-time black faculty. Of this total, approximately 11,178 were employed in white institutions and 8,273 in TBIs. What is most interesting about this contemporary distributional pattern is that the problems associated with professional growth are fundamentally different depending on which of these academic environments black faculty find themselves in.

The data implies that access and stability of employment are much greater for black faculty in the TBI settings than in the white institutions. However, employment in these TBI environments tends to isolate faculty members both physically and professionally from the mainstream of academia. For instance, within the TBIs, black faculty represent almost 66 percent of the total faculty pool as compared to only 2.4 percent of the total faculty pool in white institutions.[10] Additionally, approximately 44 percent of the full-time black faculty in TBIs had tenure as compared to only 32 percent of the full-time black faculty in non-TBIs.[11] On the other hand, a survey of black faculty employed in TBIs indicated that over 66 percent had little or no sustained contact with their white counterparts in their immediate community or with those in the larger academic disciplines in which they specialized.[12]

It has been argued that this rather negative consequence of employment at a TBI is due primarily to the basic focus of the TBIs and the resources that are available to them.[13] That is, it is a commonly held perception that the prime obligation of most TBIs is not the creation of knowledge, but rather its diffusion. Their purposes and programs show that with few exceptions their primary services are related to the teaching of undergraduate students, not research or the many activities associated with its occurrence. In the majority of instances these schools (i.e., TBIs) are unable to provide their faculties with either the opportunity of, or the resources essential to, a program of research.[14]

These contentions are supported in part by the internal problems of the TBIs, as well as the amount of research funds available for pure research. In 1962–63 black land grant institutions reported expenditures of $318,276 for the purpose of organized research.[15] This figure constituted only 0.04 percent of the research funds spent by the nation's eighty-seven land grant institutions during this particular academic year.[16] This scenario has not changed dramatically over the years. Over the past few years an extremely negligible number of TBIs have received grants awarded by the National Institutes of Health.[17] In fact, the National Science Foundation was reported to have given less than 0.4 percent of its funds to TBIs in 1984, with not one black college being in the top one hundred of the foundation's grant recipients.[18]

Even if black faculty within these TBIs resolved themselves to the fact that research funds are not forthcoming, major internal problems still exist that make it extremely difficult for many to just stay abreast of developments in their disciplines. In most cases, funds for travel to conferences, symposiums and the like are nonexistent or significantly lacking. Similarly, salaries in TBIs have averaged about 10 percent less than salaries in comparable white institutions for approximately the last twenty years, thereby further reducing the likelihood that these faculty could or would finance their own travel to these important events.[19]

These problems associated with research funding and its subsequent effect on becoming active participants in the creation of knowledge are apparently not the only problems that tend to affect the professional growth of black faculty in TBIs. The evidence also indicates that many of these faculty members believe that the mere internal dynamics of their particular organizations are of such a nature that their professional growth is outright stifled.

For instance, a recent survey of TBI faculty reported that 20 percent or more of those surveyed identified twelve of twenty-five items as "quite a problem" or "a major problem" with their employment. These areas identified and their percentages in descending order were as follows:

Adequacy of facilities	34%
Time for personal study	32%
Opportunities to attend professional meetings	30%
Salaries	29%
Red tape	29%
Student motivation	29%
Research Opportunities	25%
Promotional opportunities	25%
Appreciation for personal contributions	24%
Responsiveness of administration to problems	22%
Committee work	22%
Recognition for good teaching	21%[20]

In addition to this it has also been reported that there is a general sense of powerlessness among these black faculty.[21] There is the general belief that there is too much power concentrated in the hands of the president and, as a result, faculty members have no meaningful input into the functioning of the organization. Black faculty in TBIs therefore have an overwhelming tendency to feel viewed as lower level workers rather than colleagues in the enterprise of creating and disseminating knowledge.[22]

Thus, even though access and stability may appear to be more attractive in the TBI setting, problems associated with academic isolation and scholarly development and internal problems of status tend to push many black faculty toward the white institutions. This is evident in the relatively recent major reversal of patterns in the distribution of black faculty across these two environments.

On the other hand, employment within these white institutions is also quite problematic, and, as one would expect, of a different nature and quality due to the more direct influence of race. Although theoretically within the mainstream of academia, black faculty in white institutions are also quite isolated. However, this type of isolation is more of the interpersonal variety and, in a sense, more devastating from an individual psychosocial point of view.

The evidence indicates that not only are black faculty in white institutions isolated socially from their white colleagues, they also tend to be isolated from each other, even when there is some modicum of black presence on a given white campus.[23] The consequences of such a state are that when black faculty find themselves in isolated circumstances, problems associated with institutional and individual racism become even more dominant than they otherwise would be.[24] Because there are no meaningful support groups of people operating under similar circumstances, frustrations begin to mount. Accordingly, black faculty find themselves subjected to the most aggravating aspects of the white environment without enjoying some of its more rewarding benefits.[25]

Given the above, one might go so far as to state that these isolated circumstances are likely to produce feelings of distrust, or in some cases, outright hostility toward the institution and its intention in and commitment to hiring black faculty members.

In a study of over four hundred black faculty in white institutions in ten southern and border states, it was found that a substantial proportion of black faculty thought that their institutions were just outright racist.[26] In response to an open-ended question that asked what were some of the most significant barriers to black faculty employment in their present institution, over 41 percent indicated that it was racism. In contrast to this fairly high percentage, only 17 percent indicated that the problem with more black faculty employment was the limited supply of potential black faculty members. Similarly, a substantial percentage (56 percent) of these black faculty was of the opinion that black candidates must be "outstanding in their field" in order to be hired by the institution.

In a similar sense, one would also think that the situation of isolation would have a tendency to manifest itself in feelings of detachment or estrangement from the present institutional context once an individual is actually employed. Again there is partial support for this position.

Approximately 40 percent of a sample of black faculty in non-TBIs who were nontenured assistant professors with less than six years of experience indicated that they did not identify with their present department[27]—a situation not uncharacteristic of any individual in the probationary stage of his career. On the other hand, those who had had an opportunity to serve on important institutional committees and had a clear understanding of the promotion and tenure process were less likely to feel detached.[28] This seems to imply that the more individuals are involved with the day-to-day activities of the institution (i.e., not isolated), the less likely they are to feel detached or alienated—again a situation that seems totally consistent with organizational behavior.

However, it is interesting to note that even though black faculty as a whole tended to feel some degree of attachment to their present departments (e.g., 60 percent indicated that they had some identification with their department), over half still believed that the promotion and tenure process was racially biased.[29] Thus, even though many of the black faculty do not feel detached and are indeed active participants in the operations of the institutions, they still have a tendency to believe that the activities and contributions of blacks are not judged in a fair and impartial manner.

An explanation of this situation may very well lie in the institutional perception of scholarly activities as practiced by most black scholars. That is, black faculty have a tendency to challenge the contemporary conceptions of scholarship in terms of content, theoretical paradigms, philosophies and methodology.[30] As a result, their scholarship presents new or unfamiliar knowledge that is developed through unconventional perspectives. The result, from the point of view of the existing institutional structure, is the evaluation of new and different perspectives and methodologies by the standards of what has existed in the past.[31] This has a tendency to make the scholarly activities of black faculty foreign to the status quo and decreases the likelihood of any meaningful and sustained scholarly collaboration with those who adhere to the traditional mode of academic production. In the end, black faculty suffer when promotion and tenure decisions are to be made.

Additionally, the scholarly perceptions and activities of black faculty also make it difficult for them to participate in the "right" networks such that they may reduce their rather invisible status in a scholarly sense.[32] Because of their perceptions, their procedures and the issues that they investigate, black faculty not only suffer internally in terms of university-wide participation, they also suffer in terms of participation in those relevant networks that result in access to "mainstream" journals and other publication outlets,[33] which in most major universities is extremely critical for promotion and tenure.

It should also be pointed out that this visibility in terms of university activities and participation in the right networks is a double-edged sword that appears to have racial consequences that are more of the institutional variety.

In many cases, because black faculty are so few in number on a given campus, they are asked to serve on an extremely large number of committees requiring some black presence, do community service activities, teach, advise and serve as sympathetic mentors for black students.[34] The result is a workload that leaves very little time or energy for scholarly research and other traditional academic activities that appear to be weighted more heavily in terms of promotion and tenure.[35]

SUMMARY

Based on the data that presently exists, it appears, then, that there is some validity to both of the major arguments concerning the rather low representation of black faculty in academia. That is, there is ample evidence that indicates that the pool of potential black candidates for faculty positions is indeed relatively small and in the process of getting smaller. Additionally, there is also evidence that indicates that racist perceptions, both in an individual and institutional sense, are still rather dominant, and subsequently have a tendency to not only restrict access for those who possess the requisite credentials but to also stifle the professional growth of those already in academia such that they become less visible signs of success.

On the other hand, what is more important about these observations than the mere fact that evidence exists to substantiate each contention, is that they do not appear to be unrelated occurrences. That is, the experiences surrounding the fairly small number of black faculty presently in academia significantly impacts the decision of potential candidates to choose academia as a career option. In turn, there are fewer individuals to help alleviate the isolated conditions and subsequent experiences of those black faculty presently in the system such that more individuals would see this profession as a positive career option. What one has then, is a cycle of sorts. A cycle that tends to feed on itself in such a manner that not only is a smaller pool of black faculty produced, but at the same time conditions surrounding those presently in academia get progressively worse in terms of professional growth. This interrelatedness implies that solutions directed solely toward increasing the number of black students enrolled in graduate programs, thereby increasing the number of potential faculty members, may be overly simplistic.

Given that more black students are now attending white institutions, it would seem that white institutions need to become more sensitive to the needs and aspirations of black students if these students are indeed to graduate and continue on to graduate school. Additionally, these white institutions must provide visible signs of success as exemplified in a quite realistic sense by black faculty who are presently employed in these institutions. If these black faculty are alienated and display feelings of hostility toward their environments, it is quite inconceivable that black students would choose to subject themselves to similar circumstances, even if they were enrolled in record numbers. Thus, a mere increase in black student enrollment will not in itself break the cycle. There must be a simultaneous effort to reduce the isolated circumstances of black faculty who are presently in these white institutions such that positions in academia are viewed by the students as a positive career option.

Further, TBIs and their faculties must be brought into the mainstream of the academic environment. It is still the case that a significant proportion of black students attend these colleges and universities. In fact, they are still one of the major pipelines that provide potential faculty members. On the other hand, their ability to produce even more potential candidates is becoming progressively more restricted due to the many internal and external constraints imposed upon them and their faculties. It is imperative, then, that they be supported professionally and, perhaps more importantly, financially. If they are allowed to fade away, or are just outright closed as some education policy makers would have it, then we can expect the pool of potential black faculty to get even smaller and the problems of black representation to get worse.

In essence, if we as professional scholars do not find ways to deal with these problems, fewer and fewer black individuals will enter academia and those who are there will become increasingly more disenchanted. The result will be a major institution founded on principles of merit and objectivity that systematically excludes its largest minority group from participation. This is a situation that will surely break the already tenuous social fabric that binds this society together.

NOTES

1. W. E. B. DuBois, "Two Hundred Years of Segregated Schools," in *W. E. B. DuBois Speaks,* ed. P. Foner (New York: Pathfinder Press, 1970); Henry A. Bullock, *A History of Negro Education in the South* (Cambridge: Harvard University Press, 1967); David B. Tyack, *The One Best System* (Cambridge: Harvard University Press, 1974).

2. James A. Moss, "Negro Teachers in Predominantly White Colleges," *Journal of Negro Education* 27 (1958): 451–462; David M. Rafky, "The Black Scholar in the Academic Marketplace," *Teachers College Record* 74 (1972): 225–260.

3. J. A. Moss, "Negro Teachers."

4. Ibid.

5. Walter A. Allen, "Black Colleges vs. White Colleges: The Fork in the Road for Black Students," *Change* 19 (1987): 28–34.

6. Ibid.

7. Ibid.

8. Elias Blake, "Equality for Blacks," *Change* 19 (1987): 10–13.

9. Herman R. Branson, "The Hazards in Black Higher Education: Program and Commitment Needs," *Journal of Negro Education* 56 (1987): 129–136.

10. Susan T. Hill, *The Traditionally Black Institutions of Higher Education 1860 to 1982* (Washington, DC: National Center for Education Statistics, 1982).

11. Ibid.

12. Daniel C. Thompson, *Private Black Colleges at the Crossroads* (Westport: Greenwood Press, 1973).

13. Earl J. McGrath, *The Predominantly Negro Colleges and Universities in Transition* (New York: Institute of Higher Education, 1965).

14. Ibid.

15. Ibid.

16. Ibid.

17. H. R. Branson, *op. cit.*

18. Ibid.

19. Luther H. Foster, "The Hazards in Black Higher Education: Institutional Management," *Journal of Negro Education* 56 (1987): 137–144.

20. Thomas Diener, "Job Satisfaction and College Faculty in Two Predominantly Black Institutions," *Journal of Negro Education* 54 (1985): 558–565.

21. Thompson, *Private Black Colleges.*

22. Ibid.

23. William Moore and Lonnie Wagstaff, *Black Faculty in White Colleges* (San Francisco: Jossey-Bass, 1974); Henry T. Frierson, "Plights of Black Academicians in Educational Research and Development" (unpublished manuscript, 1986); William B. Harvey and Diane Scott-Jones, "We Can't Find Any: The Elusiveness of Black Faculty Members in American Higher Education" *Issues in Education* 3 (1985): 68–76.

24. Harvey and Scott-Jones, "Elusiveness of Black Faculty Members."

25. Ibid.

26. Kenneth W. Jackson, *A Profile of Black Faculty in Traditionally White Institutions* (final report to Southern Education Foundation, Atlanta, 1988).

27. Ibid.

28. Ibid.

29. Ibid.

30. William H. Exum, "Climbing the Crystal Stair: Values, Affirmative Action, and Minority Faculty," *Social Problems* 30 (1983): 383–399.

31. Ibid.

32. Ibid.

33. Ibid.

34. Robert J. Menges and William H. Exum, "Barriers to the Progress of Women and Minority Faculty," *Journal of Higher Education* 54 (1983): 123–144.

35. Harvey and Scott-Jones, "Elusiveness of Black Faculty Members."

ROSLYN ARLIN MICKELSON AND
MELVIN L. OLIVER

Chapter Eight

Making the Short List: Black Candidates and the Faculty Recruitment Process

The reappearance of overt racism on the campuses of the nation's predominantly white universities is merely a symptom of structural racism in higher education.[1] This situation is reflected by the declining number of minority enrollees and graduates, cutbacks in financial assistance, battles over multicultural curricula and over the broadening of canons to include the scholarship and artistry of women and members of minorities, and the precarious status of minority faculty.[2] Minority faculty members are declining in number; many who are hired fail to be tenured and promoted, and those who remain are frequently ghettoized in the lower ranks of the academic hierarchy.[3]

The number of minority Ph.D.'s who serve on university faculties depends on a three-phase process: (1) the production of Ph.D.'s (the so-called academic pipeline); (2) the search and hiring process in academic

A different version of this essay appears in *College in Black and White: Black Students on Black and White Campuses,* Walter R. Allen, Edgar Epps and Nesha Haniff, eds. (in press, SUNY Press). The authors wish to thank Rodney D. Coates for his helpful comments on an earlier draft and Angela Detlev and Ginny G. Smith for their technical assistance in the preparation of this essay.

departments; and (3) the tenure and promotion process at individual institutions. In this essay we focus on the second issue as it pertains to black Ph.D.'s, specifically the process of recruiting prospective candidates for academic positions. Although a great deal has been written about this multistep process,[4] we argue that one additional factor, overlooked in other treatments of the hiring process, contributes to the small numbers of blacks who are ultimately hired by university faculties. This factor is the fallacious assumption that "qualified" new Ph.D. candidates can be found only in the graduate departments of elite research universities.

According to this assumption, if black candidates are not trained in the graduate departments of universities considered to be the best in a field, it is concluded, often incorrectly, that no qualified black candidates are available. Search committees, often faced with a large volume of applications, frequently use the national reputation of a prospective candidate's Ph.D. department as a proxy for initially screening the individual's qualifications. "We know which are the top twenty economics departments in the country, and if an applicant was not trained at one of these schools, we are not interested in him [sic]," a department chair told one of the researchers. In this way many black Ph.D.'s from nonelite graduate programs are summarily disqualified from making the "short lists" of many university searches.

Although the assumption that the best potential academics are trained primarily at flagship research universities may be true for white, middle-class Protestant males, who until approximately 1950 filled most positions in the United States professoriate,[5] we argue that it is not true for blacks, members of other minorities and most women. We present evidence based on our analysis of data from the National Study of Black College Students (NSBCS),[6] which suggests that high-quality black Ph.D. students are found not only in premier institutions but also in a wide variety of graduate departments. We argue further that one way in which universities can increase their minority faculty is to abandon the fallacious notion that a graduate department's reputation is a suitable proxy for a candidate's potential, and to include on recruitment short lists qualified black Ph.D.'s from lesser-known universities. The results of our data analyses suggest that such a practice will enhance the likelihood of increasing the number of black academics in the coming decade without sacrificing the quality of the black professoriate.

THE CRISIS: DEMOGRAPHICS OF BLACK ACADEMICS

As this society enters the last decade of the twentieth century, a decade after the *Adams* case was first argued in federal courts, the proportion of minority faculty members at predominantly white institutions remains minuscule.[7] The proportion of black faculty members in these institutions has fluctuated from a mere handful before the 1960s to very low levels during the last three decades.[8] In the early 1960s blacks accounted for 3 percent of professors. This proportion dropped to 2.2 percent in the early 1970s, rose again in the early 1980s to the 4 percent shown in table 1, and has fallen in 1989 to an estimated 3.3 percent.[9]

The representation of black faculty members at predominantly white universities is actually poorer than these figures suggest. Faculty members are stratified both by rank and by type of institution. The higher the rank, the less likely it is that a black person will be found in it. The same is true at more prestigious schools. These unpublished estimates, however, include faculty at both four-year and two-year schools, and thus suggest that the actual proportion of black faculty at four-year universities is overestimated in the 3.3 percent figure cited above. Unfortunately, available data from the Equal Employment Opportunity Commission (EEOC) do not control for type of college. Data from a nonrandom but comprehensively researched survey of 158 four-year colleges in *The Black Student's Guide to Colleges* show that black faculty at predominantly white universities average about 2 percent of the total, while nonblack faculty at historically black colleges averages about 30 percent.[10] This finding suggests that if the data analysis reported in table 1 controlled for employment in historically black colleges, where large numbers of blacks teach, the representation of black faculty at predominantly white institutions would be even more disproportional than it already appears to be.

We are not suggesting that the significant numbers of black faculty members at historically black colleges are unwisely or poorly using their academic talent. On the contrary, the presence of large numbers of black

TABLE 1

U.S. Full-time Faculty in Four-Year Institutions, 1983

Rank	White	Blacks	All Races
Professor	119,219	2,857	128,142
Assoc. professor	102,246	3,969	111,887
Asst. professor	100,176	5,847	113,330
Instructor	73,206	5,117	82,211
Lecturer	8,274	618	9,480
Other	22,570	1,043	25,623
Totals			
N	425,691	19,451	470,673
%	90	4	100

SOURCE: NCES, *Digest of Educational Statistics* (Washington, DC: Government Printing Office, 1988), p. 177.

faculty members at these institutions is often an advantage to the students at those schools.[11] Instead we note this fact to illustrate the dearth of black faculty at predominantly white institutions of higher education, where the majority of all college students, both black and white, attend school and where most university faculty members must find employment.

THE NARROWING PIPELINE

Although this chapter will not explore in detail the issue of the production of black Ph.D.'s, we will address briefly the importance of the educational pipeline for understanding the racial crisis in higher education. The absolute number of black Ph.D.'s produced each year in this country, as well as the proportion of the total degrees granted to blacks, declined between 1975 and 1985.[12] According to the U.S. Department of Education, 1,253 blacks received Ph.D.'s in 1975 (3.8 percent of the total doctorates awarded), as compared to 1,154 in 1985 (3.5 percent). Moreover, the rates at which blacks received bachelor's and master's degrees also declined during this period. This decrease is most dramatic at the master's level, where proportions of total master's degrees dropped from 6.6 percent in 1975 to 4.9 percent in 1985.[13] When we consider that more than 50 percent of all blacks' doctorates are in education, the actual pool of potential faculty members for academic positions in the physical and natural sciences, the humanities and the social sciences is actually smaller than the data initially suggest. Taken together, these statistics reflect a deepening crisis in the black academic pipeline.

GRADUATE DEPARTMENT'S REPUTATION AS A PROXY FOR INDIVIDUAL MERIT

As we stated earlier, the available pool of black Ph.D.'s is not the only factor that inhibits schools from identifying and making offers to qualified blacks. The process by which candidates are identified, screened and selected is guided by a set of meritocratic norms and untested assumptions that work against the selection of qualified minority Ph.D.'s who are not graduates of the leading institutions.

It is well-established that merit is the overriding consideration guiding the selection process of university faculty members. Even so, one can question the ability of search committees to select new faculty on the basis of judgments of meritocratic criteria that do not inherently bias the decision-making process against minorities. Seen in its sociological context, the process of selection turns out to be less an expression of positive choices than the result of negative choices,[14] whereby inappropriate and supposedly less-qualified candidates are cast aside while the most appropriate and best-qualified candidates rise to the top of the list. At almost every turn, members of minorities seem to be excluded disproportionately by criteria that appear on the surface to be universalistic, but actually serve to decrease the probability of a minority candidate's rising to the top of the short list.

Proponents of the present system, which allows an autonomous faculty to choose its peers in the context of meritocratic values, argue that this system is minorities' best protection against biases in the selection process.[15] When selection is based on neutral, objective and universalistic criteria, the argument goes, blacks and other disadvantaged minorities are protected against the intrusion of particularistic and biased criteria that previously excluded them from participation in the academy. This view, however, disregards an established literature that finds the search process to be plagued by precisely the opposite situation:[16] "Objective standards are often vague, inconsistent, and weighted toward subjective judgments."[17] The implementation of meritocratic principles is thwarted somewhere between rhetoric and reality.

To understand where this disjuncture occurs, we look more closely at the search process itself. Several good studies offer considerable insight into this process.[18] Previous research indicates that affirmative action is one factor which has affected faculty recruitment. Affirmative action has made a marked difference in the initial stage of the search process, but unfortunately not in the results. Because of affirmative action, academic positions are now advertised more widely than ever. Advertisements are written to encourage women and minority candidates to apply. Studies and demographic data, however, show that the outcome of these searches continues to be largely the same as in the past. Those who rise to the top of the lists of qualified candidates are graduate students who studied at the most elite universities, who are recommended by the most eminent people in their field, and who were encouraged to apply, in many cases, by members of the hiring faculty. From the outset, then, the search process does not focus on candidates' individual qualifications, as the ideology of meritocracy would have us believe. Instead it focuses on institutional prestige. A graduate department's reputation becomes the proxy for a candidate's potential.

To aggravate the problem of reliance on institutional sources of merit in preliminary evaluations of candidates, faculties tend to rely heavily on the source of the recommendations that accompany an applicant's file. Because recruiting faculties cannot evaluate autonomously a candidate's record in light of conflicting or unclear standards, the nature and the source of an applicant's supporting letters become important. While they testify to candidates' abilities and potentials, they also locate the candidates in important disciplinary networks or exclude them from those networks. Thus Caplow and McGhee argue that "personal influence among networks of colleagues" is the most important carrier of the prestige that really counts.[19] This suggests that the academic market is not an objective, competitive system based on merit but a system of "sponsored mobility" in which patronage from established scholars at elite institutions is a key factor in determining who makes the short list.[20]

In this context blacks seem to suffer more acutely because they lack the momentum generated by initial privilege. Blacks have severe difficulties in conquering the personal and institutional barriers they face in their quest for academic success. In the demography of higher education, they are more likely to attend the least prestigious and least elite institutions of advanced training. A 1977 report of the National Academy of Sciences states that blacks are least likely to earn their Ph.D.'s from the top-rated institutions and that the proportion of degrees earned by blacks from the top tier is less than the proportion of total degrees granted to blacks.[21] Recent evidence shows that this is still the case; blacks continue to be found in less prestigious graduate departments.[22] If graduation from top institutions is a prerequisite even for consideration by search committees in major colleges and universities, it is clear that blacks will be excluded systematically from short lists and ultimately from employment.

In view of these past findings, we address the following questions here: Are there differences in quality among black graduate students in variously ranked graduate institutions? Do the backgrounds of these students differ, so as to confirm the notion that students from better institutions also come from more advantaged backgrounds? Do students from variously ranked graduate schools differ in aspirations regarding successful careers?

These questions test directly the assumptions that undergird present-day academic searchers. To the degree that we find differences in the present study, the current search process may well be the best way to identify minority talent. To the degree that we do not find such differences, we argue that the search process may affect blacks unfairly by overlooking an important source of black scholarly resources in nonelite institutions of graduate training.

METHODS

Data Sources

Data used in this essay come from surveys administered to participants in the National Study of Black College Students. From 1981 through 1985 the NSBCS collected data on black undergraduates, graduates and professional students who attended eight predominantly white state-supported universities. Separate questionnaires were administered to graduate and professional students and to undergraduates. The instrument gathered comprehensive information on the respondents' background, achievements, experiences, attitudes and aspirations.[23] For more details about the methods, sample and data see Allen et al.'s *College in Black and White*.[24]

Sample

Our sample consists of all graduate and professional school students enrolled in the universities that contributed to the NSBCS in 1981 and 1982. Institutions that participated in this study were chosen on the basis of regional representation, diversity in the proportion of black enrollment, and accessibility of data and school records. Participants were the University of Michigan at Ann Arbor; Eastern Michigan University; the University of Wisconsin at Madison; the University of North Carolina at Chapel Hill; Memphis State University; Arizona State University; the University of California at Los Angeles; and the State University of New York (SUNY) at Stony Brook. We drew a simple random sample of black students from computerized lists of graduate and professional students provided by each school's registrar. The overall response rate was 43 percent. The sample consists disproportionately of first-year graduate students and professional students.[25] We combined the 1981 and 1982 data sets primarily because of the small number of respondents in each year who attended schools in the lowest-ranked category. Without combining the two data sets we risked having too few cases in the lowest rank of colleges to make meaningful comparisons. (We discuss the basis for institutional ranking below.) Our sample consists of 387 students from the top rank of universities, 224 students from the middle rank and 122 students from the lower group, a total of 733 students.

A potential problem arises from combining data sets from two separate years. There is a possibility that respondents from each year have different histories. The subjects from both years, however, are distributed throughout the three ranks. This situation compensates for any bias that may occur because our analyses are conducted across rather than between years.[26]

Variables

We used a performance-based model to examine the issues of quality differences among black graduate students. What skills are necessary for success in academia? What factors are academic search committees likely to examine? Four factors come to mind. First, we considered the student's academic performance as measured by grade point average. Outstanding grades indicate that a student has mastered the necessary coursework and subsequently has obtained the skills, theoretical background and knowledge to do good work in an academic discipline.[27] Second, we looked at the receipt of fellowships, research assistantships and grants; this step is a precursor to the competitive process of securing the grants and the prized fellowships that are a part of a successful academic career. Third, we noted the presentation of scholarly papers at conferences and professional meetings. Finally, we considered the publication of scholarly articles and books. A combination of these four factors constitutes our indicator of quality.

Because the students in the NSBCS sample range from first-year graduate students to those in the process of writing a dissertation, it would be inappropriate to demand that first-year students meet the same standards in our measure of quality as fourth- or fifth-year students. Therefore we used a sliding scale that takes into account the natural history, the development and the maturation of students in graduate school. Because first-year students do little more than take courses, we weight the criteria they are most likely to meet—a high grade point average and the receipt of a fellowship or grant—more heavily for them than for more advanced graduate students. For third- and fourth-year students all the criteria are applicable; in these cases excellence is based on a wider range of factors. Ideally we would like to factor into this formula the number of papers presented and articles published, but the data do not permit this elaboration.

Respondents' quality index scores (QUALITY), our dependent variable, range from a low of 0.5 to a high of 8.0. The formula for ascertaining each student's score on our quality index works as follows: a first-year student with a high grade point average and a research grant would receive a score of 4.5 (GPA > 3.0 [2.0] + grant [2.5] = 4.5), whereas a third-year student would receive a score of 3.5 for the same accomplishments (GPA > 3.0 [1.5] + grant [2.0] = 3.5). In this way we weight the scale to the length of our respondents' graduate careers. We also adapt this formula to the extremes of our scale, however. Extraordinary first-year graduate students with high grades, grants, publications and a paper presentation or two can surpass the 8.0 scale. In these circumstances we truncate their scores to 8. Certain respondents, primarily a few first-year graduate students, show no papers, grants of publications and have a grade point average below 3.0. To prevent their quality index score from receiving a value of zero, which would cause their cases to be dropped from the data analysis, we assign them a score of 0.5 in order to retain their cases. Table 2 presents our formula for creating the students' quality index score.

We created our university rank variable (RANK) by dividing the eight graduate training institutions from the NSBCS into three groups based on the national reputations of their graduate departments. The top group represents

TABLE 2

Construction of Values of Quality Index

Year in Program	GPA*		Grant**		Paper***		Publication***	
	>3.0	<3.0	Yes	No	Yes	No	Yes	No
First or second	2.0	.5	2.5	0	2.5	0	2.5	0
Third	1.5	.5	2.0	0	2.5	0	2.5	0
Fourth or fifth	1.0	.5	1.5	0	2.0	0	2.5	0

   * Missing values were assigned the value for first year.
  ** Missing values were assigned the value for undergraduate grade point averages.
*** Missing values were assigned the value for no.

institutions which in our sample of schools, across every discipline, have highly ranked departments whose size and influence have made them traditional suppliers of faculty for other elite institutions. This group includes the universities of Michigan at Ann Arbor, Wisconsin at Madison, and North Carolina at Chapel Hill. The middle group contains institutions that are ranked nationally in particular departments but are not consistently as strong as those in the first group. This group includes the University of California at Los Angeles, Arizona State, and SUNY at Stony Brook.[28] The lowest-ranked group, which includes Memphis State and Eastern Michigan University, represents schools without national reputations and with relatively new graduate programs. These institutions, located for the most part in urban areas, developed most rapidly during the 1960s, when expansion in higher education was common. Although they have recruited high-quality faculty, they have yet to gain more than regional (and in some cases local) recognition as important institutions of graduate training.

In addition to these key variables we introduced into our analyses a series of individual and structural variables, traditionally related to academic achievement, in order to elaborate our model. These variables are student's gender (GENDER), marital status (MARITAL), presence of young children in the home (KIDS), father's educational (DADED) and occupational attainment (DADOCC), mother's educational (MOMED) and occupational attainment (MOMOCC), respondent's age at first full-time job (AGE), the type of first job (FIRST JOB), and the respondent's motivation to succeed in a chosen career (HUNGER).

FINDINGS

Differences in Quality

We began our data analysis with a series of analyses of variance (ANOVA), which examined mean differences in quality index scores for students who attended differently ranked graduate institutions. The first ANOVA revealed that the average score on the quality measure for students from the lower-ranked schools (3.35) was only slightly lower than for those from the middle- and top-ranked schools (3.51 and 3.59). Table 3 shows that the differences were not statistically significant.

The analyses of variance also showed that institutional differences are less important than certain individual attributes in predicting how well students will perform in graduate school. Two such important attributes are gender and marital status. As table 3 shows, men and married graduate students have higher mean scores on our index of quality than do women and single graduate students. Both gender and marital status differences in graduate students' performance are statistically significant (gender, p <.0001; marital status, p <.05). Overall, the analyses of variance show that high-caliber black graduate students are found not only in the highest-ranking institutions but also in the lower-ranked schools. Indeed, gender and marital status are better predictors of quality.

Differences in Background

Implicit in the academic search process is the assumption that the best and brightest black students attend the best universities and become the best Ph.D.'s. This assumption implies that the educational attainment process for blacks in academia is similar to that for whites. The evidence regarding white students reveals a strong relationship among family background, academic achievement and the prestige of the university.[29] Thus the better white students are likely to come from more privileged backgrounds and to attend better graduate schools. Can we find evidence of this educational attainment process in our sample of black graduate students? If the same social forces are at work, we should find that the very best black graduate scholars come from more affluent families and are trained at the most elite research institutions. This is not the case, however.

Among black students at the variously ranked schools, the parents' educational and occupational backgrounds can be quite diverse (see table 3). For example, the mean educational level of the mothers and fathers of students from the highest- and lowest-ranked graduate schools in our study are virtually the same (2.93 versus 2.95 for father's education and 3.10 compared to 3.00 for mother's education). Black students attending the middle-ranked schools appear to come from social backgrounds in which the parents are less well-educated and hold lower-status jobs than parents of blacks from both lower- and higher-ranked schools.

Black graduate students from all social backgrounds appear to attend a variety of graduate schools, possibly because the paths to graduate education

TABLE 3

Summary of Means and Standard Deviations of Selected Variables

Dependent Variable	N	Mean	Standard Deviation	F
Student Quality Index				.492
High rank	387	3.51	2.16	
Medium rank	224	3.59	2.11	
Low rank	122	3.35	2.23	
Student Quality Index				10.48***
Male	320	3.80	2.28	
Female	413	3.28	4.14	
Student Quality Index				4.28*
Single	427	3.37	4.53	
Married	219	3.74	5.01	
Father's Education (1 to 6 scale)				4.13**
High rank	375	2.93	1.48	
Medium rank	219	2.59	2.12	
Low rank	118	2.95	2.20	
Mother's Education (1 to 6 scale)				9.79***
High rank	386	3.10	1.31	
Medium rank	221	2.67	1.32	
Low rank	126	3.00	1.34	
Father's Occupation (Duncan SEI)				.82
High rank	345	40.40	28.75	
Medium rank	194	36.18	26.17	
Low rank	106	42.30	28.75	
Mother's Occupation (Duncan SEI)				1.47
High rank	338	40.51	24.94	
Medium rank	179	36.64	24.04	
Low rank	110	39.74	24.44	
Age at First Job				10.42***
High rank	285	20.40	9.78	
Medium rank	197	20.72	9.40	
Low rank	92	18.91	14.02	
Occupational Prestige of First Job (Duncan SEI)				5.57*
HIgh rank	243	51.95	21.18	
Medium rank	151	56.11	17.31	
Low rank	106	42.34	28.75	
Motivation to Succeed ("Hunger")				1.159
High rank	222	3.60	2.25	
Medium rank	127	3.61	1.91	
Low rank	76	3.88	1.51	

* p = < .05
** p = < .01
*** p = < .001

taken by blacks differ markedly from those traditionally taken by middle-class white males. Blacks do not necessarily take the usual four years of baccalaureate work and then enter graduate school directly, as demonstrated by the work experiences of the graduate students in our sample. Students from the lowest-ranked universities worked full time at a much earlier age (18.91) than did students from either the middle or high category (20.72 and 20.40). Furthermore, they were likely to have less prestigious first jobs than their counterparts at more elite universities ($p = <.05$). Yet the marked differences in students' family backgrounds do not seem to affect their quality index scores. It becomes increasingly clear that black students differ minimally in terms of our measure of faculty potential across graduate training institutions.

Motivational Differences

Inherent in the notion that the best students train at the most prestigious universities is the assumption that students at elite universities are the most highly motivated, and therefore aspire to higher accomplishments in their chosen fields. To learn whether this difference exists among graduate students in our sample we examined an item related to this theme that appeared in the NSBCS. Students were asked the following question: "After your are in the profession which will be your life's work, when do you think you will be able to consider yourself successful enough so that you can relax and stop trying so hard to get ahead?" Students could choose one of five answers, which ranged from "when you are doing well enough to stay in the profession" (scored 1) to "when you are recognized as one of the top persons in the profession" (scored 5). We labeled this the "hunger for success" questions: How hungry are these students to achieve at the highest levels possible? According to assumptions inherent in the evaluation of graduate students for jobs in the market today, the hungriest students are assumed to be found at the most elite institutions.

The data, however, demonstrate that for our sample the students from the most elite or most prestigious graduate programs are no more likely to be hungry for success than those from less prestigious universities. Although not statistically significant, mean hunger scores for students from the less highly ranked schools are higher (3.88) than for students at the most highly ranked schools (3.60). Once again, there is no evidence to support the notion that black academic resources, in the form of highly motivated black graduate students, are found exclusively in a narrow group of elite universities.

CONCLUSIONS AND POLICY IMPLICATIONS

The racial crisis in higher education demands renewed efforts to eliminate institutional racism wherever it is located. This goal cannot be reached, however, without attention to faculty. Reasons to increase the number of minority faculty members include issues of employment equity for minority Ph.D.'s, the role of minority faculty in the enrollment, retention, achievement, persistence and graduation of minority students, and the necessity for the full and unfettered participation in American society by all of its members if this nation is to survive economically, socially and spiritually. This situation can come about only if every college student learns from a professoriate that reflects the racial, ethnic, gender and class diversity of the entire society.[30]

One policy used widely to increase the number of minority faculty members is affirmative action. Yet even the most rigorously enforced affirmative action programs have limitations because greater numbers of minority faculty per se are not their direct goal. Rather their primary objective is to open up the recruitment process by advertising widely and stating explicitly the employers' nondiscriminatory intentions. Affirmative action programs have been relatively unsuccessful in increasing the proportion of minority faculty in this country precisely because of the way in which qualified candidates are identified, screened and selected for the short list, the points at which affirmative action policies are relevant and operate most directly. An affirmative action policy is of little value if no minority candidates are selected for the short list.

In this essay we have attempted to examine critically an assumption that undergirds the traditional academic search process; we believe that this assumption reduces the likelihood that minority candidates will appear on the short list from which new faculty members are hired. Faculty members charged with securing a new colleague often rely on so-called proven categories of evaluation to assess potential candidates, namely the ranking of a candidate's graduate department and the recommendations of prestigious, influential, well-known scholars. In this initial screening the candidate himself or herself is not an issue; the school and the referee's reputation are used as proxies for the applicant's merit. To the degree that members of minorities are found less often at top institutions and are left out of prestigious patronage networks, the "institution as proxy" process tends to exclude qualified black candidates from reaching many short lists.

As our research demonstrates, the assumption that the best black graduate students are found only at the most elite, most prestigious colleges is unfounded. The assumption that quality rises to the top may reflect some truth in the case of male majority students, but such an assumption is flawed in the case of blacks and other members of minorities who continue to meet barriers to obtaining the prerequisites for higher education, and to higher education itself. Because of family obligations, community ties, hostile social and racial climates on elite campuses, inadequate social and psychological support systems at leading schools or limited financial support, well-qualified minority groups members may enroll in a wide variety of schools rather than following the path that leads to elite universities. The data we present in this essay suggest that one direct strategy to increase the number of minority faculty members is for recruitment committees to cast their nets more widely. This process will entail a critical assessment, and ultimately the rejection, of traditional reliance on institutional proxies (such as departments' reputation and referees' prestige) as indicators of minority candidates' potential.

A second strategy to make better use of the minority academic resources found in nonelite universities is the greater use of postdoctoral training programs at elite universities. These programs can be designed to provide black scholars with some of the resources to which they allegedly had limited access during their training in lesser schools. Minority Ph.D.'s can then become stronger candidates for positions at the university where they take their postdoctoral training or in the job market in general. in this way universities can assess for themselves whether a candidate from a lower-ranked school has the abilities, aptitude and skills necessary to contribute to the discipline at the highest levels.

We offer our research as a preliminary examination of this aspect of the minority faculty crisis in higher education. This study suffers from several problems, however. First, the sample of respondents relies too heavily on professional and first-year graduate students, and the sample of schools from which the subjects are drawn is not completely representative of all universities. Perhaps if we had included in our sample the most prestigious and most elite institutions, such as Harvard, Yale, the University of Chicago and Stanford, we would have found significant differences in our measure of students' quality. Moreover, problems always arise when researchers attempt to quantify or operationalize concepts such as student quality. Our dependent variable assumes that grades across institutions are equivalent. The results might have been different if we had controlled for the discipline or for the number and quality of the respondents' articles and presentations. Yet even with these flaws we submit this research as evidence that fresh, new, black academic talent is not isolated in prestigious graduate programs but is dispersed broadly throughout higher education. Future research into this topic must address these problems.

The issue at stake here is the subtle institutional racism inherent in the faculty recruitment and search processes. Access to top research institutions and to eminent professors, whose reputations in turn attract the interest of search committees, is not yet free of discrimination. Thus to rely primarily on these criteria as the test of merit for new black scholars is essentially a racist practice. As long as "sponsored mobility" and attendance at premier institutions of higher education remain proxies for individual quality, the underutilization of minority talent will continue, as will the minority faculty crisis in higher education.

NOTES

1. Walter C. Farrell, Jr. and Cloyzell K. Jones, "Racial Incidents in Higher Education: A Preliminary Perspective," *Urban Review* 20 (1988): 211–30.

2. Scott Heller, "Scholars Defend Their Efforts to Promote Literature by Women and Blacks, Decry Attack by Bennett," *Chronicle of Higher Education* 34 (February 17, 1988): A1; Scott Heller, "Stanford Professors to Vote on Altering Freshman Reading List," *Chronicle of Higher Education* 34 (February 17, 1988): A13. And Stanley Aronowitz and Henry A. Giroux, "Schooling, Culture, and Literacy in the Age of Broken Dreams: A Review of Bloom and Hirsch." *Harvard Educational Review* 58 (May 1988): 172–94.

3. National Center for Educational Statistics (NCES), *Digest of Educational Statistics* (Washington, DC: Government Printing Office, 1988); "Shortage of Black Professors Is Forecast," *Chronicle of Higher Education* 35 (April 27, 1988): A23; Debra E. Blum, "Tenure Rates for Black Professors Found to Lag at White Institutions in Nine Southern States," *Chronicle of Higher Education* 35 (September 21, 1988) A1; Howard R. Bowen and Jack H. Schuster, *American Professors: A National Resource Imperiled* (New York: Oxford University Press, 1986); Martin J. Finkelstein, *The American Academic Profession* (Columbus: Ohio University Press, 1984); Robert J. Menges and William H. Exum, "Barriers to the Progress of Women and Minority Faculty," *Journal of Higher Education* 54 (1983): pp.123–44.

4. Bowen and Schuster, *American Professors;* Finkelstein, *American Academic Profession;* Neil Smelser and Robin Content, *The Changing Academic Market Place* (Berkeley: University of California Press, 1980).

5. Philip G. Altbach, "Stark Realities: The Academic Profession in the 1980's and Beyond," in *Higher Education in American Society,* rev. ed., eds. P. G. Altbach and R. O. Berdahl (Buffalo: Prometheus Books, 1987), p. 248.

6. Walter R. Allen, Edgar G. Epps and Nesha Z. Haniff, eds., *College in Black and White: Black Students on Black and White Campuses* (Albany: SUNY Press, in press).

7. The *Adams* case, *Adams* v. *Califano,* Civil Action No. 3095–70, U.S. District Court, Washington, DC, was first heard in 1971 and continues in the federal courts today. The case is directed at the integration of public university student bodies in several states, primarily but not exclusively in the South. Over the last eighteen years, however, the many rulings in this case have alluded to faculty integration as a necessary component of institutional changes that will facilitate and solidify the integration of student bodies. (Telephone conversation between Roslyn Mickelson

and Richard Robinson, Special Assistant to the President for Legal Affairs, The University of North Carolina, July 13, 1989.) The degree to which university faculties remain segregated is discussed in Denise K. Magner, "Nineteen Private Colleges Offer Fellowships to Minority Scholars," *Chronicle of Higher Education* 35 (December 14, 1988): A13.

8. The fact that data on minority faculty are difficult to obtain reflects the magnitude of the crisis. The situation of minority faculty in higher education has yet to become the object of widespread scholarly inquiry either by university, governmental or institutional researchers. For example, data on faculty members' race by rank in the most recent volume of the *Digest of Educational Statistics* consist of one table. Moreover, the data for this table come from an unpublished 1983 Equal Employment Opportunity Commission data set. As this essay goes to press, the U.S. Department of Education has begun to analyze data from the first-of-its-kind study of faculty members' race in higher education, the National Survey of Postsecondary Faculty. Academic researchers are no more likely than the government to pursue this issue, however. As Melvin L. Oliver and James H. Johnson, Jr. note in their article, "The Challenge of Diversity in Higher Education," *Urban Review* 20 (1988): 139–46, and as Ursula Elisabeth Wagener argues in her review essay, "Quality and Equity: The Necessity for Imagination," *Harvard Educational Review* 59 (May 1989): 241, most recent books on higher education still fail to address adequately the responsibilities of institutions of higher education to recruit and educate disadvantaged students. And greater numbers of minority faculty are crucially important if universities are to achieve these goals.

9. Joanell Porter (American Department of Education) reported these estimates from the unreleased National Survey of Postsecondary Faculty to Mickelson in a telephone conversation, July 3, 1989.

Although books such as Alexander Astin's *Minorities in American Education* (San Francisco: Jossey-Bass, 1982), Michael Olivas's *Latino College Students* (New York: Teacher's College Press, 1986), and Jacqueline Fleming's *Blacks in College* (San Francisco: Jossey-Bass, 1984) address the issue of minority students, the corpus of research in higher education—with few exceptions—almost ignores the issue of minority faculty. Institutional researchers also generally fail to address the racial crisis in higher education faculty. For example, according to Maryse Eymoneri, consultant to the American Association of University Professors (AAUP) (phone conversation with Roslyn Mickelson, June 15, 1989), the AAUP collects data on faculty members' gender by rank but not by race. The Higher Education Research Institute (HERI) will launch its first survey ascertaining faculty members' race and ethnicity in fall 1989 (phone conversation between Mickelson and Guadalupe Anaya of HERI, June 15, 1989). We present these details to illustrate the depth of the problem, which we hope this volume will address.

10. Barry Beckham, ed., *The Black Student's Guide to College*, 2nd ed. (Providence: Beckham House Publishers, 1984).

11. Fleming, *Blacks in College;* Patricia Gurin and Edgar Epps, *Black Consciousness, Identity, and Achievement* (New York: John Wiley, 1975).

12. Michael W. Hirschorn, "Doctorates Earned by Blacks Decline 26.5 Percent in Decade," *Chronicle of Higher Education* 35 (February 3, 1988): A1; William Trombley, "Faculties Still Largely White," *Los Angeles Times* (July 6, 1986), p. A34. Actually, both the absolute number and the proportion of total doctorates awarded have declined more drastically for whites than for minorities during this period. According to the *Digest of Educational Statistics* (1988) the proportion of doctorates awarded to foreign students has increased steadily during the last decade.

13. NCES, *Digest of Educational Statistics*.

14. Smelser and Content, *Changing Academic Market Place*.

15. Nathan Glazer, *Affirmative Discrimination* (New York: Basic Books, 1978); Thomes Sowell, *Affirmative Action Reconsidered: Was It Necessary in Academia?* (Washington, DC: American Enterprise Institute, 1975).

16. Dorothy M. Gilford and Joan Snyder, *Women and Minority Ph.D.s in the 1970's: A Data Book* (Washington, DC: National Research Council, 1977); Troy Duster, "The Structure of Privilege and Its Universe of Discourse," *American Sociologist* 11 (May) 73–78; Lionel S. Lewis, *Scaling the Ivory Tower* (Baltimore: Johns Hopkins University Press, 1975); Bowen and Schuster, *American Professors;* Finkelstein, *American Academic Profession*.

17. William H. Exum, "Climbing the Crystal Stair: Values, Affirmative Action and Minority Faculty," *Social Problems* 30 (1983) 383.

18. Theodore Caplow and Reece McGhee, *The Academic Marketplace* (New York: Basic Books, 1958); Finkelstein, *The American Academic Profession;* Smelser and Content, *Changing Academic Market Place*.

19. Caplow and McGhee, *Academic Marketplace*, p. 120.

20. Ralph H. Turner, "Sponsored and Contest Mobility and the School System" *American Sociological Review* 25 (1960) 855–67.

21. Gilford and Snyder, *Women and Minority Ph.D.s*, p. 18.

22. Exum, "Climbing the Crystal Stair," p. 385.

23. Walter R. Allen, Angela Haddad and Mary Kirkland, *Preliminary Report: Graduate and Professional Survey* (Ann Arbor, MI: NSBCS, University of Michigan, 1982).

24. Allen, Epps and Haniff, *College in Black and White*.

25. Allen, Haddad and Kirkland, *Preliminary Report*.

26. We conducted parallel analyses with the graduate, professional and combined (graduate and professional) students with virtually identical results. We report the findings from the analyses that use the combined data set because of the greater statistical power in the larger sample.

27. Comparing grades across institutions is always difficult for researchers who seek a reliable indicator of performance. The question of whether an A from a top-tier institution means the same thing as an A from a lesser school is beyond the scope of this essay. Used as the sole indicator of graduate students' quality across institutions, GPA might be problematic. Yet because grades are only one of the elements that constitute the quality index, we believe that the measure is sufficiently reliable to test our hypothesis.

28. Although some readers may question the placement of UCLA in the second tier of universities in this sample, many observers may be unaware of the commuter character of the Westwood campus. The effects of this character on the academic climate of graduate education militates against the intense form of graduate training that takes place in university communities such as Ann Arbor, Madison or Chapel Hill. It is unfortunate that the NSBCS sample contains no other comparable commuter campuses. Yet in view of the range of schools available in that sample, it is clear that from this perspective, UCLA does not belong in the top tier.

29. Denise Gottfredson, "Black and White Differences in the Educational Attainment Process," *American Sociological Review* 46 (1981) 448–572.

30. Michele N. K. Collison, "Neglect of Minorities Seen Jeopardizing Future Prosperity," *Chronicle of Higher Education* 34 (May 25, 1988) A1, A20; Astin, *Minorities in American Higher Education,* p. 205; Fleming, *Blacks in College.* And Melvin L. Oliver, Consuelo J. Rodriguez and Roslyn A. Mickelson, "Black and Brown in White: The Social Adjustment and Academic Performance of Chicano and Black Students in a Predominantly White University," *Urban Review* 17 (November 1985) 3–24.

MARÍA DE LA LUZ REYES AND
JOHN J. HALCÓN

Chapter Nine

Practices of the Academy: Barriers to Access for Chicano Academics

INTRODUCTION

No set of data can properly set out the full range of problems that minorities face in America. Our malaise runs deep and is not easily described statistically. Since the Declaration of Independence was first written, we have lived a life unworthy of our stated ideals, and we are now paying a heavy price for our ambiguity—perhaps even our hypocrisy. We pass laws to protect minority rights and to increase minority opportunities, but too often we are satisfied with appearances.[1]

After a decade in which many of the hard-earned gains made by minorities in the 1960s and the early 1970s have been lost to ambivalence and retrenchment, the present crisis in the education of minorities has suddenly sparked a renewed sense of concern among leading educators. The call to increase opportunities for minorities in higher education is a recurring theme of the present reform movement and is now being heard on university and college campuses across the nation. The sense of urgency in that call can be best understood against the backdrop of two current education themes. On the one hand are current demographic projections which indicate that minorities are dramatically changing the face of student bodies in schools—warranting renewed efforts to improve their academic achievement.[2] On the other is the increase in racial conflict between white and minority students on university campuses, which prompts an unspoken fear of racial conflict spreading into the public elementary and secondary schools.[3]

These impending crises in higher education have led to a call for diversification among faculty and students in campuses across the nation. Most of these initiatives have not been successful and it is not surprising. We attribute this limited success to the discrepancy between the public "courting" of minorities and their actual incorporation (i.e., recruitment, retention and promotion) into institutions of higher education (IHEs). The barriers which limit minority access to IHEs under the guise of reform have proven to be among the most formidable of obstacles. With few exceptions, the renewed interest in minorities in higher education is proving to be nothing more than superficial flirtation and empty rhetoric about the value of cultural diversity. The call is intended to give the "appearance" of interest, a position powerfully captured in the opening quote by O. Meredith Wilson. Although the call for increasing the number of minorities in IHEs has gained momentum, it has been ineffective because it is rarely accompanied by a meaningful commitment to the realization of that goal. Diversification of college communities, including an increase in minority hiring, may indeed be incompatible with the current institutional power structures, which create the barriers to the attainment of those goals and perpetuate a status quo that favors majority groups.

RACISM IN ACADEMIA

Although most reports on racial conflicts focus on students, minority faculty are also victims of racism and are greatly affected by it. Accounts of racism experienced by minority academics receive less attention because racial incidents involving students are usually overt, often include racial slurs and occur in public settings. In many respects, these incidents are written off as harmless juvenile behavior, worthy only of fleeting concern. In contrast, racism involving minority faculty in institutions of higher education is generally covert and often masked by adherence to a mythical academic meritocracy regarding professional qualifications that subtly favors whites. To admit publicly that racism exists in academia is to question the very foundation of the academic enterprise.

Chicanos' experiences with racism in institutions of higher education have been well-documented and characterized as "academic colonialism."[4] Many Chicanos attribute the inability to penetrate a traditionally white male system to the existence of a pervasive racism.[5] The dismal number of Hispanics in faculty positions in institutions of higher education is ample evidence of this. Like other minorities, Hispanics have been surprised to learn that their earned doctorates have not translated into equal access or equal benefits even at the highest levels of the educational ladder, where the most educated and enlightened individuals are expected to behave fairly and treat others equitably. Instead, they have discovered that educational stratification[6] and discriminatory practices generally encountered at the lower levels of the educational pipeline are also present in academia, albeit under various disguises.[7]

A common explanation for the lack of Hispanics in academia is that the pool of Hispanics with Ph.D.'s is very small. Proportionately, this is true. Recent figures for Hispanics indicate that Hispanics represent only 2 percent of all Ph.D.'s in the country.[8] Although the overall percentage gain is small, there is a growing number of unemployed or underemployed Hispanic Ph.D.'s unable to gain access to faculty positions in institutions of higher education. Wilson and Justiz report that there are more candidates available than are finding appointments.[9] This situation makes us question whether it is realistic to talk about diversification or the elimination of racism in institutions of higher education without having provided minorities full incorporation and participation in the educational system.

The lack of public awareness of racism in academia, however, does not minimize its existence. Minorities know from personal experience that racism in higher education is vigorous and real. Nothing short of institutional racism could account for the magnitude of existing inequality and the minuscule number of minorities in academia.[10] In 1977, for example, Hispanic faculty in four-year institutions made up only 1.5 percent of the total full-time faculty, and in 1983 they represented only 1.8 percent.[11] The dearth of minorities in IHEs was underscored by the 1982 Commission on the Higher Education of Minorities which stated that "no amount of rhetorical commitment to the principles of equal opportunity, affirmative action, and pluralism can compensate for or justify the current degree of minority underrepresentation among faculty, administrators, staff members, and students in higher education."[12] Recent reports on the status of Hispanics in higher education have reached similar conclusions.[13] Institutional racism is a fundamental barrier to access and opportunity for minority faculty members.

FRAMEWORK FOR ANALYSIS

In this essay, we propose to examine institutional practices which promote racism and act as barriers to access and parity for Chicanos in academia. The framework for analysis consists of three interdependent sets of social relations: (1) the relative social status of Chicanos in American society; (2) the interactions between minority and majority faculty; and (3) the relationship between majority faculty and administrators in institutions of higher education. The term "Hispanic" as used here refers to the two major underrepresented Spanish-language background groups, primarily Chicano and Puerto Rican. To illustrate our points, we will use examples chiefly from the experiences of Chicano academics who represent the largest of the Hispanic groups in this country, but the application to other Hispanic, and non-Hispanic, minority groups will be self-evident.

The purpose of this discussion is to examine the types of interactions, attitudes and practices that must be significantly altered to permit diversification and full participation of Chicanos and other minorities in the academy. Racism will be examined in light of these social relations which individually and collectively prevent Chicanos from achieving that access.

CHICANOS IN AMERICAN SOCIETY

Although American society is rooted in the collective experiences of various immigrant groups who settled in this country, it has evolved into a monolithic system dominated by a strong ethnocentric perspective that generally views racial, cultural and linguistic differences as deficiencies and disadvantages. The dominant group in this monolithic system is composed of individuals from white, English-speaking, Anglo-Saxon backgrounds. Ramirez explains that in this system the "dominant cultural group has the power, resources, and authority to define itself in positive, normative ways and to define the out-group in negative, dysfunctional ways—thus rationalizing the continuation of vesting power in itself and away from other groups."[14] Individuals who do not belong to the dominant group, blacks, Hispanics, Native Americans and others, constitute the minority groups who occupy lower status positions, and comprise the poor and working class who have little voice in matters of government and policy-making. Not coincidentally, these same groups are also those most highly segregated in public schools and those least likely to graduate from high school, least likely to go on to college and least likely to occupy positions in academia.

The status of Hispanics relative to the dominant group in this country has been described as "second class citizenship."[15] Since the initial interactions between Mexican-Americans and Anglos in the Southwest, an attitude of "Anglo superiority" has predominated.[16] It is that attitude that has sustained prejudice and discrimination toward Mexican-origin individuals and continues to perpetuate negative stereotypes. These stereotypes suggest that Mexican-Americans are generally passive, are present-oriented, want immediate gratification, have low levels of aspirations, and are nonsuccess oriented.[17]

The notion that cultural differences imply inferiority are vestiges of those stereotypes and are reflected in educational institutions where differences are treated as deficits. In elementary and secondary schools, these stereotypes serve to rationalize such educational practices as tracking of minorities, disproportionate representation in special education classes, poor career counseling and low expectations from teachers. These practices contribute to the small pool of college graduates available to fill academic positions in higher education.

Although the general public may cling to a naive perception that academicians who constitute the nucleus of intelligentsia are above racism,[18] "there is no reason to believe that there is less racism among academics than there is among other groups in society."[19] The academy mirrors the same attitudes and generalities about cultural/racial differences that plague the larger society. The low status that Hispanics occupy relative to the dominant group in society is reflected in what Garza refers to as Hispanics in "the role of second-class academic citizens."[20]

A culturally diverse professoriate is not valued in institutions of higher education. This is evidenced by the existence of pervasive "institutional ethnocentrism that ignores the perspectives and values of other cultures"[21] and the fact that stereotyping of minority academics is a common practice. The majority of Hispanics in academe, for example, are often relegated to ethnically oriented programs: Spanish department, Chicano studies, bilingual education and student support services (e.g., EOP, Upward Bound). In a 1987 National Latino Faculty Survey conducted by Garza, one respondent, a Puerto Rican faculty member from a midwestern university, summarized the "barriorization" of Hispanics in these words:

> There seems to be the assumption that all Latinos teach or should teach ethnic studies. I work on economic development of the Caribbean and Latin America. The problem is not that Anglos consider ethnic studies inferior [although they do], but Latinos in general inferior whether they do ethnic studies or not. I teach in a program that is the academic ghetto for Latinos at this university; the Spanish department is the other Latin ghetto.[22]

The concentration of Hispanics and other minorities in ethnically oriented departments is well-documented.[23] Rochin and de la Torre also reported in a 1986 affirmative action study that a disproportionate percentage of Chicano faculty at the University of California at Davis occupied positions in Chicano studies (41 percent), and Spanish and bilingual education programs.[24] The practice of specialized minority hiring for minority slots "is a more formal cooptation of Hispanic concern which relieves the institution of the need to integrate throughout their ranks"[25] and appears to be "the unofficial way of implementing affirmative action mandates and guidelines."[26]

The diverse representation of racial and ethnic groups in the larger society is not reflected in academia. On the contrary, there is little cultural or racial diversity among those who occupy the upper echelons of the educational pipeline and those in charge of developing and implementing educational policies. Wilson and Justiz report that minorities make up only 9.6 percent of all full-time faculty in higher education. Obviously then, white academics, who make up about 90 percent of total faculty, occupy a dominant status in the academy.[27]

The absence of a large diverse professoriate causes an unfair perception and evaluation of minority faculty. In an environment where there are few minority faculty or minority students, white students have an especially difficult time relating to minority faculty. Hispanic colleagues teaching at predominantly white colleges, for example, report that their student evaluations are replete with complaints that too much attention is given to "minority" issues, that "too many of the assigned readings focus on minorities" or are "too political," and that Hispanic professors "have a chip on their shoulders." We have also personally experienced the same type of criticism and know that it can leave a sharp sting, especially when students admit that they learned a great deal in spite of alleged biases in our teaching! This negative reaction from mainstream students occurs because a focus on race, discrimination, ethnicity, etc. makes people uncomfortable.[28] In a classic example of the old "double standard," minority faculty are perceived by Anglo students as "racial," "arrogant," or "on a personal bandwagon." Yet Anglo professors who espouse a nonmainstream perspective are regarded as sensitive and liberal. They emerge as forward thinkers and are generally accorded much respect. The tragedy of this double standard for minorities, however, is that when student evaluations are part of the evaluation, retention, promotion and merit pay decision-making processes, minority faculty pay a heavy price for being racially, culturally or linguistically different.

If more professors presented diverse perspectives on issues, the views of minorities would not seem at odds with the norm and the burden would not be so heavy for minority faculty. Additionally, white students would not be deprived of a healthy exposure to ethnically diverse points of view, which are desperately needed in an increasingly pluralistic society. Without the exposure to cultural diversity, it will continue to be difficult for students to develop mutual respect and learn how to coexist peacefully with other cultural or racial groups. The current increase in racial conflict between white and minority students on college campuses reflects that deprivation.[29]

Cultural diversity is not valued by educational systems. If it were, the success rate of minority academics would be higher and faculties in institutions of higher education would be more diversified.[30] Not appreciating cultural diversity as an asset is a major barrier to the full incorporation of Hispanics in the academy because it perpetuates the kinds of stereotyping about Hispanics faculty discussed above. Furthermore, it limits Hispanic opportunities to become full members of the academy.

In contrast, when cultural diversity is valued, ethnic, racial and linguistic diversity is not only respected, but nourished, and promoted. It means that differences are celebrated and viewed as means of enriching and benefiting the lives of both faculty and students. The Commission on the Higher Education of Minorities suggests that if IHEs were measured by the degree of "value added—that is, the difference made in quality of mind and self-respect of students, if value added were to become one of the measures used in assigning status to institutions, it is likely that . . . with this change in our national value premise, we might get commitment instead of lip service to minority opportunities in higher education."[31] If cultural diversity were valued, more opportunities would open up in all departments, and these would begin to pave the way to greater access for Chicano academics.

MAJORITY-MINORITY FACULTY INTERACTIONS

The interaction between majority and minority faculty in the academy mirrors the dominant/subordinate paradigm of the larger society. Manifestations of covert racism emerge when educated "subordinates" interact within this paradigm. Although covert racism is difficult to prove, Chicanos and other minorities in academe frequently report the same type of recurring incidents against them that limit their access and opportunities for hiring, retention and promotion. In another paper, we discussed a number of typical examples of covert racism in academia.[32] Those examples can be grouped under the following categories: the "type-casting syndrome" (similar to stereotyping already discussed), tokenism, the "one-minority-per-pot syndrome", and "brown-on-brown" research taboo and the "hairsplitting concept". Each of these typify a patronizing, condescending attitude that mainstream faculty often demonstrate in interacting with minority faculty. These practices serve as barriers to parity for Chicano academics.

Although the implementation of affirmative action programs provided more access to minorities in certain job markets, it left all minority professionals and academics with a legacy of tokenism—a stigma that has been difficult to dispel. The myth that all minorities entered, and continue to enter, the system only under special admission is a result of that legacy. The fact is that the "availability pool" clause in the affirmative action regulations greatly limited the number of minority faculty who had to be hired under the guidelines. The clause was interpreted to mean that regulations applied only in cases where it could be proven that there were a significant number of available minorities who could be hired for the targeted positions. In the case of Hispanics, Holmes[33] reported this clause made it impossible for IHEs to comply with regulations because the number of Hispanics with Ph.D.'s constituted less than one percent of available persons in many academic fields at that time.[34] The former Department of Health, Education and Welfare responsible for overseeing the regulations, together with the University of California at Berkeley, for example, found that there were only three departments out of the entire campus where projected goals for minority hiring were required under affirmative action regulations.[35]

What this means is that the majority of Hispanic faculty who are now teaching in colleges and universities got there mainly by the strength of their own qualifications. There is little substance to the general assumption that they lack the appropriate qualifications to occupy their respective positions in academia. The myth that minorities are mere "tokens" and have been hired without the adequate experience or qualifications, however, still persists. In contrast, academics from the dominant group behave as if their positions were secured solely on the basis of high qualifications and merit. Our experience has taught us that this is simply not true. What is true is that doubts about a candidate's qualifications are more likely to emerge implicitly or explicitly when prospective candidates are minorities than when they are whites.[36]

Another negative result of tokenism is that it places undue pressure on minority academics to prove that they are as good as white academics. Moore contends that "Blacks are expected to be better in order to be equal."[37] The same is true for Hispanics. This sentiment begins in graduate school, where minority students report feeling "stigmatized" by their race and culture and frustrated by the continual need to prove themselves.[38] Tokenism has the added effect of reducing minority-occupied positions to second-class status providing an easy excuse for institutions to minimize and ignore Hispanic presence.

The minimizing of Hispanic presence is also manifested in the syndrome we call "one-minority-per-pot." This syndrome refers to a continued reluctance on the part of IHEs to hire more than one minority faculty per department. This common practice places an unwritten limit on minority hiring and prevents diversification of departments. The unwritten rule is that if a department has one ethnic minority, or if the department interviews without ultimately hiring a minority, the department has met its obligation. The result is that the members of the mainstream faculty are usually satisfied that "good-faith efforts" have been exerted in hiring and integrating minorities. But, with the exception of minority-related programs, few mainstream departments can boast of more than one minority professor.

When Chicanos apply for mainstream positions, they are often met with doubts about their qualifications outside of ethnically related areas or are automatically recommended for available "minority slots."[39]

This situation has happened to both authors and to many of our colleagues. In a job interview for a teacher education position where teaching reading was a requirement, one of these authors was met with the remark, "We know you teach bilingual reading, but can you teach *real* reading?" The assumption was that the teaching of reading as it applies to bilinguals is not based on the same core of processes and pedagogical principles of teaching reading to mainstream populations. That assumption is not only condescending, but absurd to those who understand that the teaching of reading to bilinguals requires additional specialization beyond the basic requirements for reading majors. In other cases where the authors have applied to separate institutions, both applications were automatically transferred or added to positions in ethnically related program areas. While it may be well-intentioned, this practice deprives Hispanics of serious consideration to qualifications in core disciplines, i.e., educational psychology, public policy, sociology, English, etc., and it classifies them according to their ethnic affiliation. The result of this practice is that Chicanos, like other minorities, are rarely recognized as full-fledged experts in their own right.[40]

The root of the one-minority-per-pot syndrome is a deep-seated belief that minorities are not as qualified as white academics. The unspoken truth is that there is an underlying fear that the presence of more than one minority faculty member in a traditionally mainstream program will lower the academic standards of the department.[41]

This syndrome is not limited to faculty positions. It also applies to administrative ranks. An example that comes to mind involved a Chicano department chair who applied for an associate deanship at his institution. In spite of his qualifications for the position, however, he was forewarned by the academic vice president, who was Anglo, that his candidacy would not likely receive serious consideration "because there were already three other Chicano administrators at the college." Convinced that submitting his application for the position was a futile exercise, he withdrew his name from consideration. It is important to note that when a non-Chicano applied for the same position, no one counted the number of Anglos already on the faculty or in administrative positions. The one-minority-per-pot syndrome prevents full integration and diversification of departments and serves to disempower and restrict the career goals and aspirations of Chicano academics.

The greatest obstacle to tenure for minority faculty is the taboo on "brown-on-brown" research.[42] This taboo refers to the practice of devaluing research on minorities when it is undertaken by minority researchers. Efforts on the part of Chicanos and other minorities to conduct research on minority-related topics, e.g., dropouts, bilingual education, second language literacy and the education of minorities, often meet with disapproval by white colleagues who sit as judges on the quality of their research and publications.[43] The research interest in these areas stems from Chicanos' need to define, label, describe and interpret their own condition from the inside out and to lend a sense of balance to existing theories about themselves. From the point of view of mainstream academics, however, brown-on-brown research is perceived to be narrow in scope and to lack objectivity. This paternal attitude is no more than a double standard which lends credibility to the research of whites on mainstream populations, but discredits minority academics who research minority issues. In fact, whites who undertake research on minorities are infinitely more likely to be admired and rewarded for the focus of their scholarship than are minorities who study the same populations. "White-on-white" research is accorded legitimacy, while brown-on-brown research is questioned and challenged.

The devaluing of research conducted by Chicanos affects promotion and tenure decisions. Although this practice has been difficult to prove, many Hispanics and blacks cite numerous examples of unfair evaluation of their research during promotion and tenure reviews.[44] The delegitimization of minority research by majority faculty is rooted in the values that undergird academe and that are characteristic of culturally monolithic systems. Those systems judge the quality of scholarship from the normative perspective of their own cultural group and thus deem deviations from the norm as inferior.[45] Under the guise of meritocracy and quality, they often sort out political, social and intellectual factors[46] that differ from traditional Eurocentric perspectives.[47]

Decisions about hiring, promoting and tenuring minority faculty are often based on what we call "hairsplitting" practices. This refers to the practice of making highly subjective and arbitrary judgment calls that frequently result in favor of whites over minorities. Many minority academics have now had opportunities to serve on faculty search committees. They have learned that final decisions are not as objective as minorities are led to believe. Far too often the best qualified candidate is not the person hired. It is not unusual for the second or third choice candidate to be hired because they are a better fit with the faculty. The minority candidate is rarely the "best fit" for a department. Because its application is so effective against minority faculty, we are convinced that the invocation of the "best fit" rule is one of the most significant barriers to access for minority candidates. The process of selecting a particular candidate is due much more to the personal preferences of the faculty committee than to the myth of objectivity or of "equal opportunity hiring." Minorities, for example, are often not hired, promoted or tenured—not for lack of required qualifications, but on the basis of paternalistic attitudes of the decision-makers.[48] Or, they might be eliminated from academic positions on a presumption that they might not be happy in a predominantly white university.[49] Hairsplitting practices are dangerous because they exclude or limit Chicanos from full incorporation into the academy simply on the basis of minor, subjective, and often inconsequential factors.

One of the major conflicts in the academy is that majority faculty view merit, albeit mythical, as the overriding value in academia, while minority faculty emphasize worth. The "worth" of an individual is defined by the value he or she can add to the academic community, for example, the diverse perspective that a minority professor can add to a department.[50] While neither merit nor worth alone is sufficient, a balance of both can provide greater opportunity for minority access and parity. As a larger number of Chicano academics move into the ranks of the tenured professoriate, the current condescending and patronizing treatment of minorities will begin to wane. It will do so because full membership in the academy brings greater participatory power in the decision-making process. Minority voices in that process will ensure greater access and opportunities for other minorities. This will occur as minority academics begin to be treated more as equals and as full-fledged experts in their fields, and as their research interests are legitimized and put on a par with interests in mainstream issues.

MAJORITY FACULTY AND ADMINISTRATION

Access and parity for minorities in IHEs lie in the hands of both majority faculty and university administrators. The call for the diversification of the faculty and greater opportunities for minorities begins at the highest levels. The typical approach is for the university president or chancellor to make a general, but public, declaration of concern for the recruitment, hiring and retention of more minorities. Sometimes this is echoed by school deans and other mid-level administrators and tacitly accepted by the general faculty. Neither administrators nor majority faculty, however, take a proactive stance in making the goal a reality. There are several reasons for this.

One reason is that the goals are set at the institutional level rather than at the individual department level. At the campus level, the entire campus community is charged with the responsibility, but no single individual or unit is held accountable. As a consequence, no minority gains are made because each department can always "pass the buck" and let another one do it, or satisfy their goal by hiring a white woman instead of an ethnic minority. "Playing off" white women against ethnic minorities in the hiring competition is a common practice that often leaves ethnic minorities on the short end.[51] Lack of performance monitoring in meeting the goals of the institution is another major reason why few institutions of higher education are successful in increasing their number of ethnic minorities.

Since departments are not individually charged with the hiring of minorities, majority faculty fall back on traditional ways of filling available positions. Without awareness of the unique educational experiences of minorities, they write the job descriptions and simply wait for ethnic minorities to apply. What they fail to recognize is that lack of flexibility and often the wording in their job descriptions (e.g., "Educational administrators with experience as public school superintendents preferred") discourage ethnic minorities from applying for positions for which they might otherwise be qualified. Then, when the national search yields no ethnic minorities, majority faculty blame the outcome on three possible reasons: (1) the pool of minority Ph.D.'s is too small; (2) minority candidates lack the appropriate qualifications for the job; or (3) the demands of minority candidates vis-a-vis their qualifications (defined in terms of publication record) are unreasonable. All these are symptoms of an internal resistance to the mission goals of the institution, and a strong indicator of a lack of a true commitment to increasing minority access to their ranks.

The excuse that the minority pool is too small to go around is a very common response. Olivas refers to this as the "high-demand/low-supply mythology" about minorities.[52] Although no one denies that the pool may indeed be small, the data indicate that the supply of minorities is greater than the number that is actually hired.[53] There is no justification for assuming or pretending that the minority pool is empty. When concerted efforts are made to recruit and hire minorities and when this goal is made a top priority, institutions always seem to be able to find enough eligible candidates to fulfill their objectives.

The experiences of Miami University of Ohio and the University of Massachusetts are potent examples of what can be done when both the faculty and university administrators are fully committed to the hiring of ethnic minorities. Under the helm of a new president, Miami University increased the number of black faculty from only seven in 1981 to twenty-seven in 1987.[54] At the University of Massachusetts blacks make up 8 percent of the faculty with 5.5 percent of them tenured. Recently, the faculty at Duke University has taken a similarly aggressive stand. It has approved a plan to require that each academic department hire at least one black faculty member by 1993.[55] These examples mitigate against the "empty pool" concept.

Majority faculty can find myriad reasons why minorities are not qualified for positions. As we discussed earlier, the qualifications of minorities alone are almost irrelevant; for sure, they are not sufficient to ensure admission into the ranks of the professoriate. Personal and political preferences, prejudices and fears of majority faculty and inaction of administrators play a larger role in the final decisions reached. The truth is that majority faculty are the "gatekeepers."[56] They have the power to confer membership on anyone they choose, but they lack a true commitment to achieving equity for ethnic minorities. When majority faculty want an individual badly enough they can find strong justification; they can bend or interpret rules as they wish. They alone determine the composition of their departments. Under the guise of objectivity, they select those who are deemed qualified, reject those who are not, and nominate their personal choices, based on highly subjective criteria reached in negotiation with other colleagues. The following excerpt by Moore clearly delineates their role:

> . . . they establish and chair search committees; they determine the criteria for selection, screen the applicants, conduct the interviews, influence the decision makers, and check their networks for nominations and references; they negotiate among themselves to determine which candidate to support if there is not a clear agreement on a specific candidate; and they submit their final subjective judgments with regard to who will be recommended to serve as faculty members in their institutions. The gatekeepers determine who is qualified and who is not; what rules to apply, break, or modify as it suits their objectives.[57]

Faculty recognize the power they have. The problem is that they do not always choose to exert that power, especially when minorities are concerned, so they deceive others into believing that opportunities for minorities are beyond their control.

A related barrier to minority hiring is the economic issue of supply and demand. Majority faculty understand the principles of supply and demand perfectly. They recognize, for example, that prominent scholars and underrepresented minority academics represent limited resources. Both bring an "added value" and, as a result, they are "worth" more than the average candidate. When majority faculty choose to hire a white prominent scholar, they readily respond to supply and demand principles. Like businesses, they understand that when the supply is low in any field, the demand for those few is high. As a consequence, they do not hesitate to engage in a "price war" to hire an individual whose presence meets the needs of the university, or enhances its prestige.

The relatively small pool of potential minority faculty and the current demands for diversification of IHEs puts minority candidates in a similar high demand category. But, when minorities demand higher compensation for the added perspective and presence that they bring to an institution, the principle of supply and demand begins to break down. Suddenly nonminority faculty who would ordinarily support the principles of supply and demand in any other context or forum, become the most vocal opponents of this fundamental law of economics. They grumble that the demands of minorities "are unreasonable," "too expensive," or that they "don't want to get into a bidding war with another university." The truth is that when the hiring of ethnic minorities is not really a priority, a double standard is applied. The end result is that minority candidates are not hired because the faculty is unwilling to pay them more than the established norm and to accord them equal consideration in the hiring process.

On the surface, the appearance of concern with increasing the number of minorities on the faculty is sufficient for satisfying the public. Satisfying occurs, for example, when minority candidates are invited for interviews but, for various reasons which we discussed earlier, they do not get hired. Majority faculty pat themselves on the back for having tried and administrators justify the outcome by rationalizing that selection of colleagues is, after all, the prerogative of faculty—an academic freedom with which they refuse to interfere. So both majority faculty and administrators get off the hook, and the status quo remains undisturbed. The justification is unanimous: (1) there are few minority candidates in the available pool; (2) those who are available are either not fully qualified or they are already taken; and (3) those who are not taken are too expensive. In the end, all concerned can stand proud and united. They tried. Every effort was made. And, in the end, no minority candidate is hired. The self-fulfilling prophecy is once again fulfilled, and no one is held accountable.

There is no question that majority faculty and university administrators have the power to increase or restrict membership into the academy. Each plays an interdependent function. While the power to hire, promote and tenure may be vested in majority faculty, the power to ratify and fund those faculty decisions is the prerogative of administrators who control the budget. Administrators can make a difference in creating opportunities for minorities, as in the case of the president of Miami University in Ohio who had the courage to make a genuine commitment to increasing the number of black faculty. On the other hand, unwillingness of administrators to hold individual departments and their faculty accountable for the failure to hire minorities reinforces existing barriers to access and parity for all minority academics.

CONCLUSIONS

In this essay we have presented a framework for examining institutional structures that function as barriers to access and parity for Chicanos in academia. Ensuring equity and increasing opportunities for Hispanics in institutions of higher learning will not be easy. We have seen that the major roadblocks to full membership in the academy center around three different but interdependent sets of social relations. The first of these describes the relatively low status that Hispanics occupy in the larger society and the negative attitudes toward those who are culturally, racially or linguistically different. The deficit perspective that colors all interactions between the dominant group and the minority groups in the larger society are mirrored in the academy.

Those manifestations of racism can be examined more closely in light of minority-majority interactions because it is in those interactions that they emerge. The practice of hiring underrepresented minorities only for certain specialized ethnic departments, of limiting their number in mainstream departments, of fueling and perpetuating the myth that they are not fully qualified for academic positions, the continual devaluing of minority research, and numerous other hairsplitting practices are all manifestations of covert racism that constitute roadblocks to full incorporation into the academy.

The interplay between majority faculty and university administrators constitutes the third set of social relations that affects minority access to the ranks of the professoriate. It is clear that majority faculty can play a major role in helping Hispanics to achieve parity. In their role as gatekeepers they can offer or deny membership to whomever they wish. University administrators share in this power. With the budget under their control they can persuade majority faculty to hire more minorities. They can hold individual departments accountable for achieving parity or setting specific goals and deadlines for increasing the number of underrepresented ethnic minorities on the faculty.

To be effective in providing greater opportunities to minorities, institutions (administrators, majority and minority faculty) must take a more aggressive and proactive stand in opening and creating opportunities for groups whose members are severely underrepresented in the system. Diversification of colleges and universities will not happen by chance or merely in time. The status quo contains too many loopholes that serve as internal resistance to equity, and work against the empowerment of minorities.

Universities must recognize that Chicano faculty are the key to recruitment, retention and promotion of other Chicanos, both students and other Hispanic faculty. Without full incorporation and integration into the various branches of the institution, not just in minority slots, they will be unable to empower other minorities to move successfully through the series of rituals necessary to achieve professional and academic success. The educational history of Chicanos in this country strongly suggests that without minority role models at all levels of the educational system, but especially in the centers of power—the ranks of the tenured professoriate—it will be difficult to extend membership in the academy to other minorities. So IHEs must learn how to market minority faculty so that they can serve as "educational brokers" who will attract large numbers of other capable minorities.

In order to reduce the existing racism in academia, leaders in higher education must recognize that the consequence of excluding a major segment of the population from taking an active participatory role in the educational design of the future will be a major catastrophe for a nation moving into the twenty-first century. Without full access to the ranks of the tenured professors where decisions are made, the numbers of minority faculty in tenure-line positions will be reduced even further, because minorities will not have the required votes to hire, promote and tenure others like them.

It is not sufficient to recognize that the sheer numbers of minorities in the larger society require greater diversification of educational institutions. Anyone can have a vision of what is needed for the future, anyone can pay lip service to the call for increased opportunities and access for minorities. Words are cheap. But it will take bold courage on the part of majority faculty, administrators and minority faculty to push for unpopular measures that have proven effective in other institutions, like setting quotas and deadlines for hiring and promoting minorities. A strong and genuine commitment to helping minorities achieve equity in higher education is needed, not only on grounds of justice, but because a minority presence will truly enrich the perspectives of all those engaged in attaining, sharing or imparting knowledge. That commitment, however, carries both a financial and moral price tag that few institutions may be ready to make.

NOTES

1. Meredith Wilson, *The Commission on Higher Education of Minorities* (San Francisco, CA: Jossey-Bass, 1982), p. 5.

2. *From Minority to Majority: Education and the Future of the Southwest* (Boulder, CO: Western Interstate Commission of Higher Education, WICHE, 1987).

3. C. S. Farrell, "Black Students Seen Facing 'New Racism' On Many Campuses," *Chronicle of Higher Education* (January 27, 1988), pp. A1, A37–A38; C. S. Farrell, "Stung by Racial Incidents and Charges of Indifference, Berkeley to Become Model Integrated University," *Chronicle of Higher Education* (January 27, 1988), pp. A37–A38; C. S. Farrell, "Rising Concerns Over Campus Racial Bias Marked at Northern Illinois University," *Chronicle of Higher Education* (February

17, 1988), pp. A37–A38; C. S. Farrell, "Students Protesting Racial Bias at U. of Massachusetts End Occupation of Campus Building After Five Days," *Chronicle of Higher Education* (February 24, 1988), p. A41; J. McCurdy, "Nullification of Latino Students' Election Sparks Melee at UCLA," *Chronicle of Higher Education* (June 8, 1988), p. A23; Anita A. Williams, "Advice/Dissent," *Colorado Daily,* Oct. 12, 1987.

4. Carlos Ornelas, C. B. Ramirez and F. V. Padilla, *Decolonizing the Interpretation of the Chicano Political Experience* (Los Angeles: UCLA Chicano Studies Center Publications, 1975); Leonard Valverde, "Prohibitive Trends in Chicano Faculty Employment," *Chicanos in Higher Education*, H. J. Casso and G. D. Roman, eds. (Albuquerque, NM: University of New Mexico Press, 1975), pp. 106–114; Carlos Arce, "Chicano Participation in Academe: A Case of Academic Colonialism," *Grito del Sol: A Chicano Quarterly* 3 (1978): 75–104.

5. Casso and Roman, eds. *Chicanos in Higher Education;* Ornelas, Ramirez and Padilla, *Decolonizing the Interpretation;* Leonard Valverde, "Prohibitive Trends in Chicano Faculty Employment," pp. 106–114; Cordelia Candelaria, "Women in the Academy," *Rendezvous: Journal of Arts and Letters* 12 no. 1 (1978): 9–18; Steven F. Arvizu, "Critical Reflections and Consciousness," *Grito del Sol: A Chicano Quarterly* 3 (1978): 119–123; Albert Ramirez, "Racism Toward Hispanics: The Culturally Monolithic Society," in *Eliminating Racism: Profiles in Controversy.* P. A. Katz and D. A. Taylor, eds. (New York: Plenum Press, 1988), pp. 137–157.

6. Richard R. Verdugo, "Educational Stratification and Hispanics," in *Latino College Students,* M. A. Olivas, ed. (New York: Teachers College Press, 1986), pp. 325–347.

7. María de la Luz Reyes & John J. Halcón, "Racism in Academia: The Old Wolf Revisited," *Harvard Educational Review* 58 (August, 1988): 3.

8. *Minorities in Higher Education,* Sixth Annual Status Report (Washington, DC: American Council on Education, 1987).

9. Reginald Wilson and Manuel Justiz, "Minorities in Higher Education: Confronting a Time Bomb," *Educational Record* (Fall 1987–Winter 1988), pp. 9–14.

10. de la Luz Reyes and Halcón, "Racism in Academia," p. 3.

11. *Minorities in Higher Education.*

12. *The Commission on the Higher Education of Minorities* (San Francisco, CA: Jossey-Bass, 1982), pp. 5, 37.

13. R. J. Menges and W. H. Exum, "Barriers to the Progress of Women and Minority Faculty," *Journal of Higher Education* 54, no. 2 (1983): 123–144; Tomas Arciniega and Ann I. Morey, *Hispanics and Higher Education: A CSU Imperative* (Long Beach, CA: Office of the Chancellor, California State University, 1985); *Minorities in Higher Education; Minorities and Strategic Planning at the University of Colorado,* (Boulder: Office of the Associate Vice President for Human Resources,

University of Colorado, 1987); Tomas Arciniega, *Hispanic Underrepresentation: A Call for Reinvestment and Innovation,* Hispanic Commission Follow-up Report (Long Beach, CA: Office of the Chancellor, California State University, 1988); L. Gordon, "Second Report Criticizes UC on Its Policy Towards Hiring Latinos," *Los Angeles Times,* June 14, 1988, p. 3; C. M. Fields, "Hispanics, State's Fastest-Growing Minority, Shut Out of Top Positions at U. of California, Leaders Say," *Chronicle of Higher Education* (May 11, 1988), pp. A9–A10.

14. Albert Ramirez, "Racism Toward Hispanics," p. 138.

15. U.S. Commission on Civil Rights, "Stranger in One's Land" (Washington, DC: U.S. Commission on Civil Rights Clearinghouse, May 1970).

16. Julian Samora and P. V. Simon, *A History of the Mexican-American People* (Notre Dame, Indiana: Notre Dame press, 1977).

17. Albert Ramirez, "Racism Toward Hispanics," pp. 137–157.

18. de la Luz Reyes and Halcón, "Racism in Academia," p. 3.

19. William Moore, Jr., "Black Faculty in White Colleges: A Dream Deferred," *Educational Record* (Fall 1987–Winter 1988), pp. 117–121.

20. Hisauro Garza, "The 'Barriorization' of Hispanic Faculty," *Educational Record* (Fall 1987–Winter 1988): 123.

21. *Commission on the Higher Education of Minorities,* p. 22.

22. Garza, "The 'Barriorization' of Hispanic Faculty," p. 124.

23. Arciniega, *Hispanic Underrepresentation;* Gordon, "Second Report Criticizes UC," p. 3; Fields, "Hispanics, State's Fastest-Growing Minority," pp. A9–A10; de la Luz Reyes and Halcón, "Racism in Academia," p. 3; Garza, "The 'Barriorization' of Hispanic Faculty"; Wilson and Justiz, "Minorities in Higher Education"; Arciniega and Morey, *Hispanics and Higher Education;* Michael A. Olivas, "Research on Latino College Students: A Theoretical Framework and Inquiry," in *Latino College Students,* pp. 1–25; Arce, "Chicano Participation in Academe," pp. 75–104.

24. Rufio I. Rochin and Adela de la Torre in Garza, "The 'Barriorization' of Hispanic Faculty," pp. 122–124.

25. Olivas, "Research on Latino College Students," p. 14.

26. Garza, "The 'Barriorization' of Hispanic Faculty," pp. 122–124.

27. Wilson and Justiz, "Minorities in Higher Education," pp. 9–14.

28. Moore, "Black Faculty in White Colleges."

29. Farrell, "Black Students Seen Facing 'New Racism'," pp. A1, A37–A38; Farrell, "Berkeley to Become Model Integrated University"; Farrell, "Rising

Concerns Over Campus Racial Bias"; Farrell, "Racial Bias at U. of Massachusetts"; McCurdy, "Nullification of Latino Students' Election"; Williams, "Advice/Dissent."

30. Moore, "Black Faculty in White Colleges"; D. Carter, C. Pearson and D. Shavlik, "Double Jeopardy: Women of Color in Higher Education," *Educational Record* (Fall 1987–Winter 1988), 98–102.

31. *The Commission on the Higher Education of Minorities*, p. 5.

32. de la Luz Reyes and Halcón, "Racism in Academia."

33. Peter Holmes, "The Ineffective Mechanism of Affirmative Action Plans in an Academic Setting," in *Chicanos in Higher Education*, pp. 76–83.

34. *Minorities in Higher Education*.

35. Holmes, "The Ineffective Mechanism of Affirmative Action Plans."

36. D. E. Blum, "Black Woman Scholar at Emory U. Loses Three-year Battle to Overturn Tenure Denial, But Vows to Fight On," *Chronicle of Higher Education* (June 22, 1988), pp. A15–A17; S. Heller, "Some Colleges Find Aggressive Affirmative Action Efforts Are Starting to Pay Off, Despite Scarcity of Candidates," *Chronicle of Higher Education* (February 10, 1988) p. A12.

37. Moore, "Black Faculty in White Colleges:" p. 120.

38. *Commission on the Higher Education of Minorities*.

39. Garza, "The 'Barriorization' of Hispanic Faculty"; de la Luz Reyes and Halcón, "Racism in Academia."

40. Garza, "The 'Barriorization' of Hispanic Faculty"; Blum, "Black Woman Scholar at Emory."

41. Blum, "Black Woman Scholar at Emory"; Heller, "Aggressive Affirmative Action Efforts"; Garza, "The 'Barriorization' of Hispanic Faculty"; Moore, "Black Faculty in White Colleges."

42. de la Luz Reyes and Halcón, "Racism in Academia."

43. Blum, "Black Woman Scholar at Emory"; D. E. Blum, "To Get Ahead in Research, Some Minority Scholars Choose to 'Play the Game'," *Chronicle of Higher Education* (June 22, 1988) p. A17; A. Ramirez, "Racism Toward Hispanics."

44. Blum, "To Get Ahead in Research"; Fields, "Hispanics, State's Fastest-Growing Minority"; Angela Simone, *Academic Women Working Towards Equality* (South Hadley, MA: Bergin and Garvey Publishers, Inc., 1987); M. D. Tryman, "Reversing Affirmative Action: A Theoretical Construct," *Journal of Negro Education* 55, no. 2 (1986): 185–199; Menges and Exum, "Barriers to the Progress of Women and Minority Faculty."

45. Ramirez, "Racism Toward Hispanics."

46. Simone, *Academic Women Working Towards Equality.*

47. Reginald Wilson in Blum, "To Get Ahead in Research."

48. Heller, "Aggressive Affirmative Action Efforts."

49. Wilson in Blum, "To Get Ahead in Research"; Fields, "Hispanics, State's Fastest-Growing Minority", Heller, "Aggressive Affirmative Action Efforts."

50. Menges and Exum, "Barriers to the Progress of Women and Minority Faculty."

51. Ibid.

52. Michael A. Olivas, "Latino Faculty at the Border," *Increasing Numbers Key to More Hispanic Access,* "Change" (May/June 1988), pp. 6–9.

53. Ibid.; Wilson and Justiz, "Minorities in Higher Education"; Moore, "Black Faculty in White Colleges"; Arciniega and Morey, *Hispanics and Higher Education;* Fields, "Hispanics, State's Fastest-Growing Minority."

54. Moore, "Black Faculty in White Colleges."

55. Heller, "Aggressive Affirmative Action Efforts."

56. Moore, "Black Faculty in White Colleges."

57. Ibid., p. 118.

JOSEPH KATZ

Chapter Ten

White Faculty Struggling with the Effects of Racism*

Many decades ago, the Swedish economist Gunnar Myrdal and his American associates jolted the conscience of Americans with a book titled *An American Dilemma*.[1] Myrdal pointed out the discrepancy between the American creed of equality and the continuing brutal and unequal treatment of blacks in our midst. Since that time, significant changes have taken place both in the law of the country and in the behavior of its people. Yet, even the most casual observer finds persistent patterns of discrimination, including different rates of employment for blacks and whites, segregation in housing and social separation. We might expect that things would be better in today's colleges and universities, since these institutions have often been in the vanguard of social progress. Professors and students alike are dedicated not just to the pursuit of truth but to the ideal of reflective intelligence and to the task of furthering mutual understanding. The facts of university life, however, show fairly widespread racial abuse,[2] continuing underrepresentation of blacks on the faculty, social separation of black and white students and limited help for black students in coping with the effects of discriminatory prior schooling.

The project on which this chapter is based confronted me with some grim facts about the persistence of neglect, prejudice, fear and confusion

* Reprinted, with permission, from J. H. Cones III, J. F. Noonan and D. Janha, eds., *Teaching Minority Studies—New Directions in Teaching and Learning, no. 16* (San Francisco: Jossey-Bass, 1983), pp. 29–38.

among white faculty as they face black students in their classrooms. The project, which was conducted at a state institution, gave teachers an opportunity to investigate the role of racial issues in their teaching. I visited the campus on three separate occasions over a period of several days to conduct lengthy interviews with faculty and students. I repeatedly interviewed all members of project staff and participated in meetings with top administrators and university departments. The picture that emerged from my study is complex. I found no one who proudly voiced naive or vicious prejudices. Indeed, the faculty members whom I encountered were afraid and embarrassed to discover prejudicial thinking in themselves. But, many faculty tended to look away from the problems of race and thereby deprived themselves and their white students of the opportunity of becoming aware of their attitudes towards race and they deprived their black students of the essential opportunity of being treated unequivocally as equals. My experience made one major reason why racism remains an unresolved problem quite clear: One root cause of racism is passivity based on obliviousness and numbed feeling. This chapter will disentangle that obliviousness as it affects white faculty.

NEGLECT AND AVOIDANCE

It is a curious fact that the lessening of overt discrimination, the abrogation of legal barriers and enhanced access for black students to institutions of higher education have all supported neglect of the issue of racism. Many white faculty seem almost to think that the problem of racism has been solved. Occasionally, they are supported in this belief by some younger black students who, for their own spurious comfort, wish to deny the facts of the discrimination that they experience daily. The assumption that racism is waning leads many faculty to think that any special attention to their black students is itself a form of discrimination. Such professors, when asked about the distribution of grades of black students, will say that they do not want to engage in such counting. Yet, probing soon reveals that they think the grade performance of their black students is lower than that of white students. Further probing also reveals that thoughts and efforts devoted to raising the performance of underprepared students are not always pronounced. For instance, the introductory course in one science department had an unusually high failure rate; a large portion of the white students received less-than-passing grades, while the percentage of black students who received such grades was even larger. That department had rejected a proposal to improve the course by teaching it in two sections so that the failure rate due to differences in preparation could be lessened through appropriate phasing of instruction. I was told that the faculty did not want to engage in "high school kind of teaching."

As I probed further into the causes of neglect, I found that almost all faculty had been brought up under conditions in which discrimination of blacks was accepted and even endorsed by parents and other significant people in their environment. For instance, I interviewed a white professor who in high school had a black friend—a fellow football player and lover of poetry—whom he could not bring to his house. Many faculty were brought up in an environment in which there were simply no blacks; that absence suggested that there was a reason for excluding them. Almost every faculty member whom I interviewed was ashamed to find racial prejudice in herself or himself. To counter this shame, white faculty looked away from issues of race for fear of having to become more aware of their own almost unwilling prejudice. This remarkable fact helps to explain the deep impact that Myrdal's book made.[3] It touched people's conscience of finding irrational stereotypes within themselves. The feeling that prejudice is ego-alien distinguishes American racism from the antisemitic racism found in pre-Nazi and Nazi Germany, which cause neither embarrassment nor guilt for academics and nonacademics alike in regard to the stereotype of the evil Jew. This split in the American consciousness gives us a handle that can help us to clarify feelings and attitudes.

DIFFERENCES IN FACULTY ATTITUDES

There is a wide variety of attitudes among white faculty. On one end of the continuum are people like the young professor whose conscience was badly jolted when she was still in high school: Her state instituted a system of private schools in order to avoid federal requirements for racial integration. As soon as she could, she left the United States for study abroad. When she began teaching, she did so with a strong dedication to openness in the classroom. Her readiness to let black students know when they performed unsatisfactorily provided convincing evidence of her nondiscriminatory bent. (More encumbered faculty shy away from such clarity for fear that they may be thought prejudiced—perhaps as a defense against a lingering half-prejudice that they are dimly aware of in themselves.) Yet, even this professor found that her black students thought that she was not sufficiently caring. Only after she and her black and white students had shared their feelings about race did one obstacle to open communication fade. As she put it to me: "My perception of my class was that my students had been very interactive with each other. I saw the blacks as participating equally. In a group interview, black students in my class said that they perceived me to be open and receptive to discussing racial issues, but they felt that if they said everything that was on their minds it wouldn't be received well, so they didn't feel that they unfolded or revealed as much of themselves and their own value system in the course as they could have if they had felt that there was more receptivity. The issue was that, if they said what they felt, nobody really cared. The learning for me was that, even though I was being open and not shying away from issues, there was a point beyond which the black students did not feel they were willing to go. It made me aware of how much I don't know about other people—not just blacks but whites, too. I became much closer to the students as individuals. As a result of that effort, they appeared to realize that I was genuinely concerned, especially the black students, who started showing up in my office more frequently than before."

Near the other end of the continuum are professors who object to what they consider the unintelligibility of black dialect, the special clannishness of black students and the inadequacies of black students' academic performance. In the words of one professor, "I cannot communicate well with the black subpopulation. It is apparently very important for blacks to know the right handshake, to know how to talk mumbo jumbo or whatever. There are things that I don't agree with that blacks do; for example, their vocabulary when they get together. They may be doing enough of that—talking in the black jargon—that they do not have enough practice using English. In consequence, they are poorly prepared for higher education." The professor and the students speak different languages, and because translation has barely been attempted there is a sense of threat and illegitimacy.

ROOTS OF DISCRIMINATION

One asks why our society still seems compelled to continue mental and physical segregation based on skin color. Historians have explored the economic basis of discrimination. Images of black inferiority arose at the point at which exploitation of blacks became profitable for whites. As Fredrickson writes, "When it became more profitable to use black slaves rather than white indentured servants on the tobacco plantations of the Chesapeake . . . a powerful incentive was created for degrading all blacks to an inferior status."[4] But, whatever the legitimacy of economic interpretations of discrimination, they should not lead us to hide from ourselves the fact that segregation provides an opportunity for expressing malign inclinations. We know that economic reasons do little to explain the Nazis' extermination of Jews. In this country, the discrimination written into the fabric of social life had kept blacks and whites so far apart that they do not have an adequate base for learning about and testing preconceptions. Very few white faculty whom

I interviewed had acquaintance relations, not to speak of friendships, with blacks. There is thus a fertile breeding ground for the development of fears and for the projection of impulses and attitudes that are unacceptable and feared in oneself onto members of the "strange" group. Thus, a psychological walling in is added to economic segregation.

While one can view an excluded minority negatively, one can also project onto it qualities that one believes that one lacks or that one possesses to a diminished degree. Some white faculty whom I observed ascribed a depth of affect, emotional straightforwardness and directness in admitting anger to blacks that they felt to be lacking in whites. While such idealization is more benign than the projection of undesirable qualities, it constitutes another form of prejudice. It places a burden of specialness on blacks and thus hinders the intercourse of people on the basis of equality of virtue and fallibility. Racial liberals need to struggle their way through to a demystification of blacks. Attitudes towards women are comparable in this regard. Under conditions of oppression, women are both denigrated and idealized. In either case, they become an object of male projections.

There is a borderline area in which unacceptable and idealized impulses merge—the area of sexual feelings. I was struck that, not much below the surface in some academics, black people and black students aroused strong sexual feelings. In the case of women students, there was definite hedging about sexual attraction. A male professor referred to his fear (desire) that black female students would find him too attractive; hence, he had to keep a certain distance. A female black student reported that she had noticed that her white professors often stepped back a pace or two when a black female student approached them. Images of black males stressed aggression (fear of aggression), but these images, too, at times merged with sexual ones.

Other emotions were closer to the surface. Some faculty expressed their fear of discussing facts of economic discrimination and disparity of income in their classes. As one professor said, "I cannot look black students in the eye when I talk about black unemployment." Faculty said that they were afraid of encountering feelings of anger among black students and feelings of guilt among white students that presentations on the economic situation of blacks might arouse. Fear of black anger, based on the professor's own guilty identification with a long history of oppression, surfaced many times in my investigation.

Thus, underlying the routinized meeting of white professors and black students in the classroom is a tangled web of feelings and emotions. A professor's disregard of the emotional, social and intellectual situation of black students goes hand in hand with limitation of feeling, poverty of empathy, and attempts to avoid acknowledging anger and fear. Prejudice not only humiliates and dehumanizes the oppressed, it does something similar to the oppressor. However, professors who came to see their black students as full human beings were increasingly freed from the burden of alienation. Some, in the first flush of enthusiasm, seemed to want to throw content out of their classes. But, a balance was soon established. One does not need so much to talk about feelings as express them. Students want subject matter content, but they are very quick to discern and respond to caring, particularly when caring flows not from guilt but from a decently unencumbered openness to other people. The project that I observed found it necessary first to tackle the problems of white professorial attitudes before it could proceed to its initial priority, knowledge and awareness of black students.

While white professors both overidealize and disparage black students, black professors are not immune from prejudice. However, for them it takes other forms. At the very least, self-consciousness about white stereotypes can lead black professors to be sensitive if not defensive about shortcomings that black students sometimes exhibit. I found that black professors were particularly sensitive to black students' use of the allegation of discrimination as an excuse for poor performance. To quote a black professor: "A student will say to a professor, 'You didn't allow me a fair chance in this course. Your line of thinking is contrary to that of my culture, and therefore you are a racist.' The faculty member has two alternatives. one is to confront the student and say 'You are wrong. I am not a racist!' and ignore the student. The other alternative is to bend the rules and allow students to get away with this. I say *get away* in the sense that, in many cases, they had just as much of a fair chance as other students in the classroom. My bias is that at a college level we are training students to become competitive in the job market. Therefore, white faculty have the responsibility to treat all students as fairly as they can, and they should understand the games that a black or white student plays in the classroom to undermine the teaching-learning process. Fortunately, in the situation that I described, a female black student observed the conversation and said to the black student, 'You are wrong. He has been more than fair with you, and I really don't think that he should give you another chance, because it is going to dilute the learning process and the struggle that I have had to go through to obtain this grade.' The teacher did tell me that at the time he was wavering on whether or not to be more lax, but the support of the black female student helped him reaffirm his stance."

Black professors were more outspoken than white professors about manipulativeness on the part of black students. It was part of black professors' being refreshingly free of the idealization of black students that, I have suggested, is itself a subtle form of racism. At the same time, some black professors stressed what they considered the realistic needs of black students to make it in the white world—for instance, to learn the ways of competitiveness and other behaviors rewarded in the white world. In that respect, they questioned the standards of the white world less than one might expect them to, given the fact that they can look at white shortcomings from a different perspective.

In moving toward increased equality, one can also lose some of the benefits that come from the distinctive experiences of different ethnic groups. One of my white interviewees stressed his consciousness of the difference in the behavior and attitudes of white and black students. Listening to him, I asked myself whether I was trying to blur distinctions, just as the notion of unisex had tended to blur some of the differences between men and women. Differences created by ethnic backgrounds and experiences have given American society a multiplicity of customs and variegated perspectives on common experience. At the same time, some of the differences have an artificial base. Blacks were forbidden to whites. This aroused the excitement and attraction of the forbidden. The demystification of blacks—a way station in the experience of white professors as they get to know black colleagues and black students better—will also mean the loss of seductive illusions.

I have sketched some underlying factors in black-white relations— emotions that often are more exciting, crude and complex than what surface behavior shows. Surface behavior is subject to psychological censorship and dominated by rules of accommodation that make a kind of minimal coexistence possible. One has to have come to grips with the underlying trends for the surface to be different, too. Black students consistently report that white professors avoid eye contact with them and engage in other forms of behavior that limit contact and recognition of the contributions and thoughts of black students. The averted eye or ear is, among other things, an expression of the need to look away from and not hear the facts of discrimination. Indeed, it is probably not just a looking away from the black student but also from one's own felt guilt. The unconscious wish is that it would be nice, at least in the classroom, if everyone were white. That is the wish of the faculty member who says that he or she treats all students alike regardless of skin color. Once professors begin to change, they can become overly self-conscious about the transition. One faculty member almost inflicted eye contact on his students: "I have been very careful to maintain eye contact with students and to make doubly sure that I do this with black students. I have found that, in some instances, maybe I am overdoing it. It seems to make some of the black students a little uncomfortable, so that they will look away."

Black students often report that the professor's tone of voice or facial expressions display disbelief or surprise when they respond correctly or otherwise show good performance. Here, the underlying prejudice that blacks are not as good as whites shows itself against the professor's conscious will. Prejudice and bending over backwards go together, and when it comes to helping, black students report that white professors offer little guidance and criticism of black students' work. The reasons for this behavior probably differ with the individual. For some, there is the fear of being perceived as too critical—meaning prejudice. For others, a low opinion of blacks makes them feel that guidance and criticism will simply not be productive. Still others wish to minimize contact with people that their culture has stamped as pariahs. Racism is so much a part of the texture of our culture that professors will often make stereotypical comments about blacks without being aware of the hurtful impact that these comments can have on black students, particularly when they imply that blacks are less competent than whites. This is very similar to the thoughtless behavior of many professors when they address women or talk about women in class.[5] Part of the looking away involves white professors' ignorance of the contributions of blacks to society, including black literature. One of my professorial interviewees said that he assigned black writers in his literature classes but that he did so out of duty, not from a feeling for what the writers said. An economics professor described the persistent neglect of the facts of black economic life in the textbook literature of his field.

POSSIBILITIES FOR CHANGE

My observations reveal a powerful taboo: Blackness is a forbidden territory, to which badness is ascribed. Blacks stir up fears and at the same time they exert a seductive attraction, which must be compensated by the defense of rejection. Under these conditions, how might change come about? One would expect psychotherapy to be a powerful instrument. Indeed, whether they had been aided by psychotherapy or not, some of my interviewees reported that they began to grow as persons once their attitudes towards blacks underwent change. But, psychotherapy is available only in some cases. Another way of effecting change is to increase acquaintance. The process can begin by bringing about more open discussion in class, enabling students to hear about the economic, social and psychological facts of black lives. But, mere talk has its limitations. For some of the professors whom I interviewed, their behavior and attitudes to blacks began to change as a result of their having had the opportunity to become better acquainted with blacks. For instance, there was the professor referred to earlier in this chapter who had had a black friend in high school; their friendship was based on common interests and activities. In prolonged association, we can reveal to each other the depths of our being and transcend segregating rejection or romanticization. But, such friendships are difficult to initiate in the university setting, and in any case they extend beyond the confines of the classroom.

Happily, there is another means at hand: participation in a joint project. As psychological research has shown, cooperation is achieved less by talking than by working together on a joint task when objectives are shared by all members of the group, when the group's well-being depends on joint work and problem solving. Assigning projects to teams of students in one's class, defining tasks that require a mixed group of white and black students to work together encourages people to express more of themselves in a setting of solidarity. One can also expect classroom cooperation to spill over into these people's personal lives and to lead to the beginnings of friendship.

There are reasons to believe that there are more bases for friendship between blacks and whites than we realize. Black students whom I interviewed talked at first as if there were little or no communication between black and white students and indicated that they moved in entirely different social circles. When I probed, however, it emerged that many black students had at least one or two close white friends. Thus, precedents for interaction exist, but they need strengthening. It is an astonishing fact that, in a society as open as ours, attitudes persist with such vigor that the relationships between people of different color are embarrassing, distant and confused. Besides the intrinsic significance of deepening acquaintance and friendships, they are likely to enhance learning and stimulate interaction in the classroom.

The experience of the project that I studied shows that one effective way of countering racism in the classroom is to bring the facts of the black situation into the open in the classroom and to give black and white students full opportunity to express their views, attitudes and feelings about them. Such expression can increase insight and change attitudes among students and professors alike.

This chapter has explored some of the resistance that attempts to resolving the problem of racism will encounter in the classroom. The resistance is formidable and deep. If it was not, the problem would not have lasted as long as it has. But, at the same time, the resistance is not insurmountable. It can be overcome by the healing power of abandoning prejudice; by the realization of people who take the first steps that they are growing as people, that they are less defensive in their imagination, thinking and experience, and that they have a new warmth in their perception of others and—astonishingly—of themselves. The ultimate incentive is that the process enables one to become more fully human. It is an irony that the universities—those great promoters of productive social change—that have opened their doors wide to black students have in so many ways been remiss in constructing the bases for an emotional and intellectual regeneration of black-white relationships. Here, indeed, is the challenge. While there has been a great increase of commercialism and passivity in the universities over the last decade, there is also an opportunity to revivify the university's humanistic and transforming function.

NOTES

1. Gunnar Myrdal, *An American Dilemma* (New York: Harper, 1944).

2. D. A. De Coster and P. Mable, eds., *Understanding Today's Students* (New Directions for Students Services, No. 16), (San Francisco: Jossey-Bass, 1981).

3. Gunnar Myrdal, *op. cit.*

4. G. M. Frederickson, "The Black Image in the White Mind," *Arts and Sciences* 5 No. 2, (1982): 14–19.

5. R. M. Hall and B. R. Sandler, *The Classroom Climate: A Chilly One for Women?* (Washington, D.C.: Association of American Colleges, 1982).

Part 3

Case Studies

ERIC L. HIRSCH

Chapter Eleven

Columbia University: Individual and Institutional Racism

Sometime in early March of 1987, a white Columbia College undergraduate began to harass black students because of their race. On one occasion he entered a student hangout and, seeing a number of black students there, said: " 'Oh my God, the chicken wings are everywhere, let's crack a few.' "[1] His verbal and physical harassment of one particular black student continued for several weeks. At about 2 A.M. the morning of March 22, 1987, this black Columbia College student and several of his friends confronted the white student outside the student center to demand a stop to this behavior. The black student walked up to the white student and asked him for some respect. He said, " 'You've got to stop. It's got to stop. If you can't call me by my name, don't call me anything at all.' "[2] As he turned and began to walk away the white student replied " 'What's this? . . . Ah man, fuck you.' "[3]

A fight ensued between the white and black student and a number of their friends. During the course of the fight, the black student who had originally been harassed was thrown to the ground, sustained a head injury and was taken to a local hospital. Another black student was chased onto Broadway by a white student who yelled: " 'Goddam, you fucking niggers. Fucking niggers, chicken wing niggers. I'm going to get you, fucking niggers. I'm going to kill you fucking niggers.' "[4] One of the black students present when the assault occurred later said: " 'We were scared for our lives. I heard "We're going to kill all of you fucking niggers," and the way I've been raised I learned that nigger meant me.' "[5] Another student who was present went up to the white student who had yelled this and asked: " 'So this is racist?' " He replied: " 'Yes, and you go to hell!' "[6] Several black security guards were struck while trying to break up the fight.[7]

Such incidents of racially motivated harassment and assault cannot be tolerated, especially in college and university settings where a meaningful education depends on the mutual acceptance of differences. But the real problem of racism at Columbia was illustrated not by this incident itself, but by the response to it. In the days following the assault, an intense, racially polarized crisis developed on campus. Black students organized quickly to protest against the assault and institutional racism at Columbia. A small number in the Columbia community—including some white students, a few faculty members and the campus unions—supported this organizing effort. But most white students quickly came to the paradoxical conclusion that the "real racists" were the black students who had been the victims of the assault.

The Columbia administration made strong statements condemning racism, but generally refused to acknowledge the deep-seated institutional nature of the problem of racism on campus. The final outcome of the conflict was that those who protested against racism were arrested and put on disciplinary trial, while those who had engaged in the racial assault and harassment received no punishment of any kind. The lessons of Columbia's experience can only be analyzed after reviewing in detail the response to the assault of three key groups: black students, white students and the Columbia administration.

THE BLACK STUDENT RESPONSE

The black students who had been assaulted during the incident called a meeting of all black students on campus on the morning of March 22.[8] Over one hundred black students, as well as several white students and a white faculty member, attended the meeting. At the meeting the students described the harassment that led up to the racially motivated assault, the assault itself and the racial slurs which had been shouted during the incident. Other black students present felt outraged as well as threatened because the harassment and resulting violence had occurred solely because of the student's race.

Those at the meeting wanted to see those responsible punished swiftly in order to send a clear message that such behavior would not be tolerated at Columbia. The sense of the meeting was that the response to this threat had to be a firm one and that the fight against racism on campus ought to be led by students of color. An ad hoc group called the Concerned Black Students at

Columbia (CBSC) was created, and a steering committee of half a dozen was appointed.[9]

The students planned a protest for later in the afternoon. This first demonstration drew approximately two hundred black and white participants for a march to the fraternity house of several of the white students involved in the fight.[10] Speeches were made which denounced the racists and their fraternities, and which labelled Columbia a racist institution. CBSC also posted and distributed a "wanted poster" with the names of four, and the pictures of two, of the white students who had been involved in the assault. The group also disseminated information about the incident to their fellow Columbia students by having an informational table in the center of campus.

A subcommittee was appointed at this first meeting to formulate a series of demands to be presented to the Columbia administration. The students in the subcommittee and in CBSC as a whole did not define this as an isolated act by a small number of individuals. They believed that entrenched *institutional* racism at Columbia had implicitly encouraged *individual* racist acts.[11]

The CBSC suggested that white students' lack of respect for their black classmates was not based only on personal prejudices; their racist attitudes were reinforced by institutional practices at Columbia which included: (1) Columbia's failure to hire blacks and Latinos for faculty and upper level administrator jobs (in the 1986–87 academic year, only 2 percent of the Columbia University faculty was black, and 4 percent of top level administrators were black or Latino[12]); (2) the failure of the college to recruit a reasonable proportion of black students (7 percent of the college student body was black and only 6 percent was Latino in the spring semester of 1986[13]); (3) the college core curriculum—a set of intensive courses that all college students were required to take—ignored the contribution of writers of African descent; (4) Columbia was the only Ivy League school without an African-American studies major; (5) Columbia had severely alienated the Harlem community through its racist housing policies; (6) the university had not followed through sufficiently on its commitment to full divestment of South African related stock.

The Concerned Black Students at Columbia's primary response to the racial assault was to make thirteen demands of the Columbia administration. They reflected their belief that the problem of racism involved institutional practices, not just individual prejudices. The demands included: the arrest, vigorous prosecution and expulsion from Columbia of the white students involved in the attack; increases in the number of black faculty and students in the college and in the university as a whole; greater financial support for currently enrolled black students; greater emphasis on the work of black authors in the college's core curriculum and the creation of an

African-American studies major in the college; strict compliance with the
university's promise to divest its portfolio of stock in companies which do
business in South Africa; and the provision of low-income housing for the
residents of Harlem.[14]

In the next month, the CBSC organized a series of demonstrations to
protest the university's lack of response to these demands and the failure of
the authorities to arrest or discipline the white perpetrators of the racially
motivated assault. A rally and march on March 26 drew approximately one
thousand demonstrators; on April 4, approximately five hundred attended a
march to the twenty-sixth police precinct. The meetings, protest rallies and
other actions of CBSC drew support from many of the black students on
campus. More than half of the approximately two hundred Columbia College
black students attended the initial CBSC meeting; a relatively high proportion
of black undergraduate and black graduate and professional students turned
out at other CBSC events as well. As one student said to a *Columbia Daily
Spectator* reporter:

> "I think the whole incident was definitely racially motivated. As far as CBSC
> goes, I think it's important that they do what they're doing."[15]

Another suggested:

> "There's [sic] only six black professors here and that's kind of hard to accept.
> There aren't any black coaches and as far as I know only one assistant coach
> is black. There's some changes that have to be made along those lines."[16]

But support among black students on campus for CBSC was not unanimous;
a minority did not participate in protest rallies and marches and did not
support the CBSC demands. Some supported strong actions against those
involved in the assault but denied that Columbia was a racist institution. As
one black student said to a campus newspaper reporter:

> "I personally have never experienced what I would call a racist incident. . . .
> If it was a racist incident it should be attacked. But charges against the
> University I don't think are very accurate."[17]

And some others felt that the militant actions of CBSC were counterproductive. As another black student said:

> I think the whole thing was pretty trivial. It has escalated into something
> much more than it was. I wouldn't deny that there is some degree of racial
> tension here. . . . I think the issue is important to address. . . . But anyone
> who's militantly blowing this thing up is alienating people who might help
> them in terms of tolerance and more understanding."[18]

THE WHITE STUDENT RESPONSE

Perhaps the most desirable result of the racial assault would have been multiracial solidarity around the principle of fighting individual and institutional racism at Columbia. It did not happen. Rather, the incident seemed to lead to an increase in racism among many white students as they struggled to deal with their own feelings of guilt and responsibility for the assault. Thus, in the days following the assault, black students were forced to respond to an outbreak of additional racist incidents on campus. Racist statements were found on the log-in bulletin board on the university computer system. A flyer was found with black and white stick figures fighting, with the caption, "A Day at the Beach," recalling the Howard Beach assault where a black man was killed. A poster reading "Ku Klux Klan—White Power" was found on a black woman's dormitory door.[19] At one CBSC protest march, eggs, water and a wooden shelf were thrown at protestors from dormitories and student apartments near campus.[20] At another march, a confederate flag appeared in the window of a dorm room.[21] Racist groups tried to take advantage of the situation for recruiting purposes. Ku Klux Klan and National Association for the Advancement of White People (a white supremacist group) literature was found in phone booths and in a classroom.

Certainly, some white students on campus supported the CBSC; hundreds of white students participated in CBSC protests. But a few hundred white students represented a very small proportion of the over two thousand non-Latino whites in Columbia College and the approximately fifteen thousand whites at Columbia University as a whole. Most white students did not support the CBSC demands nor its methods.[22] In classroom discussions, in arguments on campus at the CBSC table, and in one-on-one conversations with friends and faculty, they reacted quite defensively to the racial assault and to the CBSC organizing effort.

The defensiveness was due to the fact that people they knew, sometimes close friends, were being accused of having participated in a racially motivated assault, and their own university was being attacked as a racist institution. Many white students assumed that this meant that they were being accused of being the kind of racist that was portrayed in old newsreels of the civil rights movement, and that Columbia was being accused of being just like the University of Mississippi in 1955. Thus, some of the same students who had supported a movement against racism in South Africa in 1985 responded quite angrily to charges of racism at Columbia in 1987.

Because they felt personally accused, many white students accepted various rationalizations which allowed them to avoid accepting responsibility for racism on campus. These arguments were made and readily accepted even when the existing evidence contradicted them. One popular interpretation was that the incident had not been racially motivated, that it had been a simple fight between two students who had had too much to drink. This interpretation was accepted despite the wide dissemination of eyewitness accounts of racial harassment, racial slurs and of the racially motivated nature of the assault itself. Some suggested that the white student who had shouted "nigger," did so because he had been drunk or angry; it had just been a slip and was not racially motivated. Others downplayed the use of the phrase "chicken wings" by saying it was not a common racial slur, or the significance of the word, "nigger" by stating that black people often use that word to refer to each other.

Some tried to delimit the impact of the fight by saying that these individuals were some of the few, or the only, racists at Columbia. One of the black student organizers of CBSC characterized this argument as follows: " 'Well, okay, that was an isolated incident that morning, but it started there and ended there, and let's not make such a big deal out of it because *I'm* not racist.' "[23]

Even those white students willing to recognize the problem of racism on campus often were unable to accept its institutional nature. Many felt that the problem could be solved by disciplining the one white student who had shouted the racial slurs. Any remaining difficulties could then be dealt with through individual white *and black* acknowledgement of personal prejudices and through better communication. As a result, proposals were made, many implemented later, to found encounter groups, where people could confront their own racism and make more black or white friends.

But the dominant white student response to the crisis was to blame the victims, to argue that the blacks in CBSC were the "real racists." "After all," the argument went, "we don't know what actually happened during the fight. It could even be that the blacks provoked it. What we do know is that the CBSC closed their initial meeting to all whites. [Of course, this was not true.] We know that they refused to allow whites to participate in decision-making in their organization. And we know that they distributed wanted posters with the pictures of the white students accused of being racists before there had even been an investigation of the incident."

Many white students thus came to the ironic conclusion that it was really the black students responding to the racial assault who were responsible for the racial problems on campus. The desirable outcome for these white students was that they did not have to deal with the fact that their classmates had engaged in racially motivated harassment and assault or the possibility that they enjoyed certain privileges in this society and at Columbia simply because of the color of their skin. The undesirable outcome for the university community was that many white students did not support the efforts of their black classmates to substantively address the issues of racial harassment, racially motivated assault and institutional racism at Columbia.

THE COLUMBIA ADMINISTRATION RESPONSE

Columbia's president made a strong statement condemning racism the day after the incident:

> There cannot be a more troublesome event on a campus like ours, which prides itself on the racial and religious diversity of its student body, than an episode of racial harassment. Our duty in response to an allegation that such an event has occurred is clear. It is the obligation of University officials to find the facts, and render swift and fair judgment on any and all offenders. . . . No incident of racism will be tolerated.[24]

The importance of this statement should not be underestimated; it is important that those in powerful positions at a university state clearly that racism will not be tolerated. But like many students, the president failed to acknowledge the underlying institutional roots of racism on campus, and he implied that such racist incidents were a product of personal misunderstandings or lack of communication among students:

> This episode has brought to the surface tensions among our students. . . . It is the responsibility of everyone at Columbia to help allay the fears and resolve the misunderstandings that lead to such tensions.[25]

The administration was also slow to act on its commitment to combat racism at Columbia. The president met with representatives of CBSC but did not respond directly or substantively to any of the group's demands.[26] And he and other administrators began what became a continual series of harsh criticisms of CBSC tactics. The major point of contention between the administration and the CBSC soon became the unwillingness of the black students who had been involved in the incident to participate in the college dean's investigation.

The investigation began in the week following the assault. The college dean's office asked all eyewitnesses to report to a dean for one-on-one discussions of the incident. Each dean—as prosecuting attorney, judge and jury—would have total discretion over which students would be disciplined and how. The black students who had been involved in the assault decided not to report for such disciplinary hearings because they did not trust the deans to be impartial; they pointed out that they were being asked to report to the same deans who had testified against many of them two years earlier at disciplinary proceedings which had resulted from a three-week divestment protest. Offers by the black students to appear as a group, or to appear as individuals with one adviser to witness the proceedings, were turned down by the college administration. Instead the deans went ahead with their investigation without the testimony of the black students who had been assaulted.

On April 21, to protest the fact that a month had gone by without any action being taken by the administration against the white students involved in the incident, fifty CBSC supporters, both black and white, chained and locked the doors to Hamilton Hall and blocked the building's entrances with their bodies.[27] Within minutes, university security officers began to videotape the demonstration so that the administration could later identify demonstrators for prosecution under the university rules of conduct. By 10:45 A.M., the university president had decided to have Columbia security officers arrest the demonstrators. Although most of the protestors were white, blacks were singled out by security for arrest.[28] One of the first to be arrested was the only junior black faculty member at Columbia College, despite the fact that he was observing and not participating in the protest. Charges against him were later dropped and the university officially apologized for the incident.[29] Another in the first group of those arrested was the very same black student who had been harassed and assaulted by white students the month before. He was dropped on the concrete steps by security officers and was again sent to a local hospital for treatment of a head injury. When this injury occurred, further arrests were called off.

After the morning arrests, the size of the demonstration grew to approximately two hundred students. At 7:30 P.M., the president decided to call in the New York City police to arrest the remaining demonstrators. One hundred and fifty mainly white protestors were detained a short distance away. Fifty mainly black protestors were arrested and charged with disorderly conduct and trespassing. Two black male students were beaten by the police and were then charged with assaulting police officers and resisting arrest. (Because the students' lawyers argued successfully that there had been a clear racial bias in the arrest and prosecution of the protestors, all of the charges against the demonstrators were later dismissed, "in the interests of justice" as the judge put it.)

The next day, the college dean's office released its report on the racial assault. It suggested that a racial incident had occurred on the morning of March 22. However, it termed the harassment which had caused this confrontation to begin "alleged," and it implied that black students had initiated the violence. The dean of the college labeled this report the "truth" despite the fact that the black students who had been assaulted had not testified before the deans. He ended his letter that introduced the report by accusing the CBSC of lying:

You have heard the chant 'No Justice, No Peace!' from a group of students and others who wish you to believe that Columbia is a racist institution. They have claimed. . . . that Columbia has covered up a racist incident on the night of March 21. These claims are false. Without truth, there can be neither justice nor peace.[30]

The student who had harassed his fellow black students prior to the assault never received any punishment of any kind. The student who shouted racial epithets during the assault was suspended as a result of the deans' investigation. But he sued Columbia, arguing that he was a victim of reverse discrimination since no black students had been punished. His lawyer also argued successfully that the black students involved in the conflict had staged the fight to gain support for their antiracist work on campus.[31] Columbia later agreed to reinstate this student if he would agree to drop any further legal action. Thus none of the perpetrators of racial harassment, no one who shouted racial epithets, no white student who assaulted a black student ever received any punishment of any kind.

But, assisted by attorneys from a New York City law firm, Columbia went ahead with its internal prosecution of the antiracist protestors who had blockaded Hamilton Hall.[32] The disciplinary trials for the forty-five student demonstrators began in late May, 1987. The students argued that their actions were necessary because institutional racism at Columbia made it impossible for them to expect justice through the college disciplinary procedures. After hearing evidence of such racism, the hearing officers found the protestors guilty of interfering with passage into Hamilton Hall for a short period of time; they received one semester disciplinary warnings. The more serious charges of disrupting a university function, punishable by suspension or expulsion, were dismissed.

LESSONS OF THE COLUMBIA UNIVERSITY EXPERIENCE

Many white Americans limit their conception of racism to the South prior to the mid-1960s civil rights movement and of racists to people like the infamous segregationist Bull Connor. An incident like this one at Columbia, a supposedly enlightened northern university, reveals the error of this view. It shows that there are people throughout our society who may act violently against others because of the color of their skin.

But racially motivated harassment and assault can easily be explained away as isolated acts by a few racists. More serious in this case was the reaction to the incident. White students and administrators quickly blamed the victims and the black students organizing against racism, rather than the perpetrators of the assault. This may have allowed them to avoid feelings of personal responsibility and guilt, but it also severely hindered efforts to punish the perpetrators and to address the more deep-seated problem of institutional racism at Columbia.

In the immediate aftermath of the incident it was important to indicate that racial harassment and assault would not be tolerated at the university by conducting an impartial, prompt and thorough investigation of the assault. Instead the college deans went ahead with an investigation without the input of the black students who had been assaulted, labeled the report that resulted "the truth," and called those in CBSC liars. Partly as a result of the lack of an adequate investigation, neither the white student who had originally harassed black students nor the student who shouted racial slurs during the fight were ever punished.

Part of the problem was Columbia College's continued use of an archaic disciplinary procedure in which deans are judge, jury and prosecutor. The black students in CBSC did not have much faith in deans whose policies they were protesting and who had testified against many of them during disciplinary hearings two years before. Disciplinary committees with student, faculty and administrator members are more likely to inspire confidence in the impartiality of the disciplinary procedure. And on those occasions when the university itself is charged with racism, it may be necessary to use an outside court or presiding officer to insure impartiality.

Punishing the individual perpetrators of racial assaults is not the only answer to the problem of racism on our campuses. The racially discriminatory practices of our universities and colleges must also be changed. Because racism affects all of our institutions and organizations, it often operates in subtle, overlapping and mutually reinforcing ways. For example, Columbia recently changed its disciplinary rules in order to be able to punish protestors who block access to buildings more severely in the future. This action is likely to affect mainly black students; all three of the most important takeovers of Hamilton Hall—in 1968, 1985 and 1987—were led by black students protesting against racism at Columbia. (And, the only white student disciplined by Columbia was later exonerated by a largely white jury who accepted the argument that his punishment was a clear case of reverse discrimination.) Finally, black students were selectively arrested and brutalized when the Columbia administration called police onto campus to arrest antiracist protestors.

Of course, there are people who accept the institutional nature of the problem of racism at Columbia and who are working to overcome it. A report by a committee appointed by the college dean accepted many of the CBSC demands recommending (among other things) that greater effort be made to recruit minority students and that greater attention be given to their financial aid needs; that more full-time minority faculty and high level administrators be hired; that the college consider more authors and ideas from non-Western cultures in core courses; that the university establish better relations with the surrounding minority communities; that a strong statement condemning racial harassment and assault be included in the college handbook; and that there be more sessions on racial awareness for administrators and students.[33] And an interim report by a Columbia University committee to study racism at Columbia emphasized an aggressive affirmative action policy which would dramatically increase the number of minority faculty and administrators at the university.[34]

Of course, it is easy to recommend changes in policy and harder to implement them. So far the signs are mixed. Columbia College did institute an African-American studies major about two weeks after the racial assault occurred, and it is trying to implement the other positive changes recommended by the college committee.[35] A month after the incident, a gift of twenty-five million dollars for minority scholarships was announced. On the negative side, however, a committee on the core curriculum submitted a set of recommendations which argued for the continuation of an emphasis on the Western cultural tradition in required courses and which failed to recommend the inclusion of authors of African-American descent.[38]

It is important for educational and moral reasons that universities make a real effort to deal aggressively with the problem of racism on our campuses. Less discriminatory institutional practices can make a difference both by giving people of color greater opportunities and by sending the message to white students that people of color and their ideas deserve respect. Fighting institutional racism will be a major challenge for colleges and universities in the 1990s.

NOTES

1. *Columbia Daily Spectator*, March 23, 1987, p. 11. The documentation of this incident and its aftermath is relatively sparse. No survey of campus attitudes was done during the course of these events. The following description and analysis of it is based in part on my own observations and on those of eyewitnesses I talked to. I was on campus at the time, teaching two large courses. I had extensive discussions with students on both sides of the conflict in classroom as well as nonclassroom settings. Other sources of information include the student newspaper, the *Columbia Daily Spectator;* the administration's official publication, the *Columbia University Record;* and various statements, reports and press releases from the student organization which responded to the assault, the Concerned Black Students at Columbia, and from the Columbia University administration.

2. *Columbia Daily Spectator*, March 23, 1987, p. 1.

3. Office of the Dean of Students, Columbia College, "Report on the Events of March 21/22, 1987."

4. Ibid.

5. *Broadway,* March 1987, p. 4.

6. Ibid.

7. *Columbia Daily Spectator,* March 23, 1987, p. 1.

8. The account of this meeting is based on my own recollection of it.

9. Several of those appointed to the steering committee had previously been active in an organization called the Coalition for a Free Southern Africa, which had led a three-week blockade of a campus building to gain university divestment of South African related stock in 1985.

10. *Columbia Daily Spectator,* March 23, 1987, p. 1.

11. Individual racism involves personal biases and negative attitudes toward those of another race. It is particularly likely to affect those in dominant racial groups who need a way to rationalize their society's negative treatment of subordinate racial groups. Institutional racism has to do with how major institutions and organizations in a society operate in complex, overlapping ways to deny equal opportunities to those in subordinate racial groups. It can have its influence on such groups regardless of the level of individual racism of those within those organizations and institutions.

12. The Task Force on Minorities, Columbia University, "Interim Report to the President," May 1989, table 1.

13. These are official Columbia College enrollment figures for the spring 1986 semester.

14. Concerned Black Students at Columbia, "Demands Issued in Response to the Racist Attacks at Columbia University," March 1987.

15. *Columbia Daily Spectator,* April 3, 1987, p. 5.

16. Ibid.

17. Ibid.

18. Ibid.

19. *Newsday* April 2, 1987, p. 38.

20. *Columbia Daily Spectator,* March 27, 1987.

21. Ibid.

22. Most of the analysis in this section is based on extensive discussions I had with white students in my classes, in small groups on campus and in one-on-one discussions.

23. *Broadway,* March 1987, p. 4, emphasis added.

24. Columbia University President's Office, "A Statement to the Columbia Community," March 23, 1987.

25. Ibid.

26. *Columbia Daily Spectator,* March 30, 1987, p. 1.

27. Columbia University press release, April 21, 1987. This action was strikingly similar to a three-week blockade of the same building in 1985, a demonstration which prompted the Columbia trustees to agree to divest from South African related stock.

28. I was an eyewitness to these arrests and to those which took place later that day.

29. *Columbia Daily Spectator,* May 13, 1987, p. 5.

30. Office of the Dean of Students, "Reports on the Events of March 21/22, 1987."

31. *Newsday,* January 13, 1988, p. 25.

32. After the 1968 building occupations, the college disciplinary procedures with regard to political protests were changed so that those charged have the option of public hearings. However, the hearing officers, who make all decisions on disciplinary action, are appointed by the executive committee of the university senate, a committee which is chaired by the university president. Unlike the disciplinary procedures which apply to nonprotest incidents (such as the deans' investigation of the racially motivated assault), the defendants have the right to have advisors or lawyers to facilitate their defense.

33. Committee on Race Relations in Columbia College, "Final Report," *Columbia University Record,* September 30, 1988, p. 6.

34. Task Force on Minorities, "Interim Report to the President."

35. *Columbia Daily Spectator,* April 9, 1987, p. 1; "Response of the Columbia College Dean to the Recommendations of the Committee on Race Relations in Columbia College," *Columbia University Record,* September 30, 1988, p. 6.

36. "Report of the Commission on the Core Curriculum." Columbia College, December 14, 1988.

SALLY COLE

Chapter Twelve

Beyond Recruitment and Retention: The Stanford Experience

We are asking young people to ignore the habits of comfort, and to seek out others with whom they are unfamiliar and sometimes ill at ease. We are exposing them and ourselves to the risk of misunderstanding and even, when sensitivities are violated as they occasionally will be, hostility. But we think it is nevertheless worth the risk, because we are among the few places in this country in which it may be possible to test the workability of the multicultural existence that will, ready or not, be the life of Californians and eventually all Americans in the twenty-first century.[1]

Who are the "young people" to whom Stanford University's president refers? They are approximately 6,460 Stanford undergraduates, over 30 percent of whom are ethnic minority students. The freshman class that entered in 1988–1989 was 16 percent Asian-American, 10 percent black, 8.6 percent Mexican-American, 1.5 percent other Hispanic, 1.1 percent American Indian and 63 percent white. All of these students arrived with both promise and significant accomplishment and they will leave in about four years with even more accomplishment and promise as they move into their adult lives. As CEOs and parents, athletes and educators—an incomplete list, to be sure—they will influence those around them in many ways and in many different settings.

When these students leave Stanford, however, do they have the experiences, the skills and the commitment to be leaders in shaping the multicultural worlds in which they will live? Are the resources of Stanford

213

University effectively directed both to creating a dynamic pluralism during students' undergraduate careers and to instilling in its graduates an enduring curiosity and respect for human differences?

These questions, among others, peppered the campus during the 1988–1989 academic year. They were discussed, debated and analyzed—but not resolved. The level of energy was high, as was the quality of thought devoted to the many points of view. The goals, by and large, are shared by the many members of the Stanford community. Most of us also agree that the goals are important. We disagree about how to obtain them.

The pages that follow present a few of the major events and themes, and actors speaking for themselves through interviews, essays and letters to campus papers. While not able to include every important event and influential campus voice in this collection, the author does hope to speak to those who share—or seek to understand—the Stanford vision of preparing its students for important roles in a fast-approaching world in which "majorities" and "minorities" have fleeting statistical lives and individual destinies are closely linked to one's knowledge, understanding and appreciation of others.

Two events, known locally as the Otero Vigil and the Ujamaa Incident, set the stage for Stanford's 1988–1989 year. Descriptions of these events have already appeared elsewhere as case studies for student affairs, staff training and graduate classes in educational administration. (This reflects a Stanford tradition, endearing to some and irritating to others, of candor carried to such an extreme that our "problems" and "incidents" become teaching tools almost as quickly as they become news stories.)

THE OTERO VIGIL

On May 25, 1988, members of the Stanford University community were dismayed to learn of events that took place the previous evening at Otero House, a predominantly white undergraduate student residence.

The following facts were determined by the assistant dean of student affairs and subsequently reported to the campus community.[2]

On Monday, May 23, an article in the *Stanford Daily* related the eviction from Otero of Mark Nilan, a freshman, for conduct in violation of the residence agreement. Specifically, Mr. Nilan had verbally attacked the resident fellow and a resident assistant, had vandalized the dorm, and had repeatedly insulted fellow residents. A central theme in the student's behavior was the apparent belief that he should not be expected to live in a residence that had a gay staff member. Mr. Nilan had been cautioned repeatedly that this conduct was out of line and that, if it persisted, his residence privilege would be revoked.

The *Daily* article was the subject of considerable discussion at the Phi Delta Theta fraternity house at lunch on Monday. Several members decided to protest the university's action in evicting the freshman. They did not know the freshman or his history of misconduct and saw the administration's action as unnecessarily heavy-handed. After further discussion, seven members decided to protest by holding a silent vigil outside of Otero House. The group included four seniors, two juniors and one sophomore. One of the seniors telephoned the *Daily* during the afternoon to say that a protest was planned that night at Otero. Another senior, Mr. Piper, was chosen to be the group's spokesman. Although Mr. Nilan had rushed Phi Delta, he was not a pledge and there is no evidence that he knew what the group planned for that night.

Shortly before midnight, the seven donned masks of various kinds (e.g., a motorcycle helmet, a hockey mask, goggles) and went with candles to Otero. Their original intention was to enter the dorm; once there, however, they instead formed a semicircle in front of the entrance of the lounge where a lengthy house meeting on the subject of Mr. Nilan's eviction had just ended. A large number of residents were around and saw the gathering on the patio: They saw seven anonymous men, faces concealed, carrying lit candles. Many residents reacted with shock and fear. At least one resident reporting seeing men in sheets bearing lighted candles. The image of the Ku Klux Klan was perceived by most if not all of the residents, and many became extremely agitated.

Otero residents called the police. A resident of a neighboring house telephoned a well-known member and past president of the Black Student Union (BSU). Three police cars arrived at 12:26 A.M., and officers questioned Mr. Piper. He declined to identify himself but assured police that what was underway was a nonviolent protest. Police cautioned the vigil participants not to be disorderly, explained to those present that since no laws were being broken vigil participants were not subject to arrest, contacted the resident fellow to relay the same information to him, and then departed. One officer remained nearby, positioned to observe any developments without being easily visible to the students. An officer checked back in with the students at 12:52 A.M. and another did so at 1:17 A.M.

Not long after midnight, a group of twenty to thirty student from various parts of the campus, many of them members of the BSU and other interested student groups, arrived on the scene. The crowd grew quickly to number about fifty to sixty students. Black Student Union members initially gathered in the lounge to check on the well-being of the dorm's black residents, two of whom were particularly upset by what was going on.

The visitors then went outside to talk directly to the vigil participants. The editor of the *Daily,* who had been present at the house meeting, remained on the scene and was joined by two photographers. Most of the residents stayed inside the dorm, although one resident assistant went out to talk to vigil participants and others. At that point, no one knew whether the men were Stanford students; nor did they know why they were there.

Over the next several minutes, students sought to learn the purpose of the vigil, the reasons for its participants' refusal to speak or to take off their masks, and the identities of the seven men. One of the participants whispered to a student nearby that this was a silent vigil. When the student provided him with paper, the vigil participant wrote that the vigil was not a racist protest, that the participants did not intend to antagonize anyone, and that they were present to protest the university's eviction of Mark Nilan. He added that it was a silent, nonviolent vigil and that its participants applauded First Amendment rights. The student who had provided the paper read the note to the assembled group.

Approximately forty-five minutes after the start of the event, the vigil participants' candles burned out and they all rose to leave. The witnesses, many of whom had sat down around the seven men and had sought to engage them in a discussion of their actions, rose too. Two of the seven men ran away from the group and hid nearby until they could return to their house unobserved. The others split up into small groups moving in various directions. Two of the small groups included students who continued to try to convince the vigil participants to remove their masks and talk with them. One man, who had removed his mask, told the students with him that he felt intimidated by their actions. Around 1:45 A.M., the groups dispersed and everybody went home.

The next day, vigil participants expressed surprise and dismay that what they had intended to be a protest was perceived as a racist act. They reported that they wore masks because they did not want to be recognized as members of Phi Delta Theta and dismissed as "frat guys." They also did not want their actions as individuals to be misattributed to their fraternity. They explained further that they had no prior experience with protests and had carried lit candles because that was how they believed protests were done. After talking with fraternity brothers, the vigil participants met with the fraternal affairs adviser. They also requested (of the resident fellow) and were given (by house vote) permission to speak to Otero residents that evening, to clarify their intentions and to apologize for the unforeseen consequences.

On Wednesday, the men went to the Black Community Services Center, again to explain their actions and to apologize for the consequences. Also on Wednesday, the fraternity published a letter disavowing the manner in which its members had chosen to protest the eviction of Mr. Nilan and apologizing to "members of minority groups, particularly the Black Student Union, [and] members of the Stanford community." On Friday, May 27, a letter of apology from the vigil participants appeared in the *Daily.*

The effect of the event on Otero residents was extreme stress. The vigil and its consequences caused some residents to feel that their home had been violated and their security breached. During the night in question, many residents found themselves fearful and confused. Many also felt that there was no one in control of the situation, which seemed volatile. A fair amount of sleep was lost by residents, vigil participants, witnesses from other residences and others involved in the event or its aftermath.

SOME RESPONSES TO THE OTERO VIGIL

The dean of student affairs was heard from almost immediately:

. . . The symbolism of the group's members choosing to mask their identities and approach silently in the dead of night bearing small "torches" cannot escape the notice of anyone who is at all aware of the history of black people in the United States.

. . . According to some witnesses, the masked group members expressed sincere surprise that their "simple vigil" had symbolized anything other than support for a fellow student's freedom of speech. Accepting that their surprise is sincere, I ask whether ignorance can be an excuse in an instance like this. The event serves to remind us all of the necessity of thinking through potential outcomes of our actions and not just intended outcomes.

. . . This is not a place that values intimidation tactics; this is a place that values learning, and the rational and thoughtful discourse that leads to learning. This is a place that finds cloaked secrecy at odds with our commitment to the open exchange of ideas. This is a place that values the feelings of members of the community, and that finds repugnant acts of viciousness or even ignorant insensitivity.

. . . Let me put it as simply and directly as I can: members of the Stanford community must know that conduct which seeks to or has the effect of discouraging the full participation in the life of this University by any student on account of his or her sex, race, color, religion, sexual orientation, or national and ethnic origin is in violation of University principle and policy.

Such conduct cannot and will not be tolerated.[3]

Some comments from the chair of the Black Student Union:

. . . These students contend that their actions were not racially motivated, but the problem is not simply their motives but the fact that these students are not sensitive enough to perceive what is and is not a racist, sexist, or homophobic action. Presently, a small group of white students had apologized and been reprimanded for their actions, but the basic problem is why white male students on this campus feel that wearing hockey masks and carrying fire is an appropriate response to minority actions. This student ignorance is a major problem.[4]

A Stanford faculty member reacts to the fact-finding report:

. . . After reading carefully the report on the Otero vigil, I and others to whom I've spoken have some serious concerns.

Perhaps most important is the following: The conduct of the vigil participants—including the "style" and "symbolic impact" and everything else about the protest—fell absolutely and totally within First Amendment protected guarantees of free speech. The participants had an absolute, unchallengeable right to do exactly what they did.

The First Amendment, and beyond that the freedom to express unpopular ideas, have to be especially important, especially treasured, and especially defended on a university campus. Educating students on this often threatened and often misunderstood issue is genuinely important—every bit as important as "combating ignorance and insensitivity in matters of racial, sexual, and sexual orientation differences." Like it or not, bigoted, homophobic or racist expressions of opinion are constitutionally protected on this campus.

I'm not defending the vigil participants; I know nothing about them, except what's in the report. But they claim they were simply, nonviolently, with total legitimacy, and using symbols often used by liberal elements on this campus, protesting a specific university action which they saw as unfair. Should not the responsibility for what ensued, or what might have ensued, be attributed as much to misperceptions, misconceptions, misapprehensions, oversensitivity, overreactions by the viewers as to anything the participants actually did?[5]

Attention soon focused on whether the seven students would be formally disciplined for violations of the university's basic code of conduct, the Fundamental Standard, which states:

Students at Stanford are expected to show both within and without the University such respect for order, morality, personal honor and the rights of others as is demanded of good citizens. Failure to do this will be sufficient cause for removal from the University.

Ultimately, the judicial affairs officer declined to prosecute the students under the Fundamental Standard, observing that the vigil participants probably did not have a monopoly on the ignorance that they displayed and that educational responses seemed more appropriate than judicial ones. The decision was controversial and is frequently revisited. The day that it was announced, however, campus papers also broke the news of trouble in Ujamaa House and attention quickly shifted to that undergraduate residence.

THE UJAMAA INCIDENT[6]

The Beethoven Conversation

In the early evening on September 29, 1988, a core of about ten Ujamaa and one Naranja house residents had a wide-ranging conversation in the main Ujamaa corridor; other residents stopped, listened, joined in for a time and moved on. At least four of the core participants were white; the remainder were black.

Freshman orientation, a major theme of which had been respect for ethnic diversity, had begun on September 22; classes began on September 28. Ujamaa is Stanford's black ethnic theme house. It has 127 residents from all four classes (65 black, 62 nonblack). Naranja is an adjacent four-class house with 65 residents (10 black, 55 nonblack).

Three participants in the conversation figure prominently in the subsequent events. Alex Burton was a freshman Ujamaa resident from Glen Ellyn, Illinois. Fred Schultz was a freshman Naranja resident. He lived in Canada from ages six to sixteen. For the two years before entering Stanford he attended an English boarding school. QC Robbins was a sophomore Ujamaa resident from the south side of Chicago. Alex and Fred are white; QC is black.

The topics of conversation that evening included black influences on music, American race relations and tribal/political differences in East Africa. The discussion was sometimes heated. Fred told us (the interviewers) that he had stopped because he saw what "looked like a debate and I like debates."

During the part of the discussion relating to black contributions to music, one of the white participants said that rap music was "violent and senseless." QC rejoined: "What about rock music? Is it violent?" He then asserted that "all music is black." QC told us that he amplified this statement by explaining that "all music listened to today in America has African origins—beats, drums and so forth." A white Ujamaa freshman challenged this statement: "What about classical music? Beethoven?" QC responded that Beethoven was black, a mulatto. Someone asked QC: "Where do you get your information?" QC responded that he had read this and was willing to provide proof. According to QC, Alex told QC to "forget it." (QC told us that he relied on two sources for his statement about Beethoven, one of which he owned and the other of which was in the Ujamaa library.)

The conversation subsequently turned to the issue of "racial purity" and a resident reportedly described herself as "pure African." Fred told us that he was "frustrated at that point and looking for something he could latch onto and win." The residents then argued about the difficulties in proving that all one's ancestors were from the same race, about current and historical definitions of black, and other aspects of this subject.

The Beethoven Poster

On the next evening, Friday, September 30th, Alex and Fred went out together. They visited a friend in a nearby residence and drank a few vodkas. They then went to a party where they had more to drink. Then they stopped at Tresidder Union and listened to music for awhile. Both told us that they were "drunk and stoned."

At some point in the evening, Alex noticed a black and white Stanford Symphony recruiting poster featuring a picture of Beethoven. Fred said, "Why don't we draw this in? Why don't we make it look like he's a black?" Fred took the poster down, folded and pocketed it. They returned to Ujamaa, went to Alex's room, where he had some crayons, and colored in the poster to make it "look like a stereotype of a black person." Fred told us that he colored the face brown; both Fred and Alex drew lines "emphasizing" the lips, and colored in "black, frizzy hair." Fred added red eyes "to give him a demonic look, because Beethoven looked demonic."

When completed, around midnight, Fred taped the defaced poster to a chalkboard which is immediately adjacent to QC's room. QC would often put sayings or notices on this board, especially quotations from and about black people. Many of the residents refer to it as QC's "food-for-thought" board.

QC found the poster on the board at about 7 A.M. on Saturday, October 1. Since he was on his way to join a cycling club trip, he simply took it down and put it in his room, not quite realizing what it was. He looked at the poster when he returned and realized that it was Beethoven. He immediately linked it to the Beethoven conversation.

Alex and Fred's Explanations for the Beethoven Poster

We asked Alex and Fred why they defaced the poster. Alex answered: "It was an emotional reaction to what it was like for me to be there [Ujamaa]. I never saw it as a bad place to live. I was learning a lot. But there were certain things about Ujamaa and certain people that didn't click . . . I had no malicious thought." He said that defacing and hanging the poster were "not thought out. I was hanging the poster because I was hanging the poster."

Alex also told us that he intended the poster as "a parody, satire, bringing forth the idea that I didn't really agree with this total concentration on being black—one quarter black makes Beethoven all black." He continued that he "knew it would evoke a reaction"; he said that he hoped that it would "reignite the discussion on the black/white distinction . . . It wasn't just Beethoven. I accepted what was being said about Beethoven. I didn't accept this black/white distinction. People were terribly caught up in it." Alex told us that defacing the poster was the result of a "lack of judgment" and "ignorance" and was "wrong."

Fred told us that he intended to make the poster image of Beethoven "look like a stereotype" of a black man: "That's why we gave him an Afro." Fred said that he "wanted to make the poster look ridiculous." He told us: "If I had really tried to draw Beethoven as a black I would not have [drawn him] as a stereotype."

Fred told us that when he and Alex defaced the poster he thought it was "tremendously funny, a witty statement." He elaborated that he was drunk and stoned and that when he drinks he "feels that all [he does] is important, relevant and right." He said that he never thought that people would be offended.

Fred also related the poster-defacing to experiences he had in England. He said that his grandfather is a German Jew. It was the custom of older students at his English school to ask new students about their weaknesses and then tease the new students about the weaknesses so the new students would not take the weaknesses so seriously. Fred had said that his "weakness" was being Jewish. The ensuing teasing included saying that "Jew means miserly" and putting a Star of David on his door. He also said that when he won arguments, the students would sometimes say "stereotypical" things about Jews in reprisal. Fred said that at first this teasing offended him, but by the time he left the school he did not take it seriously and had come to see the "humor as a release."

Fred also attributed the poster to his ignorance about the American racial situation since he had been educated in Canada and England: "The most I know about American history is the fur trade." But he also attributed it to his "arrogance and insensitivity" to others' feelings.

Reactions to the Beethoven Poster

We asked Ujamaa residents what their reactions to the defaced poster had been. QC said that his initial reaction was that he was "flabbergasted. I couldn't believe anybody would do that. . . . It's the kind of thing someone would do in their room and joke about but it didn't seem like anyone would be bold enough to put it on a door." An Ujamaa resident assistant, a senior, said the poster was "hateful, shocking. I was outraged and sickened." One of the theme associates said, "The Afro on the poster was a black stereotype. To me the red eyes had an evil connotation. No human being has eyes like that. The whole being looked very evil—devilish." But his further explanation is perhaps more illuminating of the residents' reaction to the defaced poster. He told us that the details of the poster were not important; what was important was the drawers' intent to offend by portraying a black person in a negative stereotype. Another theme associate, a sophomore, said, "Fred may have intended it as a joke but he knew, after orientation, it would piss the hell out of everyone . . . After all the programs, how could he not have known!"

Events from October 1 to October 14

Word got around among the Ujamaa staff about the defaced poster. The resident fellow and an assistant dean were informed. Opinions differed about what should be done. Some believed that "we ought to find out who did it and kick these guys out of the dorm." Others expressed more concern about the potential for negative publicity about the incident. Fred and Alex lay low, hoping it would all "blow over."

A planned meeting on October 5, with the Beethoven conversation participants, did not take place, apparently because QC and one or two of his friends who had participated in the conversation did not want to attend such a meeting. QC "was, in a sense, afraid." From past experiences he felt "the victim gets blamed" and that somehow the whole incident might "be turned against him."

At the next regular staff meeting on October 12, some argued against pursuing the matter because so much time had elapsed.

The "Niggers" Poster

Sometime on or before October 13, an Ujamaa resident hung a poster near the lounge advertising a dance at UC Berkeley, sponsored by Kappa Alpha Psi, a black fraternity. About 2:00 on the morning of Friday, October 14, he noticed the poster had fallen down. He rehung it. When he passed by a few minutes later, the poster had disappeared.

At around 2:30 A.M., QC and a friend passed a large bulletin board in the second floor crosswalk and noticed the Kappa Alpha Psi poster. Someone had scrawled the word "niggers" diagonally across it. They took the poster down, showed it to another friend and discussed whether to notify residence staff. Later that morning, when QC returned from classes, he showed the poster to a resident assistance and several of the residence staff discussed it. They decided to call an emergency house meeting for that night to discuss both the "niggers" and "Beethoven" posters.

The First Emergency House Meeting, the Identification of Fred and Alex and the Second Emergency House Meeting

About seventy-five or eighty people attended the house meeting on October 14, including Alex and QC, but not including Fred. Both posters were exhibited at the meeting which was "very intense." All of the students who spoke were clearly outraged by the posters. At some point, one of the resident assistants asked, "Does anybody want to stand up and admit to it now?"

Alex said nothing at the meeting. He told us that in his opinion the meeting was so "heated and emotional" that there was a "threat of violence" so "there was no way I was going to come forward."

Immediately after the meeting, a white Ujamaa resident told one of the theme associates that she had heard someone with an English accent say that he had defaced the Beethoven poster. The theme associate, recalling that Fred had an English accent, went to his room and asked him if he knew anything about the Beethoven poster. Fred replied that "he'd heard of it." He eventually admitted his guilt and identified Alex as the person who defaced the poster with him. He said that they were not, however, responsible for the scrawled "niggers" message.

Someone went to get Alex, and the two freshmen then met with the Ujamaa residence staff to discuss the situation. According to the resident fellow, Alex and Fred's explanations for their behavior seemed like attempts to justify or rationalize. "It didn't sell with the staff."

They discussed what Fred and Alex should do. The resident fellow told them they would have to admit to the Ujamaa community what they had done, and they would have to apologize, without trying to rationalize. An emergency house meeting for Ujamaa and Naranja residents was called for noon on Sunday, October 16. Fred and Alex were anxious for this chance to talk to the residents.

Eighty to 120 persons, including about 30 Naranja residents, crowded into the Ujamaa lounge at noon on Sunday. Alex and Fred were introduced as the persons who defaced the Beethoven poster.

Alex and Fred's Speech

Fred had suggested before the meeting, "Let me handle this. I like to speak. If only one of us speaks, maybe that's an easier way to do it." Alex agreed to this plan. Alex later told us that his agreeing to let Fred do the talking was "a big mistake."

Fred began by saying that there were "two things we want to do: . . . explain ourselves [and] hear your reaction." He continued, "I don't know if what you want is an apology. I mean 'sorry,' what the fuck does that mean, that's just a word. We know an apology won't be enough so we won't even say it."

He said he and Alex were "drunk and stoned" when they defaced the poster but this was "no excuse." He went on to say they "didn't think of themselves as racists" but that the drunken state had brought to the fore certain subconscious "things in [their] psyches," of which they had not been aware.

Fred told the crowd that he and Alex were from "multi-racial environments" where "race was not the focus of attention." He was "shocked to come [to Stanford] and find people cared so much about race." This "offended" him. He thought it was "stupid." He had been overwhelmed by the emphasis on "ethnic differences and pluralism in orientation." He spoke of his negative reaction to being "confronted" with "assertive" and "aggressive ethnicity."

Fred said that he and Alex "had got fed up with all the talk about race" and thought defacing the poster was a "good opportunity to show the black students how ridiculous it was to focus on race." He said that they had no idea that defacing the poster would be taken "seriously," that they thought of it as a "joke." He also spoke of the defaced poster as "satirical humor."

Fred offered to do a research paper on Beethoven and donate a book about Alexander Pushkin to the Ujamaa archives. He made the Pushkin offer because he had recently learned that the Russian writer had black ancestry.

An Ujamaa resident interrupted Fred's discourse with: "You arrogant bastard, how dare you come here and not even apologize. I want an apology." Fred looked toward Alex with the implied suggestion that they answer in unison. Fred responded: "Ok, 1, 2, 3, we're sorry."

Alex did not join in this remark. Immediately after Fred made it, Alex said: "I owe everyone a big apology. I hope everything can be worked out. I'm really sorry. I realize how much I hurt the house."

But the damage had been done. A resident assistant described Fred's apology, which many thought flippant, as the first "stab in the back" of the meeting. Alex's belated apology was ignored in the negative reaction that Fred's comment crystallized.

Fred told us that as soon as he made the inappropriate remark he realized that "he had lost the right to say anything else" at the meeting. In fact, Alex and Fred said little more for the remainder of the meeting.

A Summary of Subsequent Events

The Ujamaa residents with whom we spoke had extremely and consistently negative reactions to Alex and Fred's statements and manner at the meeting. One resident referred to their failure to give a sincere apology as the "big mistake"; this failure angered and surprised most of the Ujamaa residents.

Other Ujamaa residents said that when Alex and Fred spoke of their "subconscious racism" it was as if one could "feel the room heat up"; "the more they talked, the more they dug themselves into a hole"; and when they finished, it was as if a "thundercloud [was] over the room." To the Ujamaa residents, Alex and Fred seemed to be trying to "manipulate" the meeting and evade responsibility for defacing the poster with their talk of subconscious racism, drunkenness, and the impact on them of ethnicity at Stanford and the pluralism component of orientation.

The Ujamaa residents perceived Alex and Fred's attitude and "body language" as "arrogant," "insincere," "condescending," "patronizing," "not caring," and "not listening" to the black students who spoke during the discussion. Ujamaa residents were upset that Alex and Fred still did not appear to understand why they found the defacing of the poster offensive.

A white Ujamaa freshman who had not requested assignment to Ujamaa and who describes his background as "conservative," said that he first thought Alex and Fred were "sincere." But the more they talked, the more it "seemed as if they were just trying to pacify people and get it over with." He came to the Sunday meeting hoping to "see someone who recognized they had hurt" the Ujamaa residents; instead Alex and Fred's remarks made him fell "ashamed" that they were so "insensitive."

The Sunday meeting essentially disintegrated with the "1, 2, 3, we're sorry" remark. Black residents made increasingly angry and bitter statements and insisted that Alex and Fred be kicked out of their residences. A highly respected black assistant dean spoke against this reaction and was verbally attacked in return. His observation that the poster defacement was "not a big deal" compared with the racism he experienced in the 1960s was poorly received.

Then QC decided to talk, and his speech provided the emotional apex of the meeting. He described his experiences with racism at Stanford, his feelings about Fred and Alex, and his response to their comments and behavior at the meeting. He became very emotional and "choked up"; many in the room were crying. Just before the end of the meeting, QC walked toward Fred and Alex and made a violent remark to them. There are conflicting accounts about whether he then lunged at them and, if he did, whether his action was deliberate or essentially uncontrolled. There was no physical contact between the three students.

Then "all the pain broke loose." As many as sixty students were crying with varying degrees of hysteria. At least one student hyperventilated and had to be assisted in breathing. According to one resident fellow, there was "utter chaos." People were "crying, screaming," "hysterical" and "distraught." A resident assistant said "people were holding hands and crying" and "the staff was running around trying to collect people." The associate dean of student affairs, who went to the house immediately after the meeting broke up, reported that many women were sobbing, that there was "much distress, anger, and hurt."

The Naranja residents made a "mass exodus." In order to defuse the situation, Fred and Alex were promptly moved out of their residences.

There were some backlash incidents. Several white residents of Ujamaa had slipped under their doors typewritten sheets that read "NON-BLACKS LEAVE OUR HOME/YOU DO NOT BELONG IN UJAMAA." Someone punched holes in the photographs of almost all the nonblack freshmen on the welcoming picture board. In early November, a homemade sticker was found near the resident fellow's apartment which read, "AVENGE UJAAMA [sic]. SMASH THE HONKIE OPPRESSORS!" Those responsible for these acts, as well as for the "niggers" scrawl, were never identified.

SOME REACTIONS TO THE UJAMAA INCIDENT

Some students—especially those from big cities, the American South, or foreign countries torn by racial strife—were heard to wonder what the big deal was at Ujamaa and to predict that "if you can't handle a stupid poster, you'll never make it in The Real World."

A group of residential administrators asked these and other students to "pause to wonder at the term 'over-reaction,' and consider what causes someone to judge and try to invalidate the feelings of another person. How can we assess someone else's pain or grief? How can we calibrate it and decide what is just the right amount of anguish for that person to feel? On the other hand, how do we find the courage it takes to hear, accept and even empathize with another's suffering?"[7]

The university president appointed two attorneys to investigate the events of Ujamaa House and report back as soon as possible.

In January, shortly before the publication of the fact-finding report, the president released an essay entitled "Reflections on Racial Understanding." The following comments from that essay set the stage for a debate that carried well into the spring and is expected to resume in 1989–1990:

> . . . Our success [in many areas] has bred high expectations. Wherever disappointment follows, the reaction is painful, often bordering on grief. So we need to ask ourselves hard questions about our own vulnerability. Can the prospects of curricular enrichment, better management of our collective lives outside the classroom, all the other things we have talked about—can these remedies offer us immunity to incidents like the one at Ujamaa?

> I think we should not expect too much. Curricular change can broaden and deepen our understanding of difference, and of the ways in which diversity

has historically invigorated our society. It can certainly remove areas of ignorance that now promote misunderstanding. But it cannot fully protect this community, or any other, from occasional expressions of insensitivity or downright intolerance. "Ignorance is no excuse" became a well-worn phrase in the aftermath of the Ujamaa incident. That statement is true, yet unhelpful; some ignorance will survive even the best efforts at education, and it will escape in troublesome form whether we excuse it or not. Moreover, we are an open community that is characterized by rapid change, poor institutional memory, and a willingness to embrace new members at a moment's notice. It follows that some of us will always be unacquainted with the values shared by most people at Stanford. That should not discourage us.

It is worth emphasizing, in this connection, that we are dealing with a broad array of challenges and not just with affronts to the black community. Here and elsewhere, there have been counter-reactions against whites which, however understandable they may be, nonetheless represent a form of racism themselves. There has been a disturbing increase in the number of anti-Semitic expressions at universities, Stanford included. If we are to be consistent we must hold all such forms of expression to be equally unacceptable.

But what does it mean, exactly, to say that some form of expression is unacceptable? If what we mean is that most members of the community will deplore it, that leaders will speak out against it, and that those responsible will be urged to change, that is one thing. It is quite another once we begin to talk about sanctions; dismissal or suspension from the university, loss of the residential privilege, or whatever. Withdrawal of membership in the community is a penalty that requires due process and a carefully worked out balancing between the community's need for tolerance and good order and the individual's right to free expression. Freedom of speech is a powerful tradition in our society, and nowhere does it have greater or more special power than in universities, where unconventional and heterodox ideas are the very breath of life.[8]

THE FREE SPEECH DEBATE

The Ujamaa fact-finding report was released, giving its many readers a better understanding of the complexity and intensity of events during those several weeks in the fall. Then a legal analysis, "First Amendment Principles and Prosecution for Offensive Expression Under Stanford's Student Disciplinary System," was widely distributed and studied. Reviewing the characteristics of the Otero Vigil and the Ujamaa Incident in light of the university's historical commitment to First Amendment principles, the

authors presented strong arguments against university discipline in response
to either of those events.[9]

To the disappointment of some and the surprise of none, an
announcement was forthcoming that the two freshmen who defaced the
Beethoven poster would not be prosecuted under the Fundamental Standard
of student conduct. The judicial officer and the dean of student affairs
appealed to a policy-making body, the Student Conduct Legislative Council
(SCLC), to clarify the requirements of the Fundamental Standard where they
appear to conflict with the university's commitment to free expression. Thus,
after some robust criticism of the administration's unwillingness to invoke
the Fundamental Standard, campus attention and energy moved from the
judicial arena to a legislative one.

With the release of preliminary legislation by the SCLC—an effort
quickly seen to be too imprecise and broad in scope—the coast of characters
increased dramatically. The Committee for First Amendment Rights was
established overnight and collected hundreds of petition signatures, alerting
people to the dangers of the draft legislation. A computer mail file collected
hundreds of messages; dorm programs, editorials, news stories, letters to the
editor, campus radio shows—all became vehicles to involvement in the free
speech debate.

The ranks of constitutional law experts, both those with law degrees and
the self-taught, were found to represent a range of views about First
Amendment interpretations. Each debate participant, therefore, could select
and cite an expert whose testimony provided compelling support for one's
opinions.

The anti-harassment policies of other institutions also provided wide
latitude for choice—from a private university where free expression is *the*
overriding value before which everything else yields, to a state college policy
where prohibited harassment is defined to include conduct that "annoys"
another person or group. These policies are not only widely variable; those
that define and prohibit "discriminatory harassment" are also new and have
yet to face the tests of time and possible legal challenges.

The SCLC submitted for campus response a second proposed
Fundamental Standard Interpretation: Free Expression and Discriminatory
Harassment. It was widely recognized to be an improvement over the first
attempt, due in large part to the conceptual and drafting help of a member of
the Law School faculty. The author describes some of its characteristics:

> Under the proposal, it would violate the University's disciplinary code for a
> student directly and intentionally to use "fighting words" or their equivalent
> to insult someone on the basis of the characteristics ("sex, race, color,
> handicap, religion, sexual orientation, and national and ethnic origin")
> enumerated in Stanford's official non-discrimination policy. In this context,

"fighting words" are defined to include words or other symbols "commonly understood to convey, in a direct and visceral way, hatred or contempt" for people subject to pervasive discrimination on the basis of their personal characteristics. Very simply, a student would violate the standard by calling another "kike," "nigger," "faggot" and the like.

In recent years, the courts have recognized that employers must protect workers from intolerable conditions created by repeated racist or sexist insults. An employer who fails to institute reasonable disciplinary measures for dealing with a hostile work environment unlawfully discriminates against the victims of the abuse. The proposal here seeks only to bring the educator's protection of minority students to the level the law requires of employers.

Like the violence they resemble, racial epithets are not a legitimate part of the discourse at a university. They promote inarticulate rage or, worse, crushed silence, rather than free exchange and open debate. Like the defamatory and assaultive statements which they closely resemble in their individual and social consequences, "fighting words" are not protected by the First Amendment.[10]

Some critics, especially students of color, point to the requirement of the providing intent as a major problem with the second proposal because it opens a wide door for pleas of ignorance. Other concerns focus primarily on the impact of the proposed legislation. One view is that the mere presence of rules restricting expression—even narrowly defined rules—will intimidate students and chill the very discourse that the university exists to foster. A responding view is that the prohibited expression does not, in fact, promote debate and open exchange; by using a vocabulary of hatred, it angers, hurts and frequently silences its victims. A more neutral evaluation of the current proposal is that it is so narrow in scope that it may only cover offenses that would fall within the broad purview of the current Fundamental Standard.

These are empirical questions that all the eloquence in the world cannot answer in the abstract. Indeed, the questions are so complex that only with great difficulty will they be answered even empirically. The basic question is deceptively simple to state: What impact, if any, does the presence of an anti-harassment policy have upon the quantity and quality of student interactions across racial and ethnic lines?

CONCLUSION

In the area of race relations, Stanford's goals are behavioral, not environmental. In an earlier era, we articulated goals such as: "to provide a setting within which students may explore racial, sexual, and other important human differences. . . ." That goal is, of course, still important, but it is now recognized as a means to the basic goal that we really were pursuing all along: that Stanford students have positive and significant experiences with others whose racial/ethnic backgrounds are different from their own, and that they leave Stanford with the skills, the knowledge and the enthusiasm needed to contribute to the multicultural worlds that they will enter.

With respect to that basic goal, some students falter and flounder, while others thrive in the diversity of the Stanford undergraduate scene. We don't yet know what accounts for these differences, especially what environmental characteristics contribute to positive and negative outcomes. For those whose decisions shape the campus environment in significant ways, such knowledge is obviously crucial.

While we work on that research agenda, we will continue to follow several approaches that respond to common hypotheses about the major causes of racial tension and incidents on the campus.

What causes racist incidents?

- Hypothesis 1. Ignorance about races and cultures other than one's own.
- Hypothesis 2. Hostility, perhaps hatred.
- Hypothesis 3. Insensitivity and immaturity; lack of empathy.

It is likely that all three hypotheses have some truth to them; that is, any given incident is probably caused by a mixture of ignorance, malice and insensitivity. An adequate response repertory, therefore, will reflect both our limited understanding of the causes of racist incidents and the likelihood of multiple causes or motivations.

One obvious response to these hypotheses is through the academic curriculum. Confronting and correcting ignorance and its derivatives is, after all, what educational institutions are all about. As we move toward this response, however, we find that we need more and better courses about American racial and ethnic groups, as well as more faculty with the training to teach these courses.[11]

Another response to racist incidents is legislative and judicial: Prohibit the acts through the appropriate codes of conduct and then impose clear and immediate sanctions for infractions. But here, too, we confront complexity: Some acts of bigotry fall within the protection of the First Amendment and it is a delicate task to define the point at which free expression ends and harassment begins.

Orientation, residential and other nonacademic programs are probably helpful whatever the source of the problem: ignorance, hostility, or insensitivity and immaturity. These approaches recognize that eighteen to twenty-two year olds, at Stanford and elsewhere, have a lot of issues to cope with, many of them kind of scary (e.g., sex, alcohol, competition, loneliness), and that Stanford has added to their surroundings more human diversity than many of them have encountered before. Just as the other issues can be vexing, so too can diversity. Here especially, our responses to problems call for patience and optimism.

We must recognize and remember that understanding, empathy and sensitivity are *feelings*. They cannot be required, imposed, or even taught—except perhaps by example. Our job, whether in the classroom or the dormitory, is to motivate, to inspire, to encourage and to applaud. In an environment that traditionally reveres knowledge and the authority that knowledge brings, it is both ironic and humbling to admit that knowledge alone cannot make people care about other people.

As we become more analytic in evaluating our several approaches to improving race relations on campus, it is important to note that although we have a stated goal, it is not one that will ever be "achieved" in a statistical sense. That is, nowhere do our policies identify a point at which "enough" interracial understanding has occurred. Like achieving "enough" honesty, or happiness, or world peace, or good health, the very concept is elusive. Some goals can only be approached—and our measurements must be of relative progress rather than attainment.

Whatever our goals, hypotheses and approaches, we risk the whole enterprise if we ignore a group of students that generally chooses to be silent. One of these students, Stanford class of 1989, volunteered this comment in the annual senior survey:

> I have become quite worn down by Stanford's efforts at "social engineering"—i.e., controlling the ethnic mix of certain dorms, trying to create more sensitive, "pluralist" citizens. . . . Stanford is trying too hard. I have begun to feel threatened. I was once considered sensitive and liberal. The climate now is hypersensitive. I don't feel liberal enough. Insignificant acts have become multicultural tests of sensitivity. . . . I fear that if others become worn down as I am, they will be too annoyed with the trivialization of sensitivity to apply it after they leave.

Stanford's president generalizes this student's concern when he describes two forms of "backlash" that "threaten our success in achieving better racial understanding":

> The first, which might be called *hard* backlash, comes mainly from those who are seizing the racism-on-campus issue as an opportunity to advance the view that too much has already been done for minorities. It has tones of bitterness and anger, and it can be deeply disturbing. But it is not hard to recognize, and even easier to reject. Thus it poses a far less serious threat than a softer, subtler form of backlash: the disaffection of those who have believed in and have fought for equal opportunity and full minority

participation. Too many of them, I fear, are concluding that they aren't wanted, and that they should expend their energies for social improvement in other ways. That would be a tragedy; we need them, and we won't have them unless . . . they can be made to feel part of the solution instead of treated as part of the problem.[12]

As we react to problems, debate solutions and study outcomes, we encounter at every turn more questions and fewer answers. One thing, at least, is clear: To recruit, enroll and graduate a diverse student population is only a beginning, albeit an essential one. The educational opportunities—and obligations—that follow test an institution's commitment, energy, resources and imagination in profound and enduring ways.

NOTES

1. Donald Kennedy, "Reflections on Racial Understanding," January 1989, Office of the President, Stanford University.

2. "When Fundamental Values Conflict," Stanford Cases in Student Affairs Administration (November 1988), pp. 1–5, Judicial Affairs Office, Stanford University.

3. Ibid., pp. 6–7.

4. Ibid., pp. 10–11.

5. Ibid., pp. 12–13.

6. "Final Report on Incident at Ujamaa House," *Campus Report* (January 18, 1989), pp. 15–18. Edited with permission. The original report was written by Jasper Williams and Thomas F. McBride.

7. Norman W. Robinson and others, "Letter to the Editor," *Stanford Daily,* October 18, 1988.

8. Kennedy, "Reflections."

9. John J. Schwartz and Iris Brest, "First Amendment Principles and Prosecution for Offensive Expression Under Stanford's Student Disciplinary System," (no date), Office of the Vice President and General Counsel, Stanford University.

10. Thomas C. Grey, "Letter to the Editor," *Campus Report,* May 10, 1989, p. 6.

11. See, for example, the data and recommendations concerning the undergraduate curriculum in the "Final Report of the University Committee on Minority Issues," Stanford University, March 1989, pp. 5–18.

12. Kennedy, "Reflections."

LEONARD GORDON

Chapter Thirteen

Race Relations and Attitudes at Arizona State University

In the spring 1989 semester, Arizona State University (ASU) took another, if unwanted, step toward major university status beyond its substantial research and NCAA athletic developments over the past three decades. An article in the *New York Times* reported on university-based racial conflict incidents at several universities.[1] Among the racially conflicted universities explicitly discussed were Michigan, Stanford, Wisconsin and Arizona State. The article went on to note that over one hundred racial conflict incidents had occurred at American universities in recent years, encompassing every region in the nation.

In this context the racial conflict which occurred at Arizona State University has larger implications. At issue are interracial relations in the American university system and the implications this has for the larger society. To assess the specific campus situation at ASU and its broader implications, this essay has three interrelated parts:

First, the precipitating black and white violent incident and mass protest are described. The spring 1989 interracial melee and subsequent black-student–led protest aroused widespread public and mass media attention and an ongoing need to address a strained interracial campus climate.

Second, the cumulative campus racial strains that had been building up for a period of years leading toward open conflict, are explored. Presented here are multiple expressions by black students about insensitive, prejudicial and discriminatory experiences they have had on campus and the rising hostile stereotyping of blacks by white students. In this context it is understandable how a Saturday evening altercation between a few black and white students could precipitate a mass melee and protest involving hundreds of students. Discussed in this part are the broader implications of increased hostile racial stereotyping at ASU and on other college campuses.

Third, conflict resolution policy issues are addressed respecting the open campus racial conflict and the cumulative strains built up in recent years. As effective policies are dependent on the receptivity of blacks and whites on campus, considered in this part is the question of whether there has been a long-term black-white student accommodating shift away from racism of three or more decades ago. Even with the recent rise in hostilities at ASU and on many other campuses, it does appear to be the case that most students, including the majority whites, do value positive acceptance and accommodation. For that reason, the specifically formulated policies at Arizona State, if effectively implemented, have a good prospect of being accepted with positive implications for other college campuses.

First, let us consider what happened at ASU.

THE PRECIPITATING INCIDENT AND PROTEST RESPONSE

On a warm spring Saturday evening, several Sigma Alpha Epsilon Fraternity members mistakenly identified three passing black students as those who had been involved in an earlier verbal and physical altercation between one of the fraternity members and a white female student a few days earlier.[2] After misidentifying the passing black students, several fraternity members shouted racial epithets, including "nigger" and "porch monkeys," and some spat at them. Within minutes on this partying Saturday evening there were upwards of five hundred fraternity members and friends in the street. Police arrived and arrested the three identified blacks and a white friend with them, reportedly handcuffing two of the black students and macing one. When it became clear to the police that the black students were the recipients rather than the perpetrators of the violent confrontation, they were released on the university campus, away from the fraternity house. In a subsequent investigation eleven white students were cited for disorderly conduct misdemeanor offenses.

This incident resulted in extensive news coverage on and off campus. There was much discussion among black students and other students who empathized with them.[3] Reflecting this high level of student concern, within a week of the racial melee black-student–led protest activity developed. Along with the Black Student Union (BSU) there emerged an activist protest group of black, Hispanic and white students called Students Against Racism (SAR). Within a week the BSU and SAR had organized a protest rally and march, estimated by observers to be between two hundred and fifty and six hundred people strong. The protest strategy centered on a sit-in blockage of the main entrance to the Student Union. Black student protest leadership developed a set of twelve demands which were presented to the university president, J. Russell Nelson, and the board of regents president, Herman Chanin.

Technically the students were breaking the law. The university president and the regents president's decision to meet with the protesting students, rather than to call in more police or the national guard, was an important step in reducing the likelihood of violence. By coming out to meet the students in their mass sit-in a dialogue was established. In a tense campus atmosphere, both the university and regents presidents held public and private meetings with BSU and SAR students and representatives. The student representatives included BSU President Tracy Bernard Jones and SAR black leaders Vernard Bonner and Tanya Holms. Tanya Holms appeared on the local public television station beamed out of the campus with sociology chair Leonard Gordon to discuss the nature of the conflict and policy issues designed to resolve most of the campus racial conflict. These meetings and communications appeared to play a substantial role in precluding an escalation in open black-white student confrontation. Legitimacy was being provided publicly by both black representatives and university representatives to the idea of working out a new set of positive formal and informal relationships and programs on campus. The discussions centered on the list of twelve demands formulated by the BSU and SAR.

Of the twelve SAR-formulated demands a few were agreed to immediately by the university and regents presidents. Included was agreement to more effectively implement a twenty-one–point plan which had been developed the prior year by the administration. That plan was designed to promote enrollment, graduation success and the hiring of minorities. It was agreed that the demands would be considered in depth, and that more sanctions would be imposed against those involved in interracial violence, but there were academic freedom and First Amendment reservations about expulsionary demands respecting those who use verbal racial slurs.

CUMULATIVE CAMPUS RACIAL STRAINS

A common theme in theories of collective conflict and protest is that a precipitating conflict incident will not, in itself, generate a general collective reaction unless a socially combustible situation has developed over time.[4] As such, the fraternity-house precipitating incident on the ASU campus would, by itself, not in all likelihood have generated a protest march and sit-in. As with the urban racial riots in the 1960s, and organized as well as unorganized sit-ins, riots, and related actions of those years, precipitating incidents which led to those racial conflict outcomes were a consequence of cumulative interracial strains.[5]

Such cumulative interracial strains were evident at ASU over a long period. As early as the late 1960s the university had begun to encourage more black and Hispanic students to enter. They did, but as a consequence of the low income, educationally disadvantaged backgrounds they often came from, black and Hispanics students tended to socialize primarily or exclusively with other black, or other Hispanic, students, most of whom were dropping out. One student demonstrated that as many of the black, and Hispanic, student drop outs were a consequence of social isolation as were those who dropped out for academic reasons.[6] This isolation and high attrition rate tended to increase black and Hispanic students alienation on campus and to rationalize the growing negative stereotyping of white Anglo students toward minority students.

The racial brawl was an open manifestation of this growing strained campus context. As one student sit-in participant noted: "This [the fraternity house incident] was the last straw. I think we have to do something now, or this will just continue."[7] The cumulative strains referred to involved a series of incidents which circulated within the black student community. Included were racial slurs such as "nigger" directed toward black students in varying public settings and a "slave sale" fraternity fund-raising party. A few days following the incident by the fraternity house a white student entered his justice studies classroom and confronted three black students with a gun, giving a presentation with the gun before being arrested by campus police.[8]

These tension-provoking incidents are reminiscent of those occurring at other universities which have experienced open interracial conflicts. In the three years between 1986 and 1989 Howard Ehrlich, director of the National Institute Against Prejudice and Violence, reported documentation on 175 racial conflict incidents at American universities.[9] The incidents are also a reflection of a changing campus interracial climate at ASU and on many other campuses. As Ehrlich observed, this new campus climate has resulted in "[t]he kind of permission that people feel they have now to act out these racial hostilities openly."[10]

The Changing Race Relations Campus Climate at ASU and Other Campuses

Evidence of racial conflict generating changes in student attitudes is available at ASU and at other universities. Racial and ethnic stereotyping studies were conducted at ASU in 1969 and in 1982. Employing an extended version of the Katz and Braly Princeton University study of 1932,[11] replicated at Princeton by Gilbert in 1950,[12] random samples of ASU students, in the 1969 and 1982 survey studies, completed an eighty-four trait list questionnaire involving a variety of positive and negative character traits.

The survey results provide insights into the overt outbreak of racial conflict at ASU and other campuses. This broader American university meaning is evidenced in a number of ways. First, there is extensive evidence of the generalizeability of independent random samples drawn at American universities,[13] including similar stereotypical findings in independently drawn samples at ASU and at Princeton in the late 1960s.[14] Second, internal reliability of data results, with the leading traits assigned to white "Americans" are generally stable in studies spanning the half century. The traits "intelligent," "industrious," and "materialistic"—all positive in American cultural terms—were the top three selected traits in the samples drawn in 1932, 1950, 1969 and 1982. While this stability in positive perceptions toward white Americans generally persisted over the half-century period, significant change was evident in trait selections for blacks as well as for other minority status groups.[15] The changes with respect to the perceptions of blacks were particularly evident in the decline of hostile traits such as "superstitious," which was selected by 84 percent of the students in 1932 but only 10 percent by 1969, and "lazy," selected by 75 percent of the student in 1932 and 18 percent in 1969.

The 1932, 1950 and 1969 results, as seen in table 2, show a straight line decline in negative stereotypes. However, this did not continue into the 1982 study. Instead, new patterns emerged that relate to increasingly racial campus tensions which broke out in the mid- and late 1980s. These patterns were not all negative in interracial terms but were rather a complex of perceptions which included new or renewed hostile ones.

Three major patterns were (1) a new trait selection range, (2) a continued relatively low level of overall trait selections, and (3) a mixed selection of positive and negative trait perceptions of blacks.[16] The campus interracial relations implications can be seen in the nature of each of these patterns.

New Trait Selection Range. For Americans generally, who remain predominantly white Protestant,[17] marked stability was shown respecting the leading trait perceptions across the half century of reported studies. While some new top-ranked trait perceptions appeared for white Americans generally in 1982, the three leading traits remained the same in all four studies, including "industrious," "intelligent," and "materialistic." Further, in 1982, six of the top ten traits were the same as those selected in 1932.

This stability of perceptions was not the case for blacks. A majority of

TABLE 1

Trait Perceptions of White Americans (generally)
(By Percentage and Rank Order of Student Selections)

Trait	1932[1] %–Rank	1950[2] %–Rank	1969[3] %–Rank	1982[4] %–Rank
Industrious	48–1	30–3	32–3	28–3
Intelligent	47–2	32–2	33–2	39–1
Materialistic	33–3	37–1	44–1	33–2
Abitious	33–3	21–6	17–6	12–8
Progressive	27–5	5–10	9	6
Pleasure-loving	26–6	27–4	18–5	10–10
Alert	23–7	7–9	6	4
Efficient	21–8	9–7	2	1
Aggressive	20–9	8–8	10–9	15–6
Straightforward	19–10	–	1	1
Practical	19–10	–	1	2
Sportsmanlike	19–10	–	1	1
Individualistic	–	26–5	8	16–4
Scientifically minded	–	–	19–4	16–4
Sophisticated	–	–	10–9	13–7
Imaginative	–	–	16–7	12–8

NOTE: For probability significance levels see Gordon (1986), p. 202.
[1] Princeton University sample, n = 100. See Katz and Braly (1933).
[2] Princeton University sample, n = 333. See Gilbert (1951).
[3] Arizona State University sample, n = 459. See Gordon (1973).
[4] Arizona State University sample, n = 139. See Gordon (1986).

seven new trait perceptions toward blacks appeared in 1982 among the highest ten ranked trait perceptions. Only the negative trait perception of "lazy" remained in the top three perceptions.

Continued Low Level of Overall Trait Selections. The stereotypical perceptions of white Americans generally and of blacks, as well as of all other groups, showed a general significant decline by the 1969 study. While substantively important changes occurred in the 1982 study, this basic pattern of lowered general stereotyping continued. By 1982 top-ranked trait perceptions, whether positive or negative, constituted a much lower percentage of student selections, e.g., 48 to 28 percent for the "industrious" view of white Americans and 84 to 9 percent for the "superstitious" view of blacks.

The Mixed Recent Pattern. Consistent trait characterizations of white Americans generally was positive and admirable in American cultural value terms,[18] including, as noted, the top three selections in all four studies over the half-century period: "intelligent," "industrious" and "materialistic." In contrast, for blacks there has been a more modified and expanded set of trait

TABLE 2

Trait Perceptions of Blacks
(By Percentage and Rank Order of Student Selections)

Trait	1932[1] %–Rank	1950[2] %–Rank	1969[3] %–Rank	1982[4] %–Rank
Superstitious	84–1	42–1	10–6	9–10
Lazy	75–2	32–3	18–2	18–1
Happy-go-lucky	39–3	17–6	5	1
Ignorant	38–4	24–4	8–9	9–10
Musical	26–5	33–2	25–1	11–5
Ostentatious	26–5	11–8	14–3	10–8
Very religious	24–7	17–6	5	1
Stupid	22–8	10–9	2	1
Physically dirty	17–9	—	1	1
Naive	14–10	—	0	0
Sly	—	—	1	15–2
Aggressive	—	—	6	13–3
Intelligent	—	—	13–4	13–3
Loud	—	—	9–8	11–5
Materialistic	—	—	8–9	11–5
Arrogant	—	—	1	10–8
Sportsmanlike	—	—	6	9–10
Unreliable	—	—	10–6	6
Pleasure-loving	—	19–5	12–5	4
Sensitive	—	—	8–9	4

NOTE: For probability significance levels see Gordon (1986), p. 202.
[1] Princeton University sample, n = 100. See Katz and Braly (1933).
[2] Princeton University sample, n = 333. See Gilbert (1951).
[3] Arizona State University sample, n = 459. See Gordon (1973).
[4] Arizona State University sample, n = 139. See Gordon (1986).

perceptions. While positive traits perceptions also appeared, the old trait perceptions also remained. The old hostile trait perceptions toward blacks as "lazy" (18 percent) and "superstitious" (9 percent) remained among the top ten selected. New highly ranked negative trait perceptions of blacks also appeared, including "sly" and "arrogant." This more negative constellation of trait perceptions was in the context of generally more negative perceptions of racial and ethnic groups in the 1982 study compared to the results of the 1969 study. For example, in other surveys, the Irish were highly ranked as "quick-tempered," Japanese and Jews as "sly," and Chinese as "superstitious."

By these results, the campus intergroup climate in the early 1980s was more problematical than was the case in the late 1960s, when Vietnam War tensions were high but cut across racial and ethnic lines.[19] This climate provided the context in which overt interracial conflict occurred later in the

1980s at ASU. This conflict at ASU reflects a larger pattern of racial conflict on American university campuses.

The Broader Implications of Increased Hostile Racial Stereotyping

The stereotyping trend results by the 1980s provide a basis for documenting increased interracial college campus estrangement of white students from black students compared to the 1960s. The 1982 results still do not come close to the much higher levels of negative perceptions of blacks evident in the 1932 and 1950 studies, which correspond to parallel stereotyping and related social distance studies.[20] Yet, these earlier much higher levels of hostile racial stereotyping, thirty, forty and fifty years ago, did not lead to the kind of overt interracial conflict on college campuses widely evident in the mid- and late 1980s.

Why this is so is related to the increasing importance of college education in our modern cybernetic economy. As Harvard sociologist David Riesman observed about the post–World War II mid-century period, American society has become a credentials society.[21] The high general public concern with effective college and university education for the future stability and growth of the society is evidenced from such national reports in 1985 as the Association of American Colleges' *Integrity in the College Curriculum,* the National Institute of Education's *Involvement in Learning: Realizing the Potential of American Higher Education,* and the earlier, 1983, United States Department of Education's *A Nation at Risk* report.

These reports were made in a context of sharply increasing numbers of high school graduates of all races and ethnic groups going on to college. The over forty-three thousand students at ASU at the time of the spring 1989 racial conflict incidents is a reflection of this growth. Overall, the national reports indicated that the increased numbers of college students had outpaced governmental and private support of colleges needed to effectively meet the academic requirements of the mass of new students.[22]

This expansion of the American college and university system was a fundamental break from the historical pattern of American colleges having student bodies of overwhelmingly white Protestant males. This traditionally delimited college student body has changed rapidly and extensively. As the national reports document, many more white Protestant males from a broader social class range are now going on to college and being joined on college campuses by sharply increased numbers of black students, other racial and ethnic students as well as women.

This expanded and newly diverse American college student body, including ASUs, is a reflection of what colleges and universities now mean. Mass higher education has now become so central an avenue for maintenance of stable social position and socioeconomic mobility that the conditions of equality and inequality at this level of education is of extensive concern to the majority of whites, blacks and others. In this context, it is not surprising to see increased competition and interracial tension on many American college campuses.

Such a campus situation is inherently unstable. The continuing high demand for college education among white students and the growing demand for college education among black and other minority students ensures that black, white, and many other ethnic students, will increasingly interact on campuses in the future. A stable and productive collegiate environment is a prerequisite condition for both black and white students if they are to attain their educational goals. If such a collegiate environment is to be established and maintained, then effective campus policies need to be established. It is to a consideration of such policy issues and policy programs we now turn.

CONFLICT RESOLUTION POLICY ISSUES

The historic pattern of interracial tension and conflict is that it creates an inherently unstable situation for all concerned. In this case, black and white students will be increasingly adversely affected unless campus policies and practices are instituted which reduce or end interracial conflict and move Arizona State and other campuses toward productive accommodation. Such accommodation is needed to enable students across racial, ethnic and religious group identity lines, to maximize their ability to succeed at college and go on to stable and productive lives in the general society. The initial question respecting effective policy formation is whether or not students generally are receptive to accommodating changes on campus.

The Question of a Long-Term Accommodating Shift

As the ability to successfully achieve the accommodation goal is related to the general interracial orientation of most college students, an initial assessment of the stereotyping trend is useful. A central issue is whether the 1982 survey findings constitute a fundamental reversal of the long-term shift between the 1930s and 1960s toward interracial acceptance and accommodation, or a return to the long history of racism and hostile exclusion of blacks and other minorities. We know from the 1982 stereotyping results at Arizona State, and from related other campus studies cited, that there has been a rise in hostile stereotypes toward blacks. Further, although not cited in tabular form, there is also evidence that black students tend to parallel the trend among white students. There was a concurrent rise in negative stereotyping on the part of black students toward whites. This is less consequential in generating open conflict given the large campus majority of white students at ASU, as at most other large universities, but this also adds to the strained campus climate.

An overall trend assessment provides a basis for the prospects of developing accommodating policies which could be effectively implemented. Even with the rise in negative stereotyping by 1982 compared to 1969 (which was a precursor of the campus racial conflict incidents later in the 1980s), the levels of hostile perceptions were far below those evident in the 1932 and 1950 studies. Note in table 2 that the highest proportion of students selecting a negative trait toward blacks in 1982 (18 percent for "lazy"), was a small fraction of the 75 percent selecting that trait in 1932 or the 32 percent selecting the trait in 1950. The highest level attained for new hostile traits (15 percent for "sly") was also far below the high proportion of 84 percent in 1932 and 42 percent in 1950 selecting "superstitious" as a trait of blacks.

What further appears to support the long-term accommodating shift perspective is the emergence of overlapping positive trait perceptions as seen of Americans generally. The highly ranked view of blacks as "intelligent" and "sportsmanlike" is part of a context where other minority status groups—including Chinese, Japanese and Jews—also were seen to have such positive traits mixed with negative ones. A number of interracial assessments hold to the view that, for all the evident strain and conflict, there is a predominant emergent value perspective which rejects racism and accepts the American egalitarian creed in race relations.[23] This value trend becomes important with respect to accommodating policy prospects because it is well documented that the self-fulfilling prophecy for minorities of low academic achievement is often related to hostile stereotypes blacks and other students experience.[24]

Formulating Practical Policies

Policies to resolve interracial campus conflict at Arizona State took a sharp formulation and action turn following the spring 1989 racial brawl and protest demonstrations. As at Michigan, Stanford, Wisconsin and many other campuses, policy initiatives came from protest leaders.

In the heat of the racial conflict a number of policy proposals focused upon the immediate situation. The university president and other administrators and faculty senate representatives concurred on the point of having an independent investigation of "the ASU Police Department's actions in the April 14–16 brawls that took place on 'fraternity row.' Specifically, the investigation should focus on charges of policy brutality and unlawful detention of minority students involved."[25]

Some other issues in the immediate aftermath of the conflict raised administrative and faculty concerns about freedom of speech and academic freedom of expression issues. One protest policy point was that there be: "Revision of the ASU code of conduct to make racial slurs and racial violence grounds for expulsion."[26] Further, it was proposed that any ASU students involved in racial slurs during the April 14 to 16 brawls be expelled, although the ASU code of conduct had not yet been changed. There was initial agreement respecting the issue of "racial violence," but concern about expulsion for verbal expression of "racial slurs." A leading metropolitan paper reflected the administration and faculty caution in an editorial which noted:

> Aside from the inherent problem of defining [verbal] harassment, vilification and intolerance—is the racial hatred preached by [black] Louis Farrakhan and Angela Davis any worse than that of skin-head neo-Nazis?—the proposed limits on freedom of expression, no matter how well meaning, should raise caution flags.[27]

The conflict in civil rights and civil liberties on this verbal harassment policy approach was explored nationally in the *New York Times*. The conflict in principles was sharply raised in discussing similar restrictive policy proposals at other universities including Massachusetts, Michigan, Wisconsin and Stanford. A black Stanford student, a member of Stanford's Council of Student Presidents, was quoted as saying, "We don't put as many restrictions on freedom of speech as we should . . ."[28] In response, a constitutional law professor at Stanford took the Jeffersonian position that, "More speech, not less, is the proper cure for offense. . . ."[29] This latter view reflected established faculty perspectives on open expression at ASU, as on other campuses.

Less immediate contentions at ASU were the other policy proposals put forth by the ASU Black Student Union and the emergent interracial protest group of Students Against Racism. These were:

- Creation of an independent body by the ASU student government to oversee investigations done by ASUs offices of student life, residence life and the ASU Police Department.
- Revision of the ASU code of conduct to make racial violence grounds for expulsion.
- Mandatory participation in an anti-racism program for all fraternity members.
- Mandatory training for all ASU police officers on how to control and defuse racial incidents.
- Continuation of a twenty-one–point plan launched the prior year by the administration to promote the enrollment, graduation and hiring of minorities.
- Commitment of more money for minority programs.

- Establishment of a civilian review board to screen all potential appointments in the ASU Police Department.[30]

Administrative, faculty senate, Black Student Union and Students Against Racism discussions and negotiations continued beyond the spring 1989 semester. By early summer the black student representatives of BSU and SAR agreed to a revised list of demands which a SAR spokesperson characterized as ". . . successful on all points. It is not a watered-down version. It was what we wanted to accomplish."[31] The agreement, signed by the university president, provost and regents president, called for immediate changes on several points and gave the university until January 1990 to report on progress respecting other points. The agreement included the following seven provisions:

1. That the administration work with the faculty senate to propose requiring coursework about "ethnicity in the Americas" as part of the general (undergraduate) studies program by 1990–91
2. That sections of the code of conduct be amended to include language prohibiting racial and sexual harassment and violence and that anyone found guilty of code of conduct violations be subject to sanctions (note: this modified the earlier generic reference to racial slurs and automatic expulsion, as discussed earlier)
3. That all administrative staff be required to attend a racial sensitivity workshop within one year of employment
4. That a body of three community leaders unaffiliated with the university investigate the racial incidents and issue a report on its findings
5. That the Department of Public Safety director form a committee to study the possibility of establishing a police disciplinary review process and make improvements by the 1990–91 academic year
6. That the vice president for student affairs prepare an annual report on the status and treatment of minority students at ASU; and
7. That a committee representing diverse members of the university community be appointed to study the creation of a Campus Environment Team to help prevent instances of racial, sexual, religious or political intolerance at ASU.[32]

Additionally, the negotiations resulted in agreement to put more resources behind a twenty-one–point "Action Now" plan to address "the concern for underrepresentation of minorities on campus, especially as students and faculty."[33] The "Action Now" plan included minority student outreach high school programs, more aggressive graduate student and faculty recruitment of blacks, Hispanics, Native Americans and other minorities, and an annual student-staff-faculty survey to identify and assess unaddressed or emergent policy and program needs in this intergroup area of concern.

The likelihood of success of these policy initiatives in reducing interracial tensions and establishing a more productive interracial campus setting does not rest on any one of these measures. Rather, there is evidence to indicate that success will be related to cumulative effects of these various short- and long-term policies and programs.

In reviewing major studies on successful school racial integration nationally in elementary and secondary schools, sociologist Edith King observed that a number of program techniques were implemented including interracial extracurricular activities, efforts to change teacher attitudes and out-of-classroom academic assistance, among many others. King noted that there was little influence in respect to any one technique. Rather, successful interracial academic and social outcomes were a consequence of "the cumulative effect of these various social factors."[34] While far less interracial programming or reported research is available on colleges, compared to elementary and secondary schools, it is a reasonable expectation that multiple programs will need to be operating effectively to change the campus interracial strains that have widely developed.

Some other universities began earlier than ASU to address the problem of interracial campus conflict. Two are Texas A&M and the University of Texas at Austin. Their experiences may provide insight into the new ASU, as well as other campus, programs. Reported in the major higher education publication, *The Chronicle of Higher Education,* is the establishment at these two large state universities of minority outreach centers around Texas to counsel junior high and high school students about preparing for entry into college.[35] Funds were established for special summer orientation sessions for entering minority students, who also have the opportunity of being assigned to faculty mentors.

Such a program and related efforts to successfully bring into the university student body more blacks, Hispanics and other minority students, can be expected to draw opposition. This is what has occurred in Texas. A conservative University of Texas at Austin student newspaper, the *Review,* took the editorial position that programs designed to bring in and academically assist black and Hispanic students were a form of reverse discrimination toward whites. Yet, the university's vice president for student affairs reported that "she has not seen widespread resentment over minority recruitment and retention programs."[36]

This latter observation supports the long-term racial and ethnic stereotyping trends discussed earlier. Most college students at ASU and at most other campuses appear ready to accept viable racial and ethnic pluralism on campus and the programs needed to make that occur.

NOTES

1. Joseph Berger, "Campus Racial Strains Show Two Perspectives on Inequality," *New York Times,* May 22, 1989, pp. 1–2.

2. The following account of the precipitating incident draws on: Berger, "Campus Racial Strains"; Betty Bear, "Racism Persists in U.S. and Valley, Majority in Poll Agrees," *Arizona Republic,* June 12, 1989, pp. 1, 3; Mike Burgess, "Officials to Discuss Plan Against Racism," *ASU State Press,* April 24, 1989, pp. 1, 6; Michael Lacey, "Events of Deadly Relevance: An Armed Stand-Off at ASU," *New Times,* May 3, 1989, pp. 5–6; and Mary Jo Pitzl, "ASU Students Hold Sit-In, Gain Vow of Officials to Work on Anti-Bias Goals," *Arizona Republic,* April 22, 1989, pp. 1, 7.

3. Kelly Pearce, "ASU, Fraternity Must Both Learn from Racial Incidents," *ASU State Press,* June 22, 1989, p. 4.

4. E.g., see: Neil Smelser, *Theory of Collective Behavior* (New York: Free Press, 1962) or Ralph H. Turner and Lewis M. Killian, *Collective Behavior* (Englewood Cliffs, NJ: Prentice-Hall, 1987).

5. *Report of the National Advisory Commission on Civil Disorders* (Washington, DC: Government Printing Office, 1968).

6. Leonard Gordon and John W. Hudson, "College Student Attrition and the Counseling Factor," *ASU Public Affairs Bulletin* 10, no. 2 (1971): 1–3.

7. Pitzl, "ASU Students," p. 7.

8. Lacey, "Events of Deadly Relevance."

9. Denise K. Magner, "Blacks and Whites on the Campuses: Behind Ugly Racist Incidents, Student Isolation and Insensitivity," *Chronicle of Higher Education* 35 (April 26, 1989): A28–A32.

10. Quoted in Ibid., p. A28.

11. David Katz and Kenneth Braly, "Racial Stereotypes of One Hundred College Students," *Journal of Abnormal and Social Psychology* 28 (1933): 280–290.

12. G. M. Gilbert, "Stereotype Persistence and Change Among College Students," *Journal of Abnormal and Social Psychology* 46 (1951): 245–254.

13. J. P. Guilford, "Racial Preferences of a Thousand American University Students," *Journal of Social Psychology* 2 (1931): 179–204; Eugene Hartley, *Problems in Prejudice* (New York: King's Crown Press, 1946), p. 23; and John W. Hudson and L. Henze, "Campus Values in Mate Selection: A Replication," *Journal of Marriage and the Family* 31 (1969): 772.

14. Leonard Gordon, "The Fragmentization of Literary Stereotypes of Jews and of Negroes Among College Students," *Pacific Sociological Review* 16 (1973): 411–425; Marin Karlins, Thomas Coffman and Gary Walters, "On the Fading of Social Stereotypes: Studies in Three Generations of College Students," *Journal of Personality and Social Psychology* 13 (1969): 1–16.

15. Leonard Gordon, "College Student Stereotypes of Blacks and Jews on Two

Campuses: Four Studies Spanning Fifty Years," *Sociology and Social Research* 70 (1986): 201–202; Karlins et al. "Fading of Social Stereotypes."

16. Gordon, "College Student Stereotypes"; Karlins et al., "Fading of Social Stereotypes."

17. Alexander W. Astin, *Minorities in Higher Education: Recent Trends, Current Prospects, and Recommendations* (San Francisco: Jossey-Bass, 1982), pp. 174–175.

18. Robin Williams, *American Society* (New York: Knopf, 1970), pp. 501–502.

19. Todd Gitlin, *The Sixties: Years of Hope, Days of Rage* (New York: Bantam Books, 1987), pp. 261–282.

20. Emory J. Bogardus, "Comparing Racial Distance in Ethiopia, South Africa, and the United States," *Sociology and Social Research* 52 (1968): 149–156; Otis D. Duncan, "Recent Cohorts Lead Rejection of Sex Typing," *Sex Roles* 8 (1982): 127–133; Karlins et al., "Fading of Social Stereotypes."

21. David Riesman, *Constraints and Variety in American Education* (Lincoln: University of Nebraska Press, 1956).

22. Also see Dwight Lang, "Education Stratification and the Academic Hierarchy," *Research in Higher Education* 21 (1984): 329–352.

23. Leonard Gordon, "Racial and Ethnic Collegiate Stereotyping Findings Over a Half Century: Assessing the Long Term Shift and Secular Trend Interpretations" (Paper delivered at the American Sociological Association Annual Meeting in San Francisco, August 1989); Stephen Steinberg, *The Ethnic Myth: Race, Ethnicity, and Class in America* (New York: Atheneum, 1981); and William J. Wilson, *The Declining Significance of Race* (Chicago: University of Chicago Press, 1978). For a contrary view see: Charles V. Willie, "The Inclining Significance of Race," *Society* (July-August 1978), pp. 10–15.

24. Robert Rosenthal and Lenore Jacobson, *Pygmalian in the Classroom* (New York: Holt, Rinehart and Winston, 1968).

25. Pitzl, "ASU Students," p. 42.

26. "Racism on Campus: Tolerating Intolerance," *Arizona Republic,* June 7, 1989, p. A14.

27. Felicity Barringer, "Free Speech and Insults on Campus," *New York Times,* April 25, 1989, p. A11.

28. Ibid.

29. Pitzl, "ASU Students," p. A2.

30. Rochelle Mackey Cole, "Protests Results in Anti-Racism Agreement," *Arizona State Alumni* (Summer 1989), p. 6.

31. Ibid.

32. "First Phase of Action Now Successful, 10 Points Completed, Others in Motion," *Action Now* (Arizona State University) 1, no. 1 (Spring 1989): 1.

33. Ibid.

34. Edith King, "Recent Experimental Strategies for Prejudice Reduction in American Schools and Classrooms," *Journal of Curriculum Studies* 18 (1986): 331–338.

35. Magner, "Blacks and Whites on the Campuses," p. A31.

36. Cole, "Anti-Racism Agreement," p. 7.

WILLIAM D. GUROWITZ

Chapter Fourteen

Cornell Twenty Years Later

It is noon, April 19, 1989. Willard Straight Hall, the central student union on the Cornell campus, normally a bustling place with hundreds of students going in and out, sits closed, dark, silent. Only a few students walk by. A small group of staff members stand on the plaza in front of "the Straight" chatting amongst themselves and with an alumnus. After a few moments, the alumnus gets up on a low stone wall and starts to address the few onlookers, speaking as if there were hundreds of students on the plaza. He starts telling what it was like twenty years ago when he, as a leader of the Students for a Democratic Society (SDS), addressed hundreds of students on that same plaza while over one hundred black students were inside the Straight, having taken it over in the early hours of that morning. He tells of the hundreds of deputy sheriffs gathering in a downtown parking lot, ready to come to campus. He tells of the reasons for the takeover of the Straight by the black students and of the support by the SDS.

Then and now, same person, same place, same perspective. Have things changed? Then there were hundreds of students, now almost none. Then the building was occupied by more than one hundred black students, now it stands empty and silent. Then the campus had a small number of minority students, almost all black. Now almost one in five students is a minority, with approximately equal numbers of black and Hispanic students and a larger number of Asian-American students. The number of American Indian students has grown but is still small.

Have things changed? Is Cornell a better place because of the Straight

249

takeover with the famous photo of black students leaving with rifles in hand
and bandoliers over their shoulders? Is Cornell a leader or follower in
ensuring educational opportunity to minority students on the same basis as
white students? First, let us look at the academic, political and social
environment in 1969.

To say the times were tumultuous would be an understatement. The
fundamental civil rights legislation had been passed, and affirmative action
programs were beginning to be formulated. The civil rights movement was in
full swing with marches, pickets, legislation and challenges in the courts.
Civil rights and equal opportunity were on everyone's mind, and competed
on the nation's agenda with the Vietnam War.

In 1969, thousands of Americans were drafted and many of them were
killed or wounded. The war stirred American emotions—there was anger,
guilt, frustration. Those who wanted to win the war were mystified that the
strongest nation on earth could not overcome such a small and weak foe.
Others, more vocal and active, saw the war as immoral and wanted the
United States out. This included a large segment of the college age
population which was being drafted to fight what many of them saw as an
immoral war. Antiwar sentiment was expressed in rallies across the
country—draft avoidance was encouraged, draft cards were burned, and
many young men left for Canada. The federal government was successful in
prosecuting a number of those who participated in such activities.

At Cornell there were rallies against the war and against the outrageous
acts committed by some opposed to the direction of the civil rights
movement, such as the bombing of a church where several young black girls
were killed and the murder of three civil rights workers, one of whom was a
Cornell student.

Cornell, at the president's initiative, had started a program to admit
black students in 1964. Enrollment was small, but grew each year, going
from fewer than twenty to over three hundred in the fall of 1969. Capable
students were sought and found, and arrived at Cornell. They were assigned
dormitory rooms, usually with white students as roommates. The
expectation, not conscious then, was that the black students would appreciate
the efforts made to bring them to Cornell and of the opportunity to get an Ivy
League education. But of the emotions they felt in those first few months in
Ithaca, gratitude was not one. Most, while bright, were products of
educational systems inferior to those of their white counterparts. They
needed, but did not have, academic and social support systems relevant to
them, as did white students.

The minority admissions programs was set up in 1964 by the new
president, James Perkins, without the advice and consent of the faculty, and
this led to resentment. Not having been part of the program's creation, some

faculty members were quick to point out its failings. According to the "Report of the Special Trustee Committee on Campus Unrest at Cornell,"[1] some faculty complained that students were ill-prepared and unable to keep up with the work. The report also notes that the minority admissions program was started at a time when most whites believed that blacks wanted to be integrated and wanted to acquire the values and standards of the majority population. The campus was stunned to find out that this was not so. Blacks became increasingly interested in separation and less interested in becoming part of the larger campus community. They viewed a Cornell education not as a way of moving out of the black community, but as a way of gaining knowledge and skills useful to the black community, with the intent of going back to help their fellow blacks.[2]

Cornell had committed to establishing an African-American studies program the year before (1968), and was in the process of hiring a director. An advisory board had been formed and a commitment to a facility had been made. The chairman of the board of trustees had given one million dollars for minority education. There were almost three hundred black students in a total student population of about twelve thousand, and a support program was being developed in increments. There was a small residence facility housing about a dozen black women. Given this leadership in addressing black issues and concerns, why did the black students feel they had to take over the Straight, and what were their goals in doing so?

Some black students wanted an autonomous, black, degree-granting college rather than a department or center. There were demands for more relevant courses, and concern about Cornell investing in banks lending money to South Africa. Indeed, when the president was speaking during a symposium on South Africa, a black student took the stage and manhandled the president, demanding that he defend the university's policy of investing in banks lending money to South Africa. Another stood by with a two-by-four providing "protection." The Afro-American Society (AAS) expelled the two from membership as a result of their action.

Two months earlier, a group of black students went into the main library and dumped about three thousand books on the floor, saying they were not relevant to them.[3] On the same day, a group of black students, in parading around campus, knocked over some vending machines, and then danced on tables in a student cafeteria, knocking over food trays. As a result, the university moved to charge them under the judicial system. The charged students did not appear at their hearing, saying that the university was engaged in selective reprisal against the AAS, that these were political acts and so could not be judged by the university, and that the disciplinary body was racist because it had no black members (one had recently resigned). The disciplinary body met six times, each time expecting the students to show up, which they never did. At the sixth meeting, one hundred and fifty members of the AAS came and restated their position.

As the spring semester wore on, the disciplinary body realized that, by its own rules, it could try students in absentia, and it prepared to do so. Penalties handed down on April 18, 1969 were mild—a letter of reprimand sent to their parents and deans. In the early hours of the same day, unidentified persons burned a cross on the lawn of the small residence for black women. A series of false fire alarms occurred at the same time and continued for several hours. That day, Friday, was the beginning of Parent's Weekend. That night there were more false fire alarms, and a bomb threat in an auditorium where the president and many parents were watching a dance concert.

At 5:30 the next morning, about one hundred black students went into the Straight and evicted the employees and the parents who were staying in the guest rooms. The cross burning and the judicial decisions provided the justification for the takeover, which had been planned for some time. One of the AAS spokesmen later said, "Our action had been planned to occur at a critical juncture for Cornell, namely Parents' Weekend, to seize a building . . . was something that the university just couldn't ignore."[4] On hearing of the takeover, the SDS, which had been asked to come to an early morning meeting by the AAS without being told the purpose, moved to the outside of the Straight and began picketing in support of the black students. According to a black student, the takeover was intended to give the campus an emphatic warning to get off their backs, and they planned on leaving peaceably after one day.[5] The administration gathered to try to figure out how to deal with this new phenomenon.

In mid-morning, a group of fraternity men tried to get into the Straight, putatively to try to reason with the students. They were evicted quickly and vigorously. As the same time, there were reports of fraternity men drinking and threatening to take back the Straight, of carloads of armed whites coming to campus, and of a large force of deputy sheriffs and other law enforcement agencies massing downtown. Reporters from around the country began to arrive almost immediately. By late afternoon, the students inside the building were under great stress and tension. Negotiations between members of the administration and the students went on intermittently. In the late evening, based on the reports of armed posses intent on taking back the Straight by violent means, the black students inside the building decided to arm themselves. As one said later, "We were faced with a choice. There were three things we could do: we could leave at that point, surrendering to a posse, we could stay in the building, waiting for the posse to come in and get us, ok? Or we could arm ourselves, to defend ourselves against the posse. Only one choice made sense. We put our lives on the line with one provision: . . . that along with our lives on the line, everybody else's life was on the line . . ."[6]

For the first time on a college campus, guns were introduced. It was headline news and it changed the nature of the confrontation.

The administration did not move to stop the arms from being taken into the Straight for a number of reasons—they did not have enough campus police to prevent it, the Straight is on a hillside with almost two dozen entryways, and the administration feared that an attempt to stop the arms might in itself lead to violence. The administration had earlier decided not to ask for outside police help.

The students spent that Saturday night in the Straight with the lights off so as not to be a target for gunmen.

On Sunday, the administration's assessment was that unless the students left that day, there would be violence. Negotiations went on through the morning and into the afternoon. Finally, an agreement for leaving the building was reached. The students would be allowed to leave carrying their guns, but they would not be loaded. The university agreed to help the students if civil charges were filed, and they would sign a comprehensive agreement after the building was vacated. Shortly after 4:00 P.M., the students walked out, one of the leaders carrying a shotgun and two bandoliers crisscrossed over his shoulders, another carrying a rifle. A crowd of two thousand, including a large media contingent, watched. The photo of the students leaving with guns in hand won a Pulitzer Prize.

Escorted by the campus police and several members of the administration, they marched to the site of the Black Studies Center and signed a broad-ranging agreement which included a promise from the dean of the faculty that he would recommend nullification of the judicial penalties at a faculty meeting the next day, and agreements that the university would not file any civil charges or any changes in the campus judicial system, would pay for any damage to the Straight, would investigate the cross burning and the fraternity incident, and would provide a twenty-four–hour watch at the black's women's residence. The black students agreed to help devise a new judicial system.

It was over. There was no bloodshed or violence. That no one was hurt became even more remarkable as events unfolded on other campuses over the next year or so, where guns were introduced by official agencies and protesting students were gunned down.

But in many ways it was only the beginning. The next day— Monday—the faculty refused to nullify the judicial decisions, and the dean who had helped negotiate the agreement to leave the Straight resigned even though the faculty had voted overwhelmingly for him to remain. Tensions mounted, as did the number of law enforcement officials gathered downtown equipped with rifles and riot gear. The AAS and SDS were incensed. Rumors of building takeovers were rampant. A group of faculty vowed to take over a building, nonviolently, in support of the black students. The SDS called for a meeting in the huge fieldhouse on campus and thousands showed up. Faculties of various colleges met. A faculty meeting to reconsider the judicial penalties was called for Wednesday. Threats were made against some members of the administration and some faculty members. Many of them moved out of their homes.

On Wednesday, at the largest meeting of the faculty in Cornell's history, the faculty nullified the judicial penalties. Some had changed their vote to preserve the university, saying, "I had seldom in my years of life felt such bitterness of soul, as if all my thinking and working and teaching and writing had been nothing but vanity of vanities" and, "I will lose some self respect doing so; I want you to know I terribly resent this" and, "In the 800 years that they have existed, many eminent universities have come and gone and the world has survived their departure. But those that have departed because they stood for nothing have not even been missed."[7]

The mass meetings in the fieldhouse continued, and the topic turned to restructuring the university and giving the campus community more say in those aspects of campus life directly affecting them.

The trustees looked into the reasons behind the unrest and the president's handling of it. Most expected the president to continue. Soon after, however, the president asked the trustees to begin a search for another president. In reviewing the events, a trustee committee stated, "No one will ever know if this was the right way to settle this disruption. This was a matter of judgement. These men made the decision to place the protection of life above the reputation of the university. They knew the price to themselves and to Cornell was great—but was it greater than the price of human life?"[8]

* * * * * * * *

It is twenty years later, April 19, 1989. There have been racial incidents on many campuses around the country, some have involved violence. There have been none at Cornell. Good fortune or progressive programs?

How has Cornell's minority education program fared? How did the Straight takeover influence that effort and the campus as a whole?

The third version of a campus governance structure is in place, although it is invisible to much of the campus. There is involvement in the governance system by students, including minority students, employees, and to a lesser extent, faculty. Many of the earlier grievances have been addressed. The changes in the campus judicial system have often been accompanied by debate, but its authority is accepted by the campus community. The Africana Studies and Research Center, with its own faculty, is respected nationally for its scholarship. Some of its faculty have joint appointments in other departments. Students can major in Africana studies and some get master's degrees in it. Courses are available to and taken by all students, although mostly by black students. There is a large minority component of the student body. Blacks make up 3.5 percent of the 18,500-student body. There are special efforts to recruit minority students and there are academic and social support services relevant to them. Financial aid is provided that recognizes the special needs of many minority students and often is more favorable than that for nonminority students. There is a living unit committed to education about, and support of, developing communities in third world countries and in the United States. It attracts mainly black students, although all groups, including whites, are represented. There are more minority faculty and staff, and some minorities in the senior administration. Yet marches and protests still occur. There are feelings of alienation and tension, and charges of racism come up periodically. Why? Where is Cornell and higher education?

For today's students, the civil rights movement is ancient history. White students feel that legislation has taken care of the problems and do not understand why minority students are complaining. Minority students still feel like strangers on their own campuses. They feel that they are not equal partners in the educational enterprise. They sense that institutions have not come to grips with why they want minority students on the campus, other than it is the right thing to do, and, in many ways, it is mandated by the federal government. Minority students coming to campuses expect to be treated as equals. When racism rears its ugly head, and when the university does not move quickly to counteract it, they feel betrayed, and they feel the university really does not want them. It is disappointment and frustration that causes them to not trust whites, especially if they have not had much previous contact with them. This is true at Cornell and across the country.

In looking at black students at white colleges, Fleming states:

> The stress of racial tension and inadequate social lives borne by black students in white schools generate feelings of alienation that often lead to serious adjustment problems. These stresses lead to a psychological withdrawal that impairs academic functioning . . . . Consequently, black students perform below their ability levels . . . . It may be that the confusion surrounding the issue results from our faulty attempts to separate the intellectual and interpersonal components of an educational issue, components that are basically inseparable.[9]

There are several methods of coping that black students use. Gibbs describes withdrawal, affirmation, assimilation and separation.[10] In the withdrawal mode, the student wishes to avoid the conflict-producing situation. This is often the reason for what some characterize as self-segregation, but in reality it is a search for a comfortable, tension-free environment. It may be a reflection of the failure of an institution to fully accept black students. The mode of separation is characterized by rejection of whites, contempt for white values and protests against white institutions and customs. Isn't this what is now so often seen on campuses? Is this the reason for the current activism? Have institutions fully accepted minority students? Or is that acceptance contingent on black students blending into the white campus? Think of the resistance to black dorms and the comments about black students always sitting together in the dining halls. We need to be more understanding of the root causes of the withdrawal and separation, and provide remedies, not objections.

Black students expect that the university will be flexible in responding to their needs, expect that rules can be bypassed and that financial aid will be readily available. This often is not the case, and the students find that getting an education is more difficult than they imagined. They come to college expecting courses similar to those in high school in difficulty and intensity, and that out-of-classroom activities will reflect their interests as well as those of the white students. More frustration. The students expect to benefit the institution as it benefits them: "The university's acceptance of their contributions would serve as collective proof of its liberal concern, as a vehicle for diversifying the student body, and as a means of producing educated leaders to tackle the broad social problems of our society."[11]

Why are white students, at best, indifferent to the problems of minority students? As Sears said, "They know nothing of the civil rights struggle. Not only have they not lived it, but they haven't been taught it. All they have is a perception that minorities are getting more than their share."[12] On the other hand, Beckham says, "Instead of being encouraged to think of their capacity to achieve, black students are more likely to receive a totally different message: they aren't wanted and they can't make it."[13]

Have we gone to the next level in seeking equality, where many of the initial concerns which often reflected individual survival have been addressed and we are now getting to more basic, systemic issues? In the late 1960s and early 1970s the issues revolved around providing financial aid, support systems, black studies and relevant courses. A desire for more minority faculty and staff, increased numbers of minority admissions, increased financial support for programs. As recently stated in a Brown University report, "Protesting students were concerned about too few minority faculty members, too little reflection of their cultural heritage and history within the curriculum, and seeming indifference to their presence."[14]

The situation today is quite different from what it was twenty years ago.

We face new concerns and difficulties and a second civil rights movement is needed that will be quite different from that of the 1960s. A new campaign of public awareness must begin, and legislation at the state and federal level must be forthcoming. There is a need for new and more creative financial aid programs, and new ways of interesting minority students in attending college and graduate school. In carrying out these programs, minority groups must be made partners in the process and welcomed at institutions, made to feel that they are members of the institution and treated as equals.

The issues that stimulate demonstrations have much in common from one campus to the next, and they reflect broad and overriding concerns. As Steele mentioned, "much of what they are marching and rallying about seemed less a response to specific racial incidents than a call for broader action on the part of colleges and universities they were attending. . . . There is a sense in these demands that racism runs deep."[15]

At Cornell, as they have for twenty years, students are concerned about the university's investment policy as it relates to South Africa. They want the university to divest and the trustees have chosen not to do so after reviews and two votes in the last three years. Student concerns are often shared by faculty and staff. In fact, many black faculty members, after the trustee vote in January, 1989, elected to withdraw from all university committees to signify their unhappiness.

Students are also concerned about racial (and sexual) harassment even though Cornell has been fortunate to have no blatant incidents, as other campuses have. There are requests to have courses to defuse racism. Increased recruitment of minority faculty, staff and also graduate students is called for. There are also requests for more input in decisions affecting the minority education program. Students are still looking for the commitment of the university to minority programs in spite of the fact that Cornell has a large number of staff and an enormous amount of money and other resources devoted to the program.

Some attribute many of today's problems to insufficient communications, and that certainly has to be part of the problem. But is it that simple? The problem is lack of equality and full participation in the total process and the solution is equality and full participation. But are colleges and universities, with their European history and white traditions, with administrations and boards of trustees still predominantly white and male, ready to deal with minorities on an equal basis? To paraphrase novelist Peter DeVries, the danger of treating others as equals is that they might start doing the same to you.

I believe the higher education community is ready to embark on this next stage in equal opportunity, where minority students can realize their full potential in college. But help and guidance are needed by majority and minority members, especially when differences of opinion and approach arise. True community and partnership are not easily achieved. There will be difficulties, but through understanding and honesty, and a willingness to support each other, often publicly, when there are disagreements, progress can be made.

To move ahead, a number of areas must be addressed: the curriculum, the recruitment of faculty, staff and students, and the establishment of a true community. Finances, while important, must not be a barrier. The racial issue is the most important issue facing society today and priorities must reflect this. Institutions find the resources necessary to fund those things it regards as crucial—witness supercomputers, football coaches and the like.

The curriculum must be infused with the contributions of minority groups to the discipline being taught. Only in this way will the entire student body be exposed to the contributions of all groups. Separate courses can be avoided, and mandatory courses may breed more resentment than understanding. There will still be a need for ethnic studies courses and centers, mainly for research and scholarship. An ideal curriculum would be pervasive, and it would not treat minority contributions separately.

Curriculum initiative must come from the faculty. How can the faculty be enticed into undertaking such an endeavor? The president could issue such a challenge. The faculty governance system might be a logical starting point. When the faculty group comes up with their recommendations, two things will be needed. One is funds. The other is the patience not to take the recommendations and further study them. Manipulation by the administration kills the initiative and the ownership by the faculty. Such a program was highly successful in recruiting minority faculty during the 1987–88 academic year at Cornell.

The recruiting of faculty is a difficult issue. Here, too, there must be a consensus that having minority faculty is desirable. Their presence enriches the learning environment for all students and provides a vital link to black students. There are too few minority faculty now and too few eligible to be faculty members in the near future. So what can be done? In the short term, more use of visiting appointments can be made. This would not only extend the influence of current minority faculty, but could be expanded to use people in business and industry.

Too often institutions play it safe by hiring minority faculty members who are virtually ensured of getting tenure. Wanting to avoid charges of racism, they are unwilling to gamble with minority members as they often do with majority members. In the short term, "raiding" will also provide more minority faculty. If everyone takes a bit more of a risk, and as prestigious institutions hire faculty from less prestigious institutions, more openings become available.

In the long term, the problem can only be ameliorated by attracting more minority students into graduate schools. Realistically, that will require massive intervention by the federal government through a financial incentive program. A number of institutions, aided by private foundations, separately and together have started programs to attract minority students, especially in math and the sciences, but these, while important, are not sufficient. What is needed is a national program based on two priorities: to attract minorities into graduate education and to attract more students of every type into graduate education. There is a critical shortage of American students going into doctoral studies, especially in science, math and engineering. Ph.D.'s in all of these disciplines are needed for both industry and higher education. The higher education establishment must get this on the nation's agenda.

Many of the same techniques for recruiting faculty can be used for staff positions. The presence of minority staff enriches the academe, providing successful role models for students. Here, playing it safe is less of an issue since tenure is not involved, and an individual who does not work out at one position can often be tried in a different but related position. Internships can also be effective, where an individual with some, but not all, of the necessary skills can be hired and a program designed to help him or her gain the skills. The same kind of a program can be used to prepare minority staff for promotion.

The establishment of a true community may be the most daunting task of all. It is difficult enough with a homogeneous membership. In the past, diversity was often a part of the definition of community. A different term, pluralism, has now come into vogue. Its definition comes close to one for a true community. The Brown report states, "Pluralism as a social condition is that state of affairs in which several different ethnic, religious, and social communities live side by side, willing to reaffirm each other's dignity, ready to benefit from each other's experience, and quick to acknowledge each other's contributions to the common welfare."[16]

In looking at the goals universities are trying to attain, both Brown and Stanford now talk of pluralism rather than diversity.[17] Stanford talks of interactive pluralism, ". . . where all ethnic groups can engage their differences in a process of mutual enrichment, where racial minorities and the majority can acknowledge and build mutual respect for their similarities as well as their differences." Are we at a new level in seeking equality, a new level of sophistication and understanding in trying to achieve equality, in judging a person by what he or she can or cannot do rather than by his or her looks or background?

In order to do this, true partnerships must be formed with elimination of the we-they mentality. Self-segregation must be recognized for what it often is, withdrawal or separation from the institution because of discomfort and a lack of a feeling of an institutional membership. Ethnic communities within the campus community must be accepted and celebrated. Everyone must feel valued. This is a personal task for every member of the campus, but it must start with the president and his or her staff in word and in deed. They must make an official institutional commitment and then show their commitment through their everyday actions and interactions. It must be impressed on every member of the community by the president in the most positive way why this is important. If done as a continuing commitment, the ethos of the institution will change.

Conclusion

In looking at where the students who took part in the Straight takeover are now, and what they are doing, one is struck by how enormously successful many of them are. There are two judges, a few lawyers (some in very large firms), industry executives, several physicians (some with specialties), and the list goes on. Most are proud of what they did twenty years ago, but many would choose other ways to accomplish their ends today. Most are loyal to Cornell, but it is clear that the stronger loyalty is to one another and to those who will follow them at Cornell. At a recent reunion, many of the Straight participants returned to campus and took part in a weekend of activities, along with many other alumni of all ethnic backgrounds. Well over two hundred black alumni returned and pledged $100,000 to the scholarship fund.

An alumnus of the class of '73 said, "Cornell cannot move on to the next level—and cannot hope for true understanding among people of different races and ethnicities—until it comes to believe that pluralism is a necessity, not an act of goodwill. It provides not only access to opportunity for an increasingly colored citizenry, but, for the university, access to a broader spectrum of human perspectives. Such pluralism is, simply, an educational imperative no less than a social and political one."[18]

Professor Walter LaFeber of Cornell recently said, ". . . one of the most critical educational missions of our time, an ever-increasing and systematic involvement of minorities in higher education, cannot be realized without the full participation of those minorities. They must be involved fully as a matter of course, not as a matter of *noblesse oblige,* and must be understood to be representing those values that are not merely to be tolerated but are integral parts of the society."[19]

In an article written for the tenth anniversary of the Straight takeover, one of the leaders of the Straight takeover said:

> In a broader perspective, however, all participants in this sad affair were losers. We were all losers because we were students, faculty and

administrators thrust by history to center stage in the racial confrontation that has historically contained the seeds of America's destructuction, and we did no better in our selection of methods of conflict resolution than have the ugly terrorists of both races who have always exploited this issue to the detriment of the entire nation. We all failed in our responsibility to demonstrate that temperate, reasonable and ethical people of different races can work together to overcome historical injustices and animosities, and unite in pursuit of a just society.[20]

Let's not be found wanting this time around.

NOTES

1. "Report of the Special Trustee Committee on Campus Unrest at Cornell," September 1969, p. 42.

2. Ibid., p. 43.

3. *Cornell Daily Sun, Special Supplement,* April 19, 1979, pp. 13–36. This supplement provides a detailed chronology of the events surrounding the Straight takeover.

4. Ibid., p. 18.

5. Ibid., p. 19.

6. Ibid., p. 21.

7. Ibid., p. 26.

8. "Report of the Special Trustee Committee on Campus Unrest at Cornell."

9. Jacqueline Fleming, *Blacks in College* (San Francisco: Jossey-Bass, 1985), p. 3.

10. J. T. Gibbs, *American Journal of Orthopsychiatry,* 44 (1974): 728.

11. J. T. Gibbs, *Personnel and Guidance Journal,* (1973): 463.

12. S. Sears, *San Francisco Examiner,* November 13, 1988, p. 20.

13. Barry Beckham, "Strangers in a Strange Land: The Experience of Blacks on White Campuses," *Educational Record* (Fall 1987–Winter 1988), p. 74.

14. "The American University and the Pluralist Ideal," *A Report of the Visiting Committee on Minority Life and Education at Brown University,* May 1986, p. 1.

15. Shelby Steele, "The Recoloring of Campus Life," *Harper's Magazine* (February 1989), p. 47.

16. "American University and the Pluralist Ideal," p. ix.

17. "Final Report of the University Commission on Minority Issues," Stanford University, March 1989.

18. Dennis Williams, "Lessons Still Largely Unlearned," *Cornell Chronicle—Special Report,* April 20, 1989, p. 4.

19. Ibid., p. 2.

20. Tom Jones, "The Lessons of the Past: A 'Sad Affair'," *Cornell Daily Sun, Special Supplement,* p. 14.

Conclusion

RACE IN AMERICA

America is composed of several distinct ethnic, racial and cultural groups. What we have, for the most part, are different clusters—white ethnics, African-Americans, Asian-Americans, Hispanics and Native Americans—living separately, with little knowledge of, or respect for, each other. While this is not ideal in our minds, it does reflect reality; most white people prefer to live amongst other white people and most African-Americans prefer to live amongst other African-Americans, et cetera. The inevitable results of this limited ethnic and racial tolerance which dominates our society are the conflicts that we find in the workplace, in the housing market, in the precollegiate environment and indeed in our institutions of higher education. It is the conflict in this latter setting that we have attempted to address in this book.

The racial situation in American higher education has been the focus of widespread coverage in the American media. Gordon and others emphasize this point in this book. However, as Cole suggests in this volume, little analysis has been done to explain this conflict. Reports of racial incidents are invariably followed by finger-pointing, inaccurate assessments and a general lack of understanding on the part of many. Some place the blame on underrepresented students, others blame university faculty and administrators, some blame white students and still others blame society at large. All too often these assessments are too simplistic and do not derive from an adequate consideration of the context in which these incidents occur. In this volume we have attempted to provide such an assessment.

OBSERVATIONS

A few observations need to be made. First, the friction in American higher education that we describe in this book is not recent. Racial incidents

263

have been widespread in American colleges and universities since the 1960s, when large numbers of African-American, Hispanic, Native American and Asian-American students first began enrolling in predominantly white schools. Gordon describes this historical perspective well, with particular reference to the Arizona State University campus. Also, Gurowitz's assessment of Cornell twenty years after a racial conflict on that campus highlights this truism.

Equally important is the fact that this racial tension is expected to increase. As Colón points out, this is due to demographic and economic changes, which are leading to a student body that is "more colorful, older, more female and more educationally and occupationally 'at risk.' "

Prior to the 1960s, 80 percent of African-American students attended historically black colleges. Beginning in the 1960s the trend reversed; by the end of that decade, 80 percent of African-American students were attending predominantly white institutions of higher education. At the same time, similar increases in enrollment at predominantly white schools occurred for Hispanics, Native Americans and Asian-Americans. It was during this period that the racial conflict began. It was the first time that large numbers of African-American, Native American, Hispanic and Asian-American students were on these campuses. The interactions were strained and as the different groups met, the lack of understanding, appreciation and respect for differences took its toll.

In the 1960s, we addressed the conflict in a number of ways. We called for more faculty and students from these underrepresented groups. We also created black studies programs, Asian-American studies programs, Latin American studies programs and Native American studies programs. These programs were of critical importance, but they only addressed part of the problem with the curriculum. While they introduced into the curriculum, for the first time, the experiences of these groups, the introduction was tangential and peripheral. In many instances these innovations were appendages to the curriculum. What was needed, and what continues to be needed, is the wholesale overhauling of the entire curriculum so that the significant contributions of these groups are presented to all students in all disciplines.

The issues remain the same as they were in the 1960s when cultural diversity was first in vogue in American higher education—curriculum, students and faculty. It is only recently, however, that the media has seen fit to emphasize the resultant conflict and its effects on the academy.

What is also a more recent phenomenon is the increasing impact that precollegiate education has had on the condition of higher education. While we have not addressed this relationship directly in this volume, it is clear that the quality and nature of education afforded to all students in elementary and secondary school has a direct relationship to what is happening on college campuses. The increasingly poor quality of precollegiate education provided for African-American, Hispanic-American, Native American and economically disadvantaged students increases the differences that students bring to the collegiate environment, exacerbating the negative nature of intercultural relationships.

The continued failure of elementary and secondary schools (and of society in general) to provide children with an understanding and appreciation for other cultures sets the scene for the lack of understanding and appreciation and for the racial friction in higher education that we describe in this book. My own sense is that while we may be striving for a society in which differences may be less significant, as long as they are not understood and respected, there will remain a need for underrepresented groups to assert and emphasize their differences.

A second observation is that the racial controversy in American higher education is a reflection of the racial controversy in America. For example, an analogous situation arises when a Hispanic or African-American family moves into a previously all-white community. In fact, we could as easily prepare a volume on the racial conflict in American housing or in the American workplace. When viewed from a historical perspective, however, the racial conflict on campuses today has its own dynamics, derived from a social dynamic that is very different from that which was experienced in the past or indeed from that which is experienced in other arenas of American society.

Part of the cause of the racial conflict in America is in the ways institutions in America are set up. America, not unlike other societies, has set up various kinds of institutions (e.g., political, educational, economic, health, military, religious, et cetera) all of which serve unique primary functions. In America, however, these institutions have been used to serve a secondary function—the perpetuation of racism (as well as sexism and classism). Americans are not taught to respect the various cultures that comprise the citizenry. While our society is made up of many groups—some who came voluntarily, some who came involuntarily and some who were here long before the "founding parents"—what we find in America is a monolithic system dominated by an arrogant, Eurocentric or white Anglo-Saxon Protestant, male way of viewing the world that characterizes cultural and linguistic differences as deficiencies, disadvantages and pathologies.

THIS VOLUME

The interrelationship between institutions in society has been highlighted by several contributors to this volume. They stress the coexistence of

critical problems in the universities and in the larger society. In Hirsch's
assessment of the Columbia situation, he describes the racist actions of the
police against the black students whom they arrested, illustrating how
institutions (in this case, military and educational institutions) work together
in society to perpetuate racism. Altbach laments that universities are
expected to take the lead and provide a model for other societal institutions,
knowing well that such institutions are affected by society more than they
affect society.

In chapter one, Altbach begins by stating: "Race is one of the most
volatile, and divisive, issues in American higher education and has been one
of the flashpoints of crisis in the past several years." Indeed this is true and
it is the critical nature of this issue that makes this volume so important.
Katz, in viewing this issue of race and racism in higher education, argues that
one of the major reasons that racism in higher education remains a significant
problem is the passivity and reluctance of white faculty members to openly
address the issue.

We provide the lay of the land, so to speak, by initially describing, from
several perspectives, the general nature of the conflict. That discussion is
followed by a dialogue on issues of race in higher education as they relate to
faculty. Perhaps most importantly, in the third section of this volume, we
provide firsthand accounts of key racial incidents on several prominent
university campuses.

Twenty years after the big push to enroll African-American, Native
American, Hispanic and Asian-American students in higher education, the
call is still for a more culturally diverse curriculum and more faculty and
students from these underrepresented groups. Several contributors emphasize
these areas as key in improving race relations on campuses. Chan and Wang
discuss the barriers that have been put before these who have struggled to
create Asian-American studies programs over the past twenty years. Colón
highlights, from an historical perspective, the African-American pursuit of
higher education.

The most consistently raised issue in this volume, and perhaps
justifiably so, is the need for more African-American, Hispanic, Asian-
American and Native American faculty and students on American campuses.
Here, Chan and Wang discuss recent institutional attempts to limit the
number of Asian-American students on many American campuses. Trent
examines the problems of underrepresentation of African-Americans,
Hispanics, Native Americans and women students in higher education,
focusing on desegregation and affirmative action. He concludes that efforts at
increased opportunities for these groups have focused solely on recruitment
and enrollment, overlooking the importance of retention and success.

Mickelson and Oliver, Jackson, and Reyes and Halcón focus on faculty recruitment. Mickelson and Oliver and Jackson discuss African-American faculty. Mickelson and Oliver attack the widespread assumption that the best new Ph.D.'s can only be found at the major research universities. Jackson discusses two major explanations that are put forth for failures to hire adequate African-American faculty: a limited pool and the presence of institutional racism. He concludes that there is some evidence to support both arguments. Reyes and Halcón focus on the barriers put before Chicano/ Chicana scholars as they seek faculty appointments.

Solmon and Wingard point out that minuscule increases have been achieved in recent years in the number of appointments of underrepresented faculty members. They also discuss factors that have an impact on the demographics of student and faculty populations. Such factors, they argue, include the quality of precollegiate education and the changing birth rate.

While curriculum, faculty and students continue to be of concern, it is also true that our vision must go beyond them. We must consider the larger implications of our efforts in these areas. As Cole points out in this volume, "The educational opportunities—and obligations—that follow test an institution's commitment, energy, resources and imagination in profound and enduring ways."

Altbach stresses, and other contributors imply, that the achievement of racial harmony on our campuses and the realization of an understanding of and respect for cultural groups other than our own is of critical importance to all of us. Sadly, Hirsch, Cole and Gurowitz, in discussing the conflicts at Columbia, Stanford and Cornell respectively, point out that the friction only served to encourage racist attitudes.

RECOMMENDATIONS

Several recommendations can be gleaned from this volume. First, the responsibility of college and university faculty and administrators is critical and primary. If racism is to be tackled on our campuses, the initiative must come from the top. Several issues must be addressed. Related to the student enrollment, faculty recruitment and curriculum matters, are matters of student attrition, student alienation and relationships between underrepresented students and white male faculty. In this regard, Katz argues for the creation and support of opportunities for African-American and white faculty and students to closely interact in academic endeavors, allowing each group to discover the many commonalities among them and to reduce their mutual apprehensions.

Underrepresented students are still retained in higher education at a rate significantly lower than their white counterparts. Similarly, study after study has documented the feeling of loneliness, alienation and of not being wanted that these students experience on predominantly white campuses. These studies also illustrate the perceptions of many of these underrepresented students that many white faculty are insensitive and alienating. In this volume, Colón highlights the conflict that arises from the interaction between African-American culture and the European-American cultural framework that is characteristic of predominantly white colleges and universities. Committed administrators and faculty must provide the leadership in addressing these issues. This point is made repeatedly in this volume.

Second, there must be an institution-wide effort to "agitate the system"—both collegiate and societal—to bring about full participation of all of the cultural groups that make up America. For example, as Cole points out, "we need more and better courses about American racial and ethnic groups as well as more faculty with the training to teach these courses." If racial divisions are to decrease and if intercultural harmony is to be realized, increased, creative and directed energies must flow from administrators, faculty, staff and students of all ethnic, cultural and racial persuasions. In this regard, Trent argues for improvements in the quality and use of affirmative action data and for a university-wide commitment to access. He states, "we have learned that simple compliance or mere race- and sex-neutral practices will not achieve the desired results."

Finally, we hope that Gordon is correct when he says that students of today are ready to support increased cultural diversity on our campuses with the attendant institutional adjustments. Indeed, the role of students has been shown historically to be of critical importance in bringing about change in higher education. Ultimately, there is not only an educational impetus, but a moral imperative impelling us to deal with racism on American campuses and in American society. As Colón points out, the social reality of the twenty-first century will require higher education institutions to shift from a monocultural, Western European and male-dominated emphasis to a "more culturally democratic pluralism" in order to maintain the social vanguard role that many expect them to serve in American society.

In the final analysis, we must all do everything that we can to eliminate racism and the accompanying racial conflict in American higher education— and in America.

Contributors

PHILIP G. ALTBACH is a professor and director of the Comparative Education Center, State University of New York at Buffalo. He has written extensively on higher education and is co-editor of *Higher Education in American Society* and author of *The Knowledge Context*, among other books.

LEON BOTSTEIN is president of Bard College, Annandale-on-Hudson, New York.

SUCHENG CHAN is professor of history and Asian-American studies at the University of California at Santa Barbara. She is author of *The Asian Americans; An Interpretative History* and other books.

SALLY COLE is judicial affairs officer at Stanford University.

ALAN COLÓN is vice president for student affairs, Hampton University, Hampton, Virginia.

LEONARD GORDON is professor and chair of the Department of Sociology, Arizona State University, Tempe, Arizona. He has written widely on attitudes toward minorities in America.

WILLIAM D. GUROWITZ is vice president for student affairs at Cornell University.

ERIC L. HIRSCH is assistant professor of sociology at Columbia University.

JOHN J. HALCÓN is on the faculty at the University of Northern Colorado, Greeley, Colorado.

KENNETH W. JACKSON is the chairperson of the Department of Sociology and Social Work at Texas Southern University, Houston, Texas.

JOSEPH KATZ was professor of human development and director of the Research Group for Human Development and Educational Policy at the State University of New York at Stony Brook until his recent death.

CLARK KERR is president emeritus of the University of California and was chair of the Carnegie Council on Policy Studies in Higher Education.

KOFI LOMOTEY is assistant professor in the Department of Educational Organization, Administration and Policy, State University of New York at Buffalo. He is author of *African-American Principals: School Leadership and Success* and *Going to School: The African-American Experience*.

ROSLYN ARLIN MICKELSON is assistant professor of sociology and adjunct assistant professor of women's studies at the University of North Carolina at Charlotte.

MELVIN L. OLIVER is a member of the faculty in the Department of Sociology at the University of California at Los Angeles.

MARÍA DE LA LUZ REYES is on the faculty in the School of Education, University of Colorado, Boulder, Colorado.

LEWIS C. SOLMON is a professor and dean of the Graduate School of Education at the University of California at Los Angeles.

WILLIAM T. TRENT is a member of the faculty in the Department of Educational Policy Studies, University of Illinois at Urbana-Champaign.

LING-CHI WANG is associate professor of Asian American studies at the University of California at Berkeley. He is author of *The Politics of Assimilation and Repression: The Chinese in the United States, 1940–1970*.

TAMARA L. WINGARD is a doctoral student in the Graduate School of Education, University of California, Los Angeles.

Index